WOMEN AS MOTHERS

Sheila Kitzinger was born in Somerset in 1929 and was
educated at Bishop Fox's Girls' School, Taunton, and at
Ruskin and St Hugh's Colleges, Oxford. A social
anthropologist and childbirth educator, she is also the
author of *The Experience of Childbirth* (1962), *Giving
Birth – The Parents' Emotions in Childbirth* (1971),
Education and Counselling for Childbirth (1977) and, in
conjunction with John Davis, editor of *The Place of Birth*
(1977). Herself the mother of five daughters, she is a
member of both the Panel of Advisers to the National
Childbirth Trust in London and the Board of
Consultants of the International Childbirth Education
Association in the USA.

WOMEN AS MOTHERS

Sheila Kitzinger

Fontana/Collins

First published by Fontana Books 1978

Copyright © Sheila Kitzinger 1978

Made and printed in Great Britain by
William Collins Sons & Co Ltd, Glasgow

With thanks to our daughters — Celia, Nell, Tess, Polly and Jenny — who increase my knowledge and understanding, and whose growing up is an education for their mother.

Contents

1	Mothercraft or Motherhood?	13
2	The Motherhood Trap	28
3	Mothers in the Social System	51
4	Getting and Not Getting Pregnant	72
5	Childbirth — a Social Act	104
6	Ritual and Technology in Contemporary Hospital Childbirth	142
7	Bonding, Loving and Learning	163
8	Learning to be a Mother	193
9	Grandmothers	213
10	Women as Polluters and Creators	226
11	The Changing Face of Motherhood	247
12	A World Fit for Mothers?	269
	Index	277

Acknowledgements

My thanks are due to all the mothers whom I have prepared for childbirth who have taught me so much and who have helped me perceive new aspects of the experience of birth and motherhood. I should also like to express my thanks to those mothers with whom I have talked during my lecture tours with the International Childbirth Education Association of America and with the Paramedical Association for Childbirth Education of Johannesburg, South Africa, all of whom have widened my horizons.

I should also like to thank the many obstetricians, psychiatrists, paediatricians, social anthropologists and nurses who have helped me in my researches in Europe, North and South America, Israel and the Caribbean; all the British midwives and nurses who wrote to me giving me the benefit of their experience in many countries; and those members of the Medical Research Council Epidemiological Research Unit at the University of the West Indies and public health workers, doctors, nurses and teachers in Kingston, in the countryside and on the staff of the Jubilee Hospital in Jamaica who helped me during my nine months' intensive fieldwork there.

I want to thank, too, the Trustees of the Joost de Blank Memorial Fund for sponsoring my research into the challenges facing West Indian mothers in Britain, and St Mary's Hospital Medical School for giving me the facilities for talking with immigrant mothers attending their antenatal clinic.

None of this could ever have been written without the skilled deciphering of my handwriting and idiosyncratic typing by Audrey Macefield, my secretary, and the unflustered way in which she creates order out of chaos, and with the capable assistance of Barbara Morris and Susan Miller in typing the final draft.

Most of all I thank my husband, whose generosity and love have made my research and writing possible.

The Manor,
Standlake,
Near Witney,
Oxfordshire,
England.

A Wish

Often I've wished that I'd been born a woman.
It seems the one sure way to be fully human.
Think of the trouble – keeping the children fed,
Keeping your skirt down and your lips red,
Watching the calendar and the last bus home,
Being nice to all the dozens of guests in the room;
Having to change your hairstyle and your name
At least once; learning to take the blame;
Keeping your husband faithful, and your char
And all the things you're supposed to be grateful for
– Votes and proposals, chocolates and seats in the train –
Or expert with – typewriter, powderpuff, pen,
Diaphragm, needle, chequebook, casserole, bed.
It seems the one sure way to be driven mad.

So why would anyone want to be a woman?
Would you rather be the hero or the victim?
Would you rather win, seduce, and read that paper,
Or be beaten, pregnant, and have to lay the table?
Nothing is free. In order to pay the price
Isn't it simpler, really, to have no choice?
Only ill-health, recurring, inevitable,
Can teach the taste of what it is to be well.
No man has ever felt his daughter tear
The flesh he had earlier torn to plant her there.
Men know the pain of birth by a kind of theory:
No man has been a protagonist in the story,
Lying back bleeding, exhausted and in pain,
Waiting for stitches and sleep and to be alone,
And listening with tender breasts to the hesitant croak
At the bedside growing continuous as you wake.

That is the price. That is what love is worth.
It will go on twisting your heart like an afterbirth.
Whether you choose to or not you will pay and pay
Your whole life long. Nothing on earth is free.

Laurence Lerner
from *Selves*
Routledge and Kegan Paul, 1969

Mothercraft or Motherhood?

This is not a 'how to' book. It is about birth and motherhood in different cultures and historical periods so that the reader can get some idea of what it was like to have been a mother in these different societies. I am looking at birth and mothers from the point of view of social anthropology, trying to find out the process of becoming and being a mother in our own as well as in other cultures, and questioning some of the assumptions implicit in our ideas about the nature of mothering.

I have five children myself, and looking at the subject from the point of view of my own mothering role realize that anthropology, however, gives only some of the answers, and often produces little or no material just when we have the most searching questions to ask. One explanation is that anthropologists, most of whom are men, (it is very difficult to be a mother while you are studying a tribe of pastoral nomads or camping in a clearing in the bush) tend to look at mothers from the point of view of the men who run the system. They see the family through male eyes, in a perspective more readily accessible to them and which they take for granted. Social anthropology has, for the most part, neglected the private world of women and communication within the family to concentrate instead on larger issues in the public arena of tribal life. Anthropologists have tended to discuss women as objects involved in transactions between social groups and to see society largely in terms of relations between men, referring to

women only when they affect men's behaviour. In Evan
Pritchard's brilliant studies of the Nuer of the Sudan,
women come into the books rather less often than cows
This may well reflect accurately the way Nuer men them
selves think, but it means, nevertheless, that we get littl
idea of the lives of 50% of the Nuer tribe.

Cultural anthropologists, who have more often bee
women, have looked at mothers and mothering, and n
one in more detail than Margaret Mead, but cultur
anthropology has frequently been the object of scorn an
ridicule by some other anthropologists who see cultura
anthropology as the 'soft' option. In many ways the spli
which has developed in anthropology itself expresses th
contrast between the social stereotypes of male and femal
characteristics in our own society. The male is represente
as hardheaded, enumerative and rational, the female sent
mental, emotional, irrational and intuitive. Evans Pritchar
wrote about Margaret Mead's *Coming of Age in Samoa*
a study contrasting the life of adolescent girls in Samo
with that of adolescent girls in the United States, as '
discursive, or perhaps I should say chatty and feminine
book', but went on to say: 'Nevertheless, it is . . . writte
by a highly intelligent woman'.[3] It is because of this mal
bias in anthropology, and not simply because the materi
is difficult for men to obtain, that there are vast area
of social interaction involving women which are il
recorded.

Nor do the writings of psychoanalysts and psychologist
provide a complete picture. They tend to look at pre
nancy and birth as abnormal conditions producing a
kinds of pathological psychic states, and at mothers largel
from the point of view of children and their needs. I

[1] E. E. Evans Pritchard, *The Nuer*, O.U.P 1940.
[2] New York, 1928.
[3] E. E. Evans Pritchard, *Social Anthropology*, Cohen & Wes
1951.

the psychoanalytic literature, from Freud on, there is heavy emphasis on the ways in which mothers can damage their children and lay the foundations for mal-adjusted adult personality by each word, action and thought.

The psychoanalytic frame of reference tends to include mothers only as individuals who act on the child for good or ill, as objects rather than subjects of study. They are allowed to enter on the unfolding drama of child development as evil witches, or even very occasionally as good fairies, but these are bit parts and it is the child who is at the centre of the stage.

This book intends to describe mothers from another angle. Mothers not only bear and, usually, rear children, nor exist to give men descendants, but are people in their own right. I have chosen this focus not only because I think it is interesting to explore the ways in which other women mother, but also because I hope that it will provide a bit of an antidote to the 'how to' books, of which I believe there are far too many.

It is terribly easy to tell people how they ought to have their babies and run their lives and bring up their children. To give advice seems such a simple, obvious thing to do when people are confused and muddled, especially when they are eager to be given a formula for success. In my work as a childbirth educator, preparing couples not only for labour but also to some extent, I hope, for parenthood and the birth of the family, I have learned that telling people how they ought to behave creates more problems than it solves and all too often means that they are un-able to adapt to challenges confronting them, because instead of flexibility they are armed with a series of magic formulae which they hope will work when the going gets difficult.

It is much more valuable to give people information and *self-confidence* so that they can make their own in-formed choices in terms of the reality they face. To do that it is also important to get to know yourself, be honest about your own feelings and start from inside awareness rather than external mechanical acts. This is as true for bathing a baby comfortably and being able to enjoy doing it as it is for breathing through contractions at the end of the first stage of labour, or facing the sense of uselessness and the longing which a mother may feel when her child goes off to the first long day at school leaving the house empty. It applies equally to all the varied and chaotic, frustrating, tantalizing, and satisfying experiences of bringing up a family and coping with the vivid kaleidoscope of changing relationships within it.

The more that is written about parenthood, the more mothers and fathers worry about whether they are bringing up their children in the 'right' way. Much of this burden falls on mothers. They usually spend most time with children and feel that the final responsibility of somehow producing a socially acceptable, happy and reasonably bright child falls on them. Mothers are always being told, either by direct advice, or by implication, how they might mother better, if only they set their minds to it and become more tolerant, consistent, loving, wise, and at the same time more genuinely spontaneous.

In a world of experts in which training for occupations is getting more complicated and prolonged and in which new specializations pop up like mushrooms almost overnight, motherhood stands out as glaringly unspecialized and unprofessional. Mothers are not trained to do their job, and that, it is implied, is why they fail. Train them and society will be improved.

The Swedish government, for example, is planning a nationwide system of education for parenthood, and a Swedish expert has even suggested that a woman should not be *allowed* to bear a child until she has attended the course. Such is our pathetic faith in training. Only teach people things and they will be better parents and produce a better quality product – the child.

There are two flaws in this argument, however. There is no evidence whatever to suggest that simply acquiring information about the tasks which mothers usually perform, like choosing a pram, changing nappies, selecting a suitable menu for a three year old or explaining how babies are made, actually makes a woman a better mother. On the contrary, intellectualizing about parenthood may make it all rather more difficult. The things that mothers really find themselves doing are not matters only of technique but are an expression of the sort of people they are and the relationship they have with that particular child, and since mothers are usually required to act on the spur of the moment there is not time to go and consult the books and see what one ought to be doing. Kissing hurt places better, watching a two and a half year old dress in agonizing slow motion, or deciding how to act when the eighteen month old wants nothing of the carefully planned protein and vitamin-rich menu and you are scraping watercress soup, liver, yoghourt and honey off the floor, sometimes involve very powerful feelings. These emotions are valid. I think that motherhood without emotions would be a very frightening thing, and if you have the positive ones – joy, triumph, ecstasy and so on – it is certain that you will also experience the negative ones – fear, depression and rage.

Parenthood is a bit like sex in that although it is amusing to try out novelties occasionally, too much reading about goals to be attained and techniques used can superimpose a set of gimmicks, and result in a strange dissatisfaction and even resentment. Real life mothering, like spontaneous sexuality, is too precious and subtly appropriate for analysis to intercept between the thought and action, or the glow of the relationship between mother and child to be organized according to a carefully conceived plan. The inherent rightness of much that people do in relationships, and that parents do in responding to a child, if they are in an environment which gives them

confidence and an opportunity to interact in a meaningful way, is only just now being discerned. Given a 'facilitating environment', that is, one that gives the *parents
themselves* emotional support and allows them to develop
confidence, most parents spontaneously enjoy their new
babies, for example, and handle and talk to them in a
manner which is tuned and synchronized in just the right
way to the baby's needs and to the non-verbal signals
which it is sending out.[4, 5] The sad thing is that our own
maternity hospitals rarely provide such a facilitating
environment.

Parent-child interaction can be studied and analysed,
of course. Such information is useful, and often fascinating, but it is not necessary to have read books about it
in order to be an adequate parent. Perhaps what is important is that experts inform rather than advise us, and
allow us as parents to make our own choices. But too
often professionals think they know the answers and seek
to impose a style of mothering which, of its essence, is
culture-bound, ephemeral, and reflects preoccupations
which are linked to fashions in child-rearing. Mothers
may be told, for example, that they must never leave
their small children lest they suffer irreparable damage
and are unable to form good relationships thereafter; or
the ethos of liberated womanhood may dictate that every
woman should work outside the home and that anyone
who does not do so will not be interesting and lively
enough to rear children satisfactorily. When lactation
is seen as the essence of mothering women are taught
that the baby who is not breast-fed is deprived and the
mother must have something wrong with her personality
if she doesn't want to breast-feed; and when 'gentle birth'
is the fashion that to greet a newborn baby with shouts

[4] Marshall H. Klaus and John H. Kennell *Maternal-infant Bonding*,
Mosby, St Louis, 1976.
[5] Rudolf Schaffer, *Mothering*, Fontana/Open Books, 1977.

of joy is to subject the child to a traumatic barrage of noise, or to cut the umbilical cord before it has stopped pulsating causes a frightening shock to the baby's system which may have effect long after it has become an adult. Since fashions are constantly changing, there are a great many women who worry that they have inflicted irreversible harm on their babies, and who feel guilty because of things they did at birth or during their children's infancy.

Put in this way, each of these theories may sound a bit one-sided. Yet in the seventies statements like these confuse and bewilder mothers who by nature of the wide variety of tasks in which they are engaged and the undervaluing of parenthood in our society, are already very unsure of what they 'should' be doing and whether they have the 'right' to do it, and who feel anxious and guilty.

Another reason why parents should be wary about the advice given in books on how to prevent children's emotional deprivation, how to ensure that you meet their psychological needs, or how to raise a more intelligent, better child than all the other, mismanaged, offspring of unenlightened families, is that experts focus on relatively restricted areas of behaviour, and no single expert is able, perhaps fortunately, to pronounce on the hazards and skills of child-rearing and relationships within the family in all their complexity. In fact we do not yet know enough even to be able to say with certainty that certain types of families are bound to produce certain types of children, and we certainly cannot assume that bowel and bladder training, for example, or swaddling or being free to explore in infancy, or carrying an infant round on the mother's back all the time, or sleeping in the parents' bed, act as blueprints for certain kinds of adult personality, although many claims have been made to this effect.

This is partly because it is not just a matter of a mother performing an action, such as suckling a baby for example, but also of how she *feels* about what she does. And whether or not she behaves in an easy, spontaneous and above all non-anxious manner may be a good deal more important than the system of child-rearing she adopts or the fact that she holds or does not hold the child, or even that she breast or bottle-feeds it.

Moreover, the minutiae of child-rearing practices in any society are a product of the total culture. They are interlaced with values which give that culture common themes and unity.

A great deal of what we take for granted as 'natural' in mothering is not natural at all, but a product of culture. It is only when we go back to the first moments and hours of life and the interaction of mother and baby which starts then that we are really at the level of the purely natural and instinctive. And that first meeting, as we shall see, is controlled by society in such a way that in many technologically orientated cultures the biological basis for the unfolding relationship is interfered with to such an extent that sometimes effective interaction between mother and neonate is made impossible. The two are strangers to each other. Natural processes have been blocked by cultural imperatives.

Values change and the culture of child-rearing changes too. We cannot alter styles of mothering without ultimately also changing the larger society and re-examining what it is to be male and female, what it is to be a child, the role of parents, and the significance of the family in that culture.

When women are urged to adopt deliberately certain styles of mothering another element is introduced into the relationship with their children, one of a goal which should be reached, a standard of which it is all too easy to fall short. This in itself can make mothering a self-conscious, joyless and even painful task in which a woman labours with the burden of her own inadequacy. A great many middle-class women who want to do the best for their children suffer under standards which other people have imposed on them, and look back on the way in which they have brought up their children feeling that they have failed them and have 'done everything wrong'.

Jean Liedloff went to work with a South American Indian tribe and was very impressed with their child-rearing practices. Children were not restrained and, as in many preliterate and peasant societies, remained close by their mothers in physical contact with them. A mother never thought of getting away from her child, and babies and toddlers were attached to the maternal body like limpets.

She believes that British mothers should behave in the same way.[6] One eminent paediatrician has picked up this theme and suggests that mothers should not put babies down, but should have them in baby carriers close to their bodies 24 hours of the day. I believe it is every baby's birthright to be close to its mother's body; but mothers sometimes need to get away from their babies. I am concerned that mothers may feel that they *ought* to keep their children close to them day and night, whatever they are doing, and may worry that they are inadequate mothers if they find this hard to do or if they do not enjoy it.

I question the value of taking any custom which is so much an integral part of a culture almost diametrically opposite to that of our modern urban society in the West and introducing it to women as yet one more goal of mothering which they ought to attain. What of the woman herself and *her* psychological needs? What of her own feelings of identity and value as something other than a mother? For many women such unbroken contact with their children might be anxiety-arousing, just as anxiety-arousing, perhaps, as similarly superimposed rules about *not* being with their children, *not* picking them up when

[6] *The Continuum Concept*, Futura, 1976.

they cry, *not* playing with them when they want to, or *not* taking a distressed child into one's bed at night.

The movement towards touching babies and having them close to you, and the whole search for greater physical contact with other human beings generally – as in encounter and sensitivity groups, for example – is probably a reaction to child-rearing customs which were at the height of popularity between-wars, which stressed the desirability of routine and of 'teaching' a baby from the very beginning that when it was put down it must stay put down, and that mothers could spoil their babies if they kissed and cuddled them and picked them up when they were unhappy. It is extraordinary how such views have persisted, long after most mothers have realized that they made the parents and rest of the family perhaps even more miserable than the baby, among members of the medical and nursing professions. In the total institution of the maternity hospital such dogmas take a long time dying, even when enlightened paediatricians and nurses plan new policies. There always seem to be some members of staff for whom freedom for mothers produces severe anxiety and just one or two people like that can destroy a whole liberal system.

Certainly most women going into hospital to have a baby can be pretty sure that however progressive the hospital there will be some people who will come between them and their babies, saying 'mothers need their rest' as they wheel the infant off to the nursery, or 'demand feeding means that you can feed any time between three and five hours after the last feed, but if you breast-feed more than that you're bound to get sore nipples' or 'if you take that child into bed with you you're making a rod for your back' or even 'you might fall asleep on it, and you wouldn't want to lose your baby, would you?'

It does not stop with hospital either. One of the great

things about being a new mother, especially of a first baby, is the amount of advice that pours in from all and sundry, people who have had children themselves and others who have not. It starts in pregnancy and carries on at least until children are of school age. Perhaps this is why mothers tend to 'compare the products' and to look anxiously at their own baby's weight, or skin condition, the number of teeth, or whether it is sitting up or crawling yet, feeling that this kind of thing can show whether they are a good-enough mother. In the past this comparison of babies' progress used to focus on weight gains. The fattest babies were the most admired. But now that we know that chubby babies tend to become chubby – and then fat – adults, the limelight is on development skills and intelligence. Is it better to thumb-suck or have a security blanket, or is a well-balanced child one who needs neither of these things? Or maybe thumb and blanket together are better than neither? The mother looks at her three year old in a tantrum, finding himself on the pavement in an orgy of rage, and feels acute shame at what she thinks must be evidence of her own failure in mothering.

Mothers of two year olds start teaching their babies to read and organize their own days round creative activities which develop the child's skills with special apparatus. It is, to say the least, exhausting, and because no one quite knows what the norm is all a mother can do is to strive to do better and better and not to miss out on providing her child with anything that any other child is getting.

This is a pattern of a certain kind of middle-class life-style. Women at the lower end of the socioeconomic scale are not so competitively involved with proving that they are adequate mothers, if only because their time and energy is taken up with getting and maintaining the more basic conditions of existence, and where rural community life is strong and childbearing customs are passed down from mother to daughter almost unchanged, as in peasant communities, the norms of mothering go unquestioned and women do not feel open to criticism, because they are doing more or less what every other woman in the same village is doing.

We cannot go back to that kind of lifestyle, because the whole context of family life has changed. The qualities our children need in order to survive in the twentieth-century world are not only those of learning the skills their father has in his workshop or on the farm, or imitating their mother's actions as she bakes bread or looks after the baby, but human qualities of adjusting without too great stress to the demands of a technological age and exploring and learning how to control a new and challenging environment. South American Indians may be perfectly adapted to their environment and African pygmies to theirs, but take them out of that environment or change it radically through culture clash by the introduction of industry and trade, and they will meet problems. I suspect that you cannot rear a child in London or Liverpool, or even Little Rollright, as if he or she were a South American Indian, without meeting new difficulties as the child grows to discover that the values of industrial society are rather different and that a peasant response is inappropriate even if only crossing a road in a big city and in a world where there is unemployment and competition for jobs.

Perhaps that is the most frightening thing of all for mothers: that the world in which they are bringing up their children is bound to be very different from the world in which the children have to live as adults. My father-in-law, who lived to see astronauts going to the moon, could remember as a young boy the excitement when the first railway linked Nuremberg with his home town of Furt. I myself am questioned by my children with something approaching amused condescension when I tell them that there are lots of interesting things to do besides watching

TV and that I remember seeing television for the first time as a child and how incredible it seemed to bring a live recording into people's sitting-rooms. I remember a discussion among the grown-ups about whether it would really 'catch on'.

But it is not only technological change, with all that that implies about change in lifestyles, but change in the nature of the relationships which bind people together in marriage, the way men's and women's roles are in process of rapid transformation. Some of these are intimately bound up with technological change. When I was a teenager sex meant possible babies, and the only reliable method of not getting pregnant was not having sex. Today sex and pregnancy are in two different categories and, largely because of the Pill and more effective contraceptives generally, one can plan for the first without the second, and is even encouraged to do so by a society deeply concerned about an overpopulated world. And when a woman does decide to have a baby she can probably fit conception, pregnancy and the early years of child-raising into a busy life in which she also has responsibilities to employers and a career. She may decide she does not need a man, and get on with motherhood alone, feeling that it is good to go to bed with a man and to have men friends but that does not necessarily mean that she wants to live with one all the time. If she shares her life with another woman they may decide to bring up children together, and a Lesbian mother may even choose to have artificial insemination.

I doubt whether the mothers of these young women had any idea of the way their daughters were going to live or thought of preparing them for a world in which male-female roles have altered so dramatically. There is not much point in teaching a girl how to cook when she is going to live with a deep freeze and a microwave oven, or to darn socks in a world of disposables or how to get a good husband if she does not want one, or how to keep one if she has other fish to fry! The *Telegraph* had an advertisement which announced something to the effect that 'Fashions change. Values don't'. Hence, read the *Telegraph*. But of course values do change, even though the fashion is just the bubble on the surface. Mothers are bringing up their children not only in a world of changing fashions but also of shifting values.

In spite of this it is extraordinary how the culture of child-rearing in our society has certain main themes which are major concerns of most, if not all, mothers. In any group of mothers of toddlers, conversation turns to potty training and food likes and dislikes and how to get the child to do things he or she doesn't really want to do. I. almost any group of mothers of teenagers discussion turns to teenage rebellion, drugs, sex, smoking, motorbikes and anxiety about their studies. Although we may differ in the way we deal with these concerns there is a universality of experience in mothering which is not so unlike that of a primitive society.

Perhaps the thing that constantly distinguishes most mothers from the rest of the world is the *quality of caring*. It starts with the anxiety which accompanies the plunge into motherhood which quite naturally occurs in the first 4–6 post-partum weeks, when the new mother is in a mental state which if it existed in anyone else we should consider bordering on the psychotic. She listens to her baby's breathing; she is roused from heavy sleep by its first cry; 24 hours of the day she is tuned in to her baby and its needs. Winnicott called it 'primary maternal preoccupation'. It is a transitional state, but nevertheless many elements of it persist right through motherhood – a kind of inner listening to the other person; perhaps the closest you can get to feeling intensely the hurt, fear and pain of another, and the hope and joy too; and the surrender of self to the needs of another. There are biological reasons for this kind of adaptation, because only thus can the young be safely nurtured. But biology apart, it leads to a relationship with them, which overlaps with the maternal role, increasingly so in our own society, but is nevertheless distinct from it.

In a world of change and shifting values maybe it is this which is the most valuable thing that anyone can give to a child. Even though a mother has done everything else 'wrong', if she has this kind of relationship with her child as he or she grows up she has probably provided the best basis for the development of adult personality and for the young person's own capacity for giving and receiving love. Martin Buber epitomized the optimum relationship between mother and child when he described the relation between I and 'Thou' rather than I and 'It', the awareness of the other in his or her own identity and reality, rather than the use of the other as an object for one's own satisfaction or as a tool to achieve one's own ends. Perhaps this is what mothering in the second half of the twentieth century is all about.

2

The Motherhood Trap

The unhappy mother, trapped within the four walls of home, anxious, depressed, or desperate, is a stock figure of the contemporary TV film and the novel. Do women find motherhood a matter of anguish, or satisfaction, or perhaps both? In this chapter I should like to look at the realities of the situation, see what motherhood is like for many women, and focus on some of the problems and challenges inherent in mothering in today's society.

For women are not only less well prepared for motherhood than were their own mothers and grandmothers, but they are also less well prepared in the West than in many pre-industrial societies which live much closer to survival level and which do not possess the elaborate and sophisticated technology of advanced industrial societies. Not only are they less aware of the reality of motherhood and what a baby is like, but they are less inclined to resign themselves dutifully to the inevitable when they discover that their fantasies have deceived them or that they have been presented with a picture far removed from the facts. Part of the problem is that we have far too little education for parenthood, for either expectant mother or father, but this is not just a question of classes in the weeks before the baby comes. To be effective, preparation for the major life crisis of becoming a parent has to take place both in adolescence, as part of learning about adult roles, and even earlier, in the prospective parents' own childhood. For many of today's mothers parenthood, however welcome, comes as a surprise.

For large sections of the educated middle class a woman is already caught up in a conflict when she has to come to a decision whether or not to come off the Pill, or to cease using whatever contraceptive method she has selected. Motherhood is no longer the inevitable and necessary sequel of marriage, whatever pressure the young couple may be under from their parents. The woman often feels caught in cross currents of pressure from co-workers and peers to continue in her job, to improve the standard of living, to enjoy holidays together and to feel free, and pressure from her own and her husband's parents, to 'settle down and have a baby'. In interviews with couples during pregnancy this subject is often discussed in answer to a question from me as to whether the baby was planned, unplanned, or half-planned. Few middle-class couples today will say that the pregnancy was unplanned, although they often hesitate between the 'planned' and 'half-planned', and they say, 'Well, planned, but . . .' We then explore together some of the conflicting feelings which both partners may have about the pregnancy, and the way in which these relate to the social context of their living, their jobs, families, friends and lifestyle.

An increasing number of couples are also deeply concerned that they are contributing to the world population crisis, and feel guilty about indulging in the luxury of having a baby. For the first time in history motherhood is considered anti-social. Car stickers in the United States proclaim: 'POLLUTION IS YOUR baby'. Fertility is seen — quite rightly — as a major world problem. Educated women even in their first pregnancies may feel guilty that they are being selfish and are denying the ideals for which they struggled, an essential tenet of which was that ours is an overpopulated world, and that if we are to feed the hungry we must stop having babies. The woman who is enjoying pregnancy and motherhood and who wants another baby may be accused of being 'pro-natalist', especially if she has exceeded her quota of two. She feels that she is being punished for being female.

The message is that if a woman is socially aware she rations herself to one or two children, and if she has any sense she probably decides against having *them*, because only if she does not have children can she really enjoy life and have a good relationship with her mate. However delighted she is personally, and however pleased her husband and mother are, the social context of childbearing has become negative and rejecting.

One result is that some educated women are becoming shamefaced and positively apologetic about becoming pregnant, as if it were a private indulgence to which they had no right. They approach birth and the initial tasks of motherhood in a businesslike spirit, determined to do it well, but concerned to get back to the real challenges of living after a few years, months, or sometimes weeks. Childbearing is an interruption of their 'real' lives. And because they intend to have only one or two babies these women may feel that it is very important that they perform perfectly. Consequently they read books about every aspect of birth and child-rearing to ensure that they bear and bring up a secure, emotionally balanced, highly intelligent, creative, human being, who can fully justify its existence in the world. This is demanding a great deal of mothers, and because the child then becomes the object of rearing and educational practices rather than a person in its own right, it is also very hard on children.

It has also the effect of removing childbirth from the normal life process, the changes and crises that occur as a matter of course in the lives of the majority of women, and turning it into a clinical condition, a pathological event, like an appendectomy or having an impacted wisdom tooth removed.

Even when couples feel that it is wrong to bring children into an already overpopulated world, they may not want to miss out on an important life experience, and are intrigued by the developing relationship with their partner and the effect which having a baby may have on it. Others again feel unsatisfied in their occupations and seek satisfaction in childbearing, hoping that they will be more successful in mothering than they have been in their jobs. Some feel personally deprived until they can have a baby, associated with a sense of lack of love from and being needed by the partner: A baby will need me. There are numerous other unconscious factors which play a part – the woman's relationship with her own mother and her desire to show her that she, too, has not only a right to take on the same role, but can do it equally well or better, or the woman's relationship with both parents and an impulse to prove to them through having a baby that she is grown up now. But today justification must be found for using one's fertility. Although for some contraceptive failure, accidental or half intended, (such as 'forgetting' the Pill) overrides the need for coming to a decision, for many couples today having a baby is a subject which entails difficult joint decision-making.

Already in the pregnancy the middle-class woman starts to seek the help of 'experts' so as to be able to fill the role of the mother. She reads books and magazine articles about babies and tries to find information on subjects which in a pre-industrial society were handed down from mothers to daughters. She is in a better position to do this, to ask the questions, and to know where to find the answers, than is the woman of lower socioeconomic class, who depends more on advice from kin and neighbours. The verbalization which Bernstein[1] and the Newsons[2]

[1] B. Bernstein, 'Theoretical studies towards a sociology of language', in *Class, Codes and Control*, Vol. I, Routledge, 1971; and 'Applied studies towards a sociology of language', in *Class, Codes and Control*, ed. Bernstein, Vol. 2, Routledge, 1973.

[2] J. and E. Newson, *Infant Care in an Urban Community*, Allen and Unwin, 1963; and *Four Year Olds in an Urban Community*, Allen and Unwin, 1968.

stressed as an important part of the middle-class woman's role in relation to her child and as a primary instrument of child-rearing is already taking place in pregnancy. She expresses her goals in mothering the new baby, and often contrasts them with methods used by her own mother or by other women who have adopted a style of mothering which is going out of fashion.

She often finds it difficult to get the information she is seeking from health care professionals, to whom she spontaneously turns because they are available in the antenatal clinic, and says they are 'too rushed', that it is 'just like a conveyor belt', 'the doctor seems so busy I don't like to bother him', 'I went in there with a lot of questions but when they had finished doing all the examinations I couldn't remember one of them', 'I wanted to ask him a whole host of things but lying with my bottom half bare and my legs up in stirrups I just couldn't', or even 'I don't think they are interested in anything except my uterus'.

During the pregnancy the relationship between husband and wife is affected by her 'tuning in' to the developing fetus inside her, and increasing awareness of and pre-occupation with it, so that the husband is sharing her with the as yet unseen baby. For some men this diversion of attention is threatening and the fetus is an invisible rival. The sexual relationship may be adversely affected by pregnancy, either as a result of an emotional withdrawal from genital sex, or of a taboo frequently medically enforce or self-imposed in intercourse in the last few weeks and in the immediate post-partum weeks and occasionally for much longer (especially if there has been difficulty in conceiving or in holding on to the pregnancy). These changed sexual attitudes can lead to a deterioration of the marriage relation.

Once the baby is born and the first few weeks of emotional support and assistance are over (and this is often severely curtailed) the mother is left coping with the

child more or less unsupported, and holds complete
responsibility for its welfare and development at a time
when she has little confidence in herself. Although the
father often helps when he is at home and may enjoy
playing with the baby for limited periods, it is she who
is accountable for everything that occurs to the baby.
She frequently finds herself living in an unfamiliar community to which they have moved on marriage, or shortly
before or after the birth, with nobody to reassure her
that she is doing the right thing, that her baby is normal,
or that she has feelings about the child and her relations
with it which other new mothers share. She is often
physically isolated and immobile, tied to the home in a
way in which she never has been before. She may be
deprived of adult company for six to eight hours a day,[3, 4]
unless she has the energy, initiative and confidence to go
out and seek social contacts, and the effects of concentrated baby care are such that she may be occupied
with the tasks of cleaning, washing, bathing and feeding
for more than ten hours a day. Even when she has put
the baby down she often starts to worry about the next
waking bout and how she will act then, and begins preparations for it. Feeding the baby alone often takes five
hours out of the twenty-four, and sometimes considerably longer. Although some babies finish a feed in half an
hour, they need six of these at least in the twenty-four
hours, and a good many take twice as long and many
demand eight feeds at shorter intervals. The sense of time
is affected, and especially if the baby is restless and
'colicky', days and nights unroll in a seemingly endless
undifferentiated ribbon of service to the baby, with no
respite, and no breathing space in which the mother feels

[3] Alice S. Rossi, 'Transition to Parenthood', *J. of Marriage and the Family*, 30, 1968.
[4] Arlene S. and Jerome H. Skolnick, editors, *Family in Transition: rethinking marriage, sexuality, child-rearing and family organiza-tion*, Little, Brown, Boston, 1971.

W.A.M. — B

she can catch up.

Helene Lopata[5] has pointed out that school and work teach the young woman to be 'task oriented, to measure accomplishments in terms of a finished product, and to organize it in blocks of time within a specialized division of labour'. 'The care of infants and socialization of children are, however, highly emotional processes . . . and there is no perfect procedure for them'. Moreover as the child grows it requires different things from its mother, and this means that she can never perfect her techniques, but must remain flexible and capable of adapting to a changed situation. In our isolated families the mother is the person who is supposed to introduce the world to the child, and communicate to it its cultural heritage, when she is herself sealed off from participating in the world outside the home and in sharing creatively in the culture. As the child grows out of babyhood she is required to be an agent of acculturation. This is one reason why the woman who may feel she can cope quite well with a new baby finds herself unable to handle a toddler, why the one who enjoys the activity of the toddler may have felt inadequate when the same child was still a small baby, and why many mothers feel themselves quite unable to handle the problems of adolescence with understanding and remain on an emotional even keel.

The dynamic nature of mothering can itself make some women feel very insecure. If there was a task they could anticipate, learn about, and then perform and see the finished product, they would feel easier about it. But mothering is not like that.

While the woman is meeting the challenges of mothering, her relationship with her husband is changing in subtle ways at a time when he is likely to be very involved with his work outside the house, and when he feels the burden of added financial responsibilities. They

[5] Helene Z. Lopata, *Occupation: Housewife*, OUP, New York, 1971.

each act out their versions of motherhood and fatherhood, and look to the other to match their performance by dovetailing with it in a smooth and harmonious way. But their ideas about what a mother and father are have been derived largely from the family of procreation from which each came. Often their pictures of the roles which the other ought to be playing are discordant with the other's role image.

The woman is also having to come to terms with her body, which has been changing dramatically and rapidly over a short period of time, first of all swelling and becoming heavier and inhabited by another life during pregnancy, and then giving birth, with all that this entails. Subsequently she is confronted with a leaking, soft maternal body, empty of the baby, but not the body with which she was familiar before the pregnancy and which she felt as uniquely her own. This is the basis of her concern, which usually starts in pregnancy, as to when she can get back to 'normal'. The return to normality also concerns life patterns generally. Childbearing is seen as an interruption. 'Children are viewed as a temporary constriction preventing desired experiences'.[6]

There are great contrasts between this experience and that which the new mother passes through and her self-image in a pre-industrial society. Information she may need about the changes involved in having a baby is there built in to her personal life experience, and she is the centre of a group of women all of whom are concerned to ensure that everything goes as it should and that no harm should befall either mother or child. Far from seeking a return to normal, she knows that by having a child she has raised her social status in her community and is now on an equal footing with other matrons. Child-rearing is not an interval in her life but its *raison d'être*.

[6] Lopata, op. cit.

In the West, before the first baby comes many women have had the freedom of being able to fill multidimensional roles in a range of social settings, experimenting and playing with how they feel in each. Their jobs, leisure occupations and social contacts all provide opportunities for making choices about what to do, where to go, how to be. But with the birth of a baby suddenly a woman finds she is fixed in one role, that of a mother, and there is little choice left because of the infant's unremitting demands on her. Komarovsky[7] believes that this is a crisis similar to that of retirement for men. This may be why so many women worry that they are turning into 'a vegetable', for in contrast to their life styles before motherhood they are both socially isolated and cut off from the intellectual stimulation they were accustomed to before.

Frequently too the woman finds that she is restricted to one place for the first time in her life, and that a relatively small one. There is no opportunity to 'pop out to the shops', to see an art exhibition, to go for a swim, and even if she makes the elaborate planning necessary to go to the library or to visit a friend across the town, she cannot be sure that it will be possible because of the lack of any 'routine' in the first weeks of the baby's life. In England the large and frequently ostentatious pram, often given by the woman's mother, is one of the impedimenta which contributes to this restriction to a limited place. Those couples who adopt equipment which allows for mobility with a small baby, such as folding carrycots and baby carriers, are in a much better position to attain an – albeit still curtailed – mobility.

The tasks which caring for a baby involve are repetitive. There is regular washing and cleaning up to be done, and the removal of waste matter in one form or another from the baby is a chore which is repeated six to ten times a day. Eyes may get 'sticky', the nose get 'snuffly', the scalp develops 'cradle cap' which has to be treated with ointments, regurgitated milk dribbles down the baby's clean clothing and also spurts on to the mother's dress. The nappies must be scraped of faeces, soaked, washed, rinsed thoroughly, dried, aired, folded, and even if they are disposed of down the lavatory, there is the massive problem of unblocking the drains, with all that that entails in stress for the husband-wife relationship. The mother can soon feel that she is on a treadmill.

In the middle of these tiring and apparently endless tasks she may catch sight of herself in a mirror and be appalled at what she sees, an exhausted and anxious mother, who has 'let herself go'. Her mother or mother-in-law is expected and she looks at the home which the couple are still furnishing and decorating together, and is appalled at the chaos she sees there, too. She has not had time to clean up and there are piles of dishes in the sink, a stain from a dirty nappy on the new carpet, all the bedding smells of milk, the oven is saturated with grease because he has been doing the cooking and only knows how to do steak, she forgot to put the dustbins out to be emptied so there is a pile of rotting refuse by the back door, and thick layers of dust sit over the furniture. She starts to cry and is told that this is because of her 'un-balanced endocrine system'. There is so little social recognition of what is actually involved in the fatiguing task of being a mother that women are usually made to explain their post-partum experience entirely in terms of internal states, their hormones, their psyches and their own inadequate personalities, instead of the realities of the situation as they adjust to the new occupational and emotional tasks of motherhood, tasks which are challenging for every woman, however experienced in housekeeping or nursing she was previously, and however 'balanced' and placid she may be.

The Health Visitor calls, neat, efficient, calm and caring, often at the worst possible time. The mother shows her into the sitting-room, and is immediately apologetic, because she is a 'visitor'. I very much doubt whether it is *visitors* the new mother needs, even expert ones. She would benefit greatly from a helper who would roll up her sleeves to clean the house, cook some food, and let mother and baby lie in bed together, like the trained maternity assistants in the Netherlands. In the United States and Britain, however, if the mother is not coping she tends to be given mere advice together with pharmacological assistance in the form of tranquillizers.

Maternal roles have to be 'service-oriented'. According to Lopata[8] the American marriage ideal focuses on 'relational and sentimental features', that is, it has to do with warmth of feeling and the quality of the relationship. But in fact more and more ideals about the maternal role also have to do with these relational and sentimental features and this in itself makes motherhood a more complicated task. A mother 'should' feel constant love for her baby. She should feel a protective tenderness under all circumstances and at all times. She should be able to understand her baby and respond to its needs appropriately. Her mothering skills should be able to stop it crying instantly and keep it contented. As these relational aspects of mothering become increasingly emphasized, the service aspects can seem even more irrelevant and tedious. The mother who does not organize her day (which must, of course, be round the baby), plan ahead (allowing for flexible adaptation to circumstances), rest when she has the chance because the baby is sleeping, get food into the house in advance, do essential chores early in the day, but is enveloped in her concern to achieve a good relationship with her baby, is the one who may be most likely to feel so completely sucked into

[8] Lopata, op. cit.

serving the infant's needs that she feels 'drained' (an appropriate image, associated with feeding problems), becomes resentful, as a result feels guilty, over-compensates by sacrificing herself to the baby still further and by watching it for every sign of discomfort or deviation from the normal, and then becomes more exhausted, anxious and depressed. This is one of the problems resulting from the highly self-conscious mothering which is typical of urban middle-class culture.

Patricia Morgan, aggressive critic of what she sees as 'the dreamy love relationship with a baby . . . in the childcare books, and in every woman's magazine and babyfood advertisement',[9] as well as of my own approach to birth and parenthood,[10] says, quite rightly, that

> . . . breast-feeding, toilet-training, cuddles and play . . . have been moved by the heirs of Freud to the very centre of civilization's hopes and aspirations. A mother must have the incalculably delicate skills of a psychological surgeon whose smallest slip could have untold consequences: by comparison with the awful responsibilities falling to a mother of children in their First Five Years, those of directors or cabinet ministers can be regarded as small beer.[9]

The very insistence upon a 'good mother-child relationship' can itself make such a relationship harder to achieve, and I suspect that some of the best relationships have emerged when the mother, happy in herself, has simply 'got on with it', as the peasant mother of necessity always had to.

In our society the new father is often in a difficult situation too. He is expected to be 'interested' in the

[9] Patricia Morgan, *Child Care: Sense and Fable*, Temple Smith, 1975.
[10] Sheila Kitzinger. *The Experience of Childbirth*, Penguin, 4th ed., 1978.

baby, and to help his wife, but has no preparation for this, and is even less likely than the woman to have had any previous experience. He often feels extraneous to the mother-child relationship, even rejected. The emotional umbilical cord linking the mother to her baby in the first six or eight weeks may worry or irritate him. He sees that all his wife's time, energy and concentration of purpose are being spent on the baby, and is often anxious lest she become worn out, and in effect, be unable to be the wife to whom he is accustomed. He may therefore be the first to respond with alacrity to every bit of confusing advice that floods in about how to get the baby to sleep longer, put on weight faster, cease crying, lose its rash, and 'go through the night'. When none of it works he tends to withdraw to work outside the home, and the wife is often left to seek solutions either in a circle of female helpers, or quite alone. Either way, the interaction between husband and wife is profoundly affected.

In peasant societies the husband's role is much more clearly defined, and he leaves most matters to the group of women who are waiting and surrounding the mother even before the baby's birth. Since male and female roles tend to be strictly differentiated anyway, the wife tending the home and the husband responsible for the farm, for instance, the birth of a baby provides a new link between previously disparate worlds.

Because the style of mothering is an expression of the culture, and embodies a value system relating both to what a woman is and also what a child is, attitudes to motherhood vary between social classes. In a study done in Chicago[11] it emerged that the least educated women were the most likely to say that they had no child-rearing problems: 'you know what you have to do and get on with it', and if they mentioned difficulties, limited them to those connected with running the house. 'Life is a round

11 Lopata, op. cit.

The Motherhood Trap   41

of work met without surprise'.

Women who had a high school education, but had not continued with their education beyond this, assessed themselves as powerless to keep their children obedient and happy. They also tended to be deeply resentful of males and their world was peopled by threatening strangers. These women were 'single dimensional' in their interests, home-bound, and often listed problems connected with money, disciplining children, children fighting and quarrelling, and the noise they made. The impression was that above all the mother was seeking to control her offspring. They were always messing up things she had just straightened out and dirtying things she had just cleaned. Such a mother is product-orientated, wishing simply for clean, quiet, and well-behaved children and a clean, neat house; so she finds it irritating that these conditions are not present for more than a few fleeting moments. She often speaks of patience but projects an aura of irritation.

Women who have been to college are much more likely to be 'relation-oriented', to worry whether they are good mothers and be concerned about emotional and creative responsibilities, and anxious that they are not realizing the full potential of the role of mother. They are not worried about daily routines or technical aspects of mothering and feel fairly competent to deal with problems of discipline, but they are concerned to develop the child's abilities to the full.

In this same study women who identified their backgrounds as Jewish in the descriptions of 'the ideal housewife' emphasized qualities of 'warmth, loving and being loved, and being respected in the community', and less educated Jewish women stressed a willingness to do menial jobs, 'giving more than receiving' and 'not complaining', sometimes almost to the point of martyrdom. Catholic women were quite different in their approach, and emphasized the duties of the woman to keep her house clean and orderly, and the children under control, rather than seeing the mother as the centre of a network of relations. They tended to mention tasks and end products, and to be oriented towards actions rather than states of mind. All these women encountered problems in being a mother but they defined them in different terms, according to their own educational and cultural backgrounds, and were really aiming at producing different kinds of people.

Following the initial accumulation of goods, the rearing of two or at most three children has become the modern family's main function. This is very different from the family operating as an economic unit as it did in the eighteenth century, when in the rural family all hands were put to work, young and old, and the survival of the family depended on the labours of all its members. Now the primary task of the parents is to concentrate on successfully bringing up their children.

> The child-rearing function of the family has given rise to the notion that the family is nothing more nor less than a vehicle of love and nurturance – a tiny enclave of loving and caring in a sea of materialism. What is forgotten is that the old, like children, also need loving care and attention . . . Where once the family was a defensive unit, with the able-bodied men and women working to support the dependent young, old and sick, it is now a unit wholly concerned with consumption and reproduction.[12]

If the home is supposed to be a haven of love and good feelings it comes as a great disappointment to many that this proves not to be so for them, for it is somewhere where the ugliest and most powerful destructive emo-

---

[12] Lee Comer, 'Functions of the Family', in *Conditions of Illusion*, op. cit.

The Motherhood Trap 43

tions are experienced, where there is disturbing interpersonal conflict at its most primitive level, and inside the
four walls of which these raw feelings are concentrated
and mixed together as if in a pressure cooker.

A woman wants to be a good mother and aims at giving herself to her children selflessly, providing them with
concentrated attention, generous care, a lively mind quick
to offer stimulus of an appropriate kind, perfectly balanced
and delicious meals, unlimited time, and unstinted love —
just as all the magazines and books say. But the con-
structive play turns into a litter of cardboard boxes all
over the kitchen, tacky flour and water paste in the coconut matting, and finger paints on the curtains. The carefully prepared food is rejected with noises of disgust from
the older child and is simply expelled from the baby's
mouth in a great glob of goo. By late afternoon she still
has not finished the jobs she planned on getting out of the
way in the morning, there is nothing to eat for the evening
meal and the baby has nappy rash because she has not had
time to change him often enough. She pushes the pro-
testing children in a pram and wheels them to the supermarket, where the older one helps by stocking up the
basket with all the things she does not want to buy, while
the younger one sweeps tins from their shelves. In the
end she slaps the baby's hand and gets a long, cool look
from an older woman who clearly thinks she is a baby
batterer. She hates what she has become and scuttles
back home, with both children whining. She gets more
food into them and propels them to the bath, where
they play happily and look cherubic and adorable. She re-
laxes for a moment, only to realize that the new game
is squeezing the sponge over the edge of the bath and
streams of water are running under the vinyl. She bends
to mop it up with the bath towel. She hears a sound at
the front door, sweeps back her hair from her face, and
in comes her husband saying cheerfully, 'Had a good day,
darling?' or worse, 'I'm ravenous. What's for supper?' or

worse still, 'I've got a bit of a headache. It's been a rotten day at the office.'

The extraordinary thing is that after trying to perform a task of these dimensions she feels uniquely a failure, convinced that she is the only woman experiencing these emotions and the only one incapable of coping. One in every six women receives psychiatric treatment for emotional disturbance at some time in her life. The high degree of minor neurosis and subclinical depression experienced by women may point to something about the role of women in modern society which produces emotional dissonance for many, and complete breakdown for some. It is possible that women may always have been this unhappy, and that it is simply increased skills in diagnosis and recognition of when help is needed that adds to the figures of those who are diagnosed as mentally ill. But if so, the fact that the conditions from which many women suffer are perceived as abnormal and as involving misery is part of an altered definition of mental conditions seen as requiring treatment, and is evidence of a change in the value system concerning sickness and health. Society cannot afford to ignore the 'cries for help' which are often expressed in the clinic visits with a request for 'something to make me sleep' or 'to help my nerves, doctor'. The busy doctor with only two minutes to spare hands out prescriptions for tranquillizers and hopes that with a pharmacological boost the phase of despair will pass.

The phase of motherhood spent with babies is not, of course, the only stressful period. Later phases in child-rearing may produce even more difficulties. Jessie Bernard,[13] describing 'low points in the natural history of parenthood' which, because motherhood does not function in a vacuum, produce great stress on the marriage, defines one of them as the whole period when the children

[13] Jessie Bernard, *The Future of Marriage*, Souvenir Press, 1972.

are at school. She discovered that children from six to fourteen 'have an especially distressing effect on the marriage . . . positive companionship is reported at its lowest level', and the mother especially feels frustrated in whatever she tries to do. Then there is the awful phase when the children become teenagers and the parents are acutely dissatisfied with the young people they have reared, and ask themselves, 'Where have we gone wrong?' Parent-child conflict exacerbates pre-existing irritants in the husband-wife relationship. The children expose their parents too, if they are delinquent and become tangled with the law, often in a public and humiliating way. The husband and wife tend to blame each other for failures in child-rearing, and this can become a major source of discord.

Following on this are the late teens and early twenties. Young unmarried sons and daughters, warns Bernard[14], can be devastating to a marriage: 'The extrusion of young adults from the family may perform a benign function for the marriages of their parents – as well, of course, as the young people themselves'.[15]

Throughout all this in contemporary Western society, husband and wife can play an elaborate game with each other over the distribution of responsibilities and the work that each does to keep the home running, a game which can turn into open warfare when they are committed to adopting shared role patterns because the woman is also working outside the home. Men have developed superior skills of gamesmanship in this particular dialogue:

'I don't mind sharing the housework, but I don't do it very well. We should each do the things we're best at.'
MEANING: Unfortunately I'm no good at things like

[14] *ibid.*
[15] Jessie Bernard, op. cit.

washing dishes or cooking. What I do best is a little light carpentry, changing light bulbs, moving furniture . . . ALSO MEANING: Historically, the lower classes . . . have had hundreds of years experience doing menial jobs. It would be a waste of manpower to train someone else to do them now. ALSO MEANING: I don't like the dull stupid boring jobs, so you should do them.

'I don't mind sharing the work, but you'll have to show me how to do it.' MEANING: I ask a lot of questions and you'll have to show me everything every time I do it . . . Also don't try to sit down and read while I'm doing my jobs because I'm going to annoy hell out of you until it's easier to do them yourself.[16]

And so on.

There is never any point at which parents can sit down and feel they have finished the tasks they have taken on, and never one at which they know they have succeeded. The only effective technique is that of being able to shift quickly in response to new challenges. Inherent in each of these challenges is an image that each has of the other as a good, adequate or bad husband and father and mother and wife. Caught in this quandary either parent may come to feel imprisoned in relationships which bind and frustrate them. But the man can escape from the home and can more easily see himself as a person in wider social relations and in his career. The woman at home with children, holding sole responsibility for their day-to-day welfare, or in conflict with adolescent sons and daughters, cannot break free in this way. Motherhood seems to have become a trap.

But it can be a trap in another way too, and this largely because of the emphasis which is put nowadays

[16] Pat Mainardi, 'The Politics of Housework', in *Sisterhood is Powerful*, edited Robin Morgan, Vintage, New York, 1970.

on self-expression, self-development, and self-fulfilment. A mother who enjoys being with her children and caring for them, and is content to centre on them for a certain phase of her life, can come to feel ashamed that she is not doing things outside the home, and is 'just a mother'. She is made to feel that she is engaged in a second-rate occupation which no intelligent, up-to-date woman could possibly endure for more than a few hours. We have already seen that there is a modern ethos which down-grades motherhood and child-rearing. It is the same atti-tude which attributes to those women who find mother-hood satisfying a mindless, sentimental form of idiocy. It is even implied that these mothers are somehow not living in the *real* world, the world of action, and the cut and thrust of exciting living that is going on without them. The arguments sound convincing and are ex-pressed so strongly that many women come to believe them themselves. It is only when they return to the office or to the schoolroom that they realize that, after all, be-ing a mother was a deeply enriching experience and taught them a great deal.

In the women's movement there is ambiguity in the approach to motherhood. It represents for some a bio-logical trap associated with the outmoded stereotype of woman as breeder and a method of ensuring her servi-tude in the home, and for others an opportunity for achieving something which a man manifestly cannot do, however hard he tries. There are on the one hand those who actually enjoy birth, breast-feeding and other aspects of biological motherhood, and on the other those who see them as traitors to the whole movement. But which-ever position they adopt they are seeking a more realistic view of the family, and are scraping away the varnish of what they believe is a 'Sunday supplement dream' held up to women as a model which leaves each one feel-ing that she cannot cope as well as all the others. This is not simply a private neurosis, they say, but an inevitable consequence of society as at present organized. They question the relevance of the more or less isolated nuclear family, at any rate in its present guise, to contemporary needs, particularly those of women, and seek alternative ways of living and working together. Some have gone further than that and have proclaimed open warfare on it, living in simmering hostility to the men who share their lives or whom they encounter at work.

One women's group used to meet regularly at a pub, but insisted that their mates, who supported their aims, waited outside in the street, whatever the weather, till they had finished, and not surprisingly after a time lost male support. Another group ran a crèche for its members, but some of them became incensed when boy babies were brought to it, and there was a power struggle between those who saw themselves as the only true champions of women's rights and the others who were simply seeking day care for their babies, whatever their sex.

These represent extreme views, but they do not affect the fundamental message of what the women are saying: 'It is up to women to stop rocking the cradle and start rocking the boat. We cannot any longer accept our passive role'.[17]

Some feminists who have families seek escape from the motherhood role by concentrating entirely on work roles and avoiding close and emotional contact with their children. Although this is possible for a man 'the constraints of conventional roles . . . have meant that similarly emotionally impoverished mothers have had maximal impact on their young'.[18] Perhaps the only solution is to ex-

[17] Michelene Wandor, in *Conditions of Illusion*, edited by Sandra Allen, Lee Sanders and Jan Wallis, Feminist Books, 1974.
[18] Alice S. Rossi, 'Maternalism, Sexuality and the New Feminism', in *Contemporary Sexual Behaviour: Critical Issues in the 1970's*, edited Joseph Zubin and John Money. John Hopkins University Press, 1973.

plore a wide range of maternal styles and to develop
social institutions which can accommodate them without
resulting in emotional deprivation of children.

There is no single tram-line to liberation for mothers,
and in different parts of the world needs have to be
assessed in the context of the existing social system.
From one point of view the introduction of machinery,
although it looked as if it were going to free women
from domestic servitude, has meant that a new treadmill
has been created by women themselves. They now try
to run the home and rear the children unaided while
doing jobs outside the home too, and their working
hours at these two jobs are much longer than a man's
working day. In the United States at present one out of
every two married women living with their husbands
work outside the home. The full-time woman worker,
however, earns about half that of the full-time male
worker. Women seem, in fact, to be getting the worst of
both worlds, and are neither getting full recognition in
their jobs nor are able to enjoy being full-time mothers.

Perhaps this is one reason why women are now examining their own roles as wives, mothers and workers outside the home with a new acuity and are beginning to see
exactly what the pay-off is. Motherhood has had a bad
press for too long, and a woman who seeks escape from
the drudgery of her home may find that there is equal
and perhaps less rewarding drudgery outside it.

Women are reaching out to help others approach
motherhood realistically and to be *people* as well as
mothers. There is an increased self-awareness among
women in general, but it is not enough. This new role
perception means that men must rethink their roles too,
and become not only providers but child-rearers alongside
women. The birth of a baby provides opportunities for
discovering new aspects of themselves, taking on responsibilities, and sharing in the growth of a family, for
both the woman and the man. Parenthood can be a

biological trap. But it can also be an education.

We have only to look at the different manifestations of the motherhood role in other cultures to realize that mothering is also a multidimensional activity. There is no formula applicable to all women which can ensure that it is a satisfying one.

3

Mothers in the Social System

Every society regulates the right to motherhood and in a way 'selects' those women who can become mothers. Even in those cultures which permit the free expression of sex among adolescent boys and girls, the right to bear a child is strictly controlled, and transgression of the rules may result in severe punishment, and the baby and mother, and sometimes both parents, may be put to death.

The dances and rituals of primitive societies and of ancient civilizations are not primarily an expression of the power of sex, but of *fertility*. In such cultures young girls learn from an early age that pregnancy is fruition and that they will become more, not less, beautiful when pregnant. The same goes for peasant cultures too. When I was doing field work in Jamaica an appropriate greeting to a woman from the public health nurse or midwife as she moved about the community was 'You be getting fat!' – meaning 'Maybe you're pregnant', or to a teenage girl, 'When you coming to clinic?' (the antenatal clinic). Both remarks caused great delight and smiles all round. It is very different from current attitudes in our own society, where women may find it difficult to come to terms with their changing bodies. As one ex-Playboy Bunny put it, 'I feel like a great hippopotamus wallowing in the mud.'

A Sanskrit poem describes a girl's loveliness as enhanced in pregnancy:

> The *romavali*'s thick stem supports a pair of
> lotuses, her close-set breasts, on which sit
> bees, the darkening nipples. These
> flowers tell of treasures hidden in
> my darling's belly.[1]

The songs that are chanted, the drums beating in rhythm, the rocking pelvises and undulating bodies, proclaim birth and renewal, of the crops that grow, the fish, herds of cattle, and wild animals brought in from the hunt, no less than of human birth.

We do not acknowledge our need for plants to sprout, trees to give fruit, animals to bear young, because most of us are so far removed from the soil and the farmyard that we expect these things to happen automatically. Our own fertility rite – incorporated into the drama of the Christian church as the harvest festival – has little relevance for most of us. Our food comes prepacked and often precooked, with a guarantee that it is identical to every other package of that kind produced by that particular manufacturer. And as for human fertility, that has become an inconvenience. Childbirth has become a clinical and potentially pathological condition which must take place in a hospital, rather than in the marriage bed over which the rice bestowing fertility on the couple was strewn on the wedding night.

In our own culture sex is the experience which launches a girl into womanhood. Peasant societies all over the world, on the other hand, stress the first pregnancy and birth as the occasion of attaining adult status. Perhaps in some ways we have lost the balance, as if sexual arousal and fulfilment were the key to being 'grown up', rather than the rights and responsibilities of bringing new life into the world, or for those who do not choose fertility, the

[1] Trans. Daniel H. H. Ingalls, *Sanskrit Poetry from Vidyakara's Treasury*, Harvard Univ. Press, 1968.

ability to accept responsibility for the lives of others.

We tend to think of our own industrialized, urban society as circumscribed by forces outside our personal control and often idealize simpler societies as allowing a greater personal freedom, a more 'natural' way of life, and the spontaneous expression of feeling. Yet there are many areas of human interaction in which the rules and regulations of primitive societies are so pervasive that people do not even notice they are there. Behaviour which breaks the rules is literally unthinkable.

The nuclear family is found in every society known to us, and this is the form that we tend to think of as 'normal'. Most people are members of two nuclear families, one from which they have come, the family of *orientation*, and one which they create, the family of *procreation*. The nuclear family fulfils sexual, economic and reproductive functions and is the primary unit in which the small child begins to be socialized. It is, of course, the mother, or occasionally someone acting in her place, who usually starts that process.

To understand the context in which she does this we shall have to look at some of the different forms which marriage takes. Polygyny means that two or more women share one husband. Polygynous marriage used to be practised by the Mormons and is the ideal over large parts of Africa. In sororal polygyny the women are sisters, and this is the type that existed among the Hebrews; Jacob worked for seven years to pay the bride price for Rachel, but had to marry Leah the older sister first, and only after that was he allowed to work another seven years to marry Rachel. In a polygynous family the women have separate households around a mud clearing or courtyard, each one cooking meals for her children, with the man sleeping with one woman after another in strict rotation, and the children all playing together in the clearing, but going back at night to sleep in their mother's hut.

Polyandry, where a woman has more than one husband, is rare, and only occurs where people are living close to starvation level. The Marquesan Islanders are polyandrous, and the Todas of Southern India practised fraternal polyandry, with the women marrying brothers. Fraternal polyandry has the advantage that the brothers retain the land handed down to them by their father, and pass it down intact to the next generation. But it is difficult to discover who is a baby's father. The Todas solved this problem by having a ceremony in which one of the brothers gives a miniature bow and arrow to his wife during her pregnancy, so claiming fatherhood. In subsequent pregnancies this can be done by one of the other brothers if he decides that he, too, would like to be a father.

When a couple set up home together they can go and live with his parents or hers, or can start a separate home of their own. What is normal for us, making a separate home, is in fact the rarest system; most people live in extended families. That is, they live in a household with their grandparents and parents, and perhaps others as well. Usually the woman goes to her husband's family. This is the pattern in most polygynous societies, and the woman's interests tend to be subordinated to those of the group which she joins as a newcomer, her 'in-laws'. In other societies it is the man who moves into his wife's parents' home, and then he is the outsider who must work for the welfare of the group he has joined. Going to live with the woman's family tends to occur in agricultural economies and also when land is owned by women.

In some societies the couple can choose whether to set up home with the husband's *or* the wife's family. When couples have a choice the society may either be a developed one in which men and women have equal property rights, or, at the other end of the scale, be a simple wandering band of gatherers. In those societies where couples make their own separate home, the pattern is usually one of monogamous marriage, with emphasis on the importance of the individual finding his own way of life and achieving personal success. These kinds of societies are also those in which – perhaps significantly – a large part of the population often lives in great poverty.

The extended family system is one in which it is easier to maintain and hand down tradition than in our own type of marriage which produces short-lived households which disintegrate when the parents die. Years before that point is reached for many families the household consists of only two people, the father and mother whose children have left home. Extended families, on the other hand, have a kind of immortality.[2]

The nuclear family, with a mother, her husband and their children, to which we are accustomed in the industrialized West, is also characteristic of hunting and gathering societies where people are living at subsistence level. But the extended family predominates in agricultural economies which also go in for rearing animals.[3]

Nuclear families are usually linked by only one member who is common to both, the person who moves from his or her family of 'orientation' (the one they grew up in) to a new family of 'procreation'. Our family system is like a long chain of beads, instead of the intricate system of sometimes incredibly geometric patterns which is characteristic of what are often called 'simpler' societies.

Child-rearing practices stem to a large extent from the size of the family. When it is as small and isolated as the modern middle-class family, the child becomes very dependent on its parents. There are no other adults to share

[2] Gerald R. Leslie, *The Family in Social Context*, 2nd ed., OUP, N.Y., 1973.
[3] Meyer F. Nimkoff and Russel Middleton, 'Types of family and types of economy', *American Journal of Sociology* 66, Nov., 1960.

responsibility and care. In an extended family, where there are aunts and uncles, cousins, grandparents and others to turn to, the parents' power over their children is modified and checked by the opinions of others. In the modern family, however, the mother is all in all to the young child, and since the father is usually absent from the house because of his job, she is the one with complete responsibility, who is supposed to control and bring up the child and to represent the world to it.

The white, middle-class urban family is especially isolated from any other kin, whereas in extended families, blood ties between parents and children and brothers and sisters are stressed. Our own society underplays all this and stresses instead the links between people with whom one is in daily contact. Usually there are no names for people who in most societies would be considered relatives in one way or another, what anthropologists call 'classificatory kinship terminology'. Although we in the West have aunts and uncles, we do not, for example, have a word for 'my mother's maternal aunt's paternal nephew', whereas in many other societies they know exactly who this is, and have a special name for him.

Inside small nuclear families there is usually a strict apportioning of rights and responsibilities. The couple making a new home are careful to invite his parents and her parents an equal number of times, and not to show favouritism to one or the other. One consequence of this impartiality towards the two families is that the young couple tend to move farther away from *both* as they establish their independent family unit.

What some writers see as dysfunction in the modern family, Talcott-Parsons[4] believes is effective adaptation to the demands of an industrial economy. Although the nuclear family operates more or less without suppor

[4] With Robert F. Bales, *Family, Socialization and Interaction Process*, Free Press, Illinois, 1955.

from other kin and in structural isolation, it is integrated with the occupational system of an industrialized society. The status of the family depends on the husband's occupation. Inside the family a father may be very different from the sort of man he is in his job, and he keeps these two worlds separate. This contrasts with the system in a primitive or peasant society, where the father works in and around the home, where activities he engages in outside the home intermesh with occupations he has inside it, and where he takes his children with him to the fields and teaches them how to do some of the simple tasks which are a part of the work he does.

As a result of the importance of the father's occupation in modern industrial society, all family needs are subordinated to those of his job. When marriages break up it is often because the woman's interests no longer tally with the man's occupation. From one point of view marriage breakdown is not just a pathological event, but a readjustment to meet the challenges of the occupational system in which the man works. Individuals may get broken in the process, but the society goes on functioning.

Some pre-industrialized societies put special emphasis on the mother-child bond. They are mother-focused in the sense that the mother has functions central to the kinship system; there is relative equality between the sexes, and women are important economically and ritually. The role taken by many black women in the United States, especially in the deep South, as mothers and wage earners, if necessary without the support of a male, is often, probably incorrectly, assumed to be the product of a breakdown in the system[5]. Matrifocality is to some degree characteristic of all West African societies. The Ibo of Eastern

[5] Daniel P. Moynihan, *The Negro Family*, the case for national action. Office of Policy Planning and Research, Dept. of Labour, Washington DC, 1965.

Nigeria have, for example, a patrilineal system, but the smallest social unit consists not of a man, a woman and their children, but a woman and her children, which has been described as 'an eating unit'[6]. There is a male head of the polygynous household, but the day-to-day running of the home operates almost independently of him.

Legitimacy of offspring implies the possibility of illegitimacy, and the unmarried mother is at a disadvantage in most societies. Even in those rural communities where illegitimate children are absorbed with little fuss into their mothers' parents' families – extra mouths to feed, but later also extra hands in the fields – the bearing of children before marriage is considered unfortunate unless it serves to precipitate the marriage ceremony, offering the bridegroom proof of fertility. Historically, in some societies, in farming communities in Scandinavia, for example, evidence of fertility was thought essential before a man married the woman. The Banaro of New Guinea only allow sexual intercourse between husband and wife after she has had a child by a man selected for insemination.[7]

In many parts of the world, including the black ghettos of the United States, Bantu townships in South Africa, the West Indies and Latin America, girls bargain for a man with their fertility, and use sex in what is sometimes called 'consensual courtship', either risking the birth of a child, or actually bearing children 'for' a man, in a short-term, often highly unstable relationship, whether or not it involves legal marriage. In these societies birth outside marriage is considered normal, though usually, at least in economic terms, regrettable.

[6] Victor Uchendu, quoted by Nancy Tanner in *Woman, Culture and Society*, ed. Michelle Z. Rosaldo and Louise Lamphere, Stanford Univ. Press, 1974.
[7] George P. Murdock, *Social Structure*, Macmillan, N.Y., 1949.

In England and Wales, illegitimacy dropped steadily from a peak in the mid-nineteenth century until the 1930s, and then began to climb again. In modern industrialized societies the incidence of illegitimacy is higher at the lower end of the social class scale, and those in the lower socio-economic groups bear more children outside marriage or within eight months of the wedding. People working on the land also have more conceptions outside marriage than do workers in big cities.

There are, as might be expected, more illegitimate births when the baby's father is away from home for long periods, and this accounts for the hight rate in Aberdeen in cases where the father is a trawler fisherman in the North Sea, or a long-distance lorry driver, or where he is in the armed services.

Women can have babies over a longer span of their lives today than they could a hundred years ago. Girls start menstruating earlier and the menopause comes later. Their health is better on the whole and they live in better social conditions. But fertility has, in fact, declined. Women are able to, but they do not. The childbearing period has become a much shorter part of each woman's life and fewer children are born within it. In the United States, for instance, the span of childbearing is now half as long as it was two generations ago.

All this has implications for the relationship between husband and wife and parents and children, and for women's image of themselves. When she has finished childbearing there is a long period of life in which a woman's maternal role becomes gradually less necessary and is no longer central to her view of herself. We really have to create a new kind of motherhood if we are to adapt to the demands of present day society and the radically changed family development cycle with which we are living today. It is not just a question of mothering techniques being different from those used by a woman's mother and grandmother in their day, but of motherhood having to adapt itself to a dramatically changed social context. And that means that not only motherhood must change, but fatherhood too.

The danger is that because motherhood is occupying less time the skills which come with experience may never be learned. The problem of the oldest child in a family is well known. This is the one with the feeding and the sleeping and the potty training problems. This is the one whom the parents practise on, and also the one they very often become anxious about. When the second baby comes along they are much more relaxed, and confident in themselves as parents.

As families become smaller, children do not get the opportunity to learn parenting skills in caring for younger brothers and sisters, and so start out on parenthood themselves without any idea as to what it is all about. In antenatal classes expectant mothers often say that they have never held a baby in their arms, never even seen a newborn infant, nor had the opportunity of watching a mother look after a small baby. No amount of lessons in child care or practising with a rubber doll in a bathtub in the few weeks before a baby is born can ever make up for this deprivation.

In the last twenty years or so there has been a good deal of discussion about the 'disintegrating' family. People speak nostalgically of the joys of the extended family, although they themselves have never had to live with their mother-in-law and aunts and cousins by marriage. Yet the nuclear family of a man and wife and their children has been with us a long time and is not simply a modern deterioration in the form of the family. The family is infinitely flexible to adapt to changed conditions and challenges presented by the larger society around it. Margaret Mead believes that it is 'the toughest institution we have'.

To find out about motherhood it is also important to look at what might be called 'biological anthropology'. Women's biological endowment has, to a large extent, especially before the advent of effective contraceptive techniques and human milk substitutes, defined her social roles.

Her physiological state, in particular menstruation and the moon rhythm of her life, and childbearing, governed her existence, her day to day activities plotted according to the things she might or might not do when she had her period, or was pregnant or lactating. The jobs she could do, the illnesses from which she suffered (some mental illnesses for example are still entirely explained in terms of a woman possessing or having lost her uterus or passing through the menopause) the manner in which she could worship, the books she could read, the way in which she walked and sat, her speech and forms of language, the games she could play, and the way in which she was educated were all those considered suitable for or inalienably associated with the feminine state. From infancy and the time when the newborn baby is dressed in pink or blue according to sex, and admired as strong and a 'real boy' or pretty and 'very feminine', sexual roles are inculcated by society.

Yet in biological terms all mammalian organisms have potential for bisexuality. During fetal and early neonatal life the baby's development as a boy or a girl is largely dependent on a delicate balance between hormones. When androgen is present masculine behaviour potential exists, and the basic female component of sexuality is suppressed according to the amount of androgen circulating in the body.[8] Studies have been done which indicate that girls who have been exposed to abnormally high levels of fetal

[3] Arnold A. Gerall, 'Influence of perinatal androgen on reproductive capacity', *Contemporary Sexual Behaviour*, Ed. Joseph Zubin and John Money, John Hopkins, University Press, Baltimore, 1973.

androgen tend to show little 'maternal behaviour' as expressed in playing with dolls and other activities which might be thought of as a 'rehearsal' for later motherhood.[9] But so great is the effect of social conditioning that there is no evidence at all to suggest that they do not go on to make perfectly good mothers, even if they are unable to bear babies themselves and have to adopt a family.

One very important stage in the development of gender identity is the attainment of language between eighteen months and two and a half years. From that point the child knows that it is a boy or a girl with no hesitation, and it is impossible to change gender after this without a major upheaval.

In many ways mammalian evolution has been accompanied by an increased sexual autonomy.[10] Intercourse in human beings is not, for example, dependent on the female being on heat, as it is in lower mammals. Behaviour in mating is no longer an almost automatic response to copulatory behaviour on the part of the male. Higher functions of the brain are increasingly concerned with sexual activity and controlling the release of hormones. In the progress up the evolutionary ladder genital sex and reproductive behaviour become differentiated. Human beings, to a greater extent than any other creature, are emancipated from their hormones.

Yet universally society enforces the duality of the sexes, and it seems almost as if social order is dependent upon their strict differentiation. When change occurs and there is greater flexibility about sex roles, as in many contemporary lifestyles, critics of change express anxiety about loss of gender identity, and perhaps most of all are

[9] Anke A. Erhardt, 'Materialism in Fetal hormonal and related syndromes', in Zubin and Money, op cit.
[10] Saul Rosenzweig, 'Human sexual autonomy and evolutionary attainment', in Zubin and Money, op. cit.

anxious that women will not be able to be adequate mothers and that the family, the very basis of culture, will somehow be threatened.

Traditionally woman's most important role has been that of a disseminator of culture through mothering. The fact that she has a uterus and lactates means that she not only bears the children but is largely responsible for their care while they are babies, and sometimes for much longer. She is the first and most important channel through which the culture is communicated to her baby. She introduces the world to her children and teaches the basic differences in sex roles, and often does all this quite unconsciously. She begins the socialization of the small child, and in most cultures continues it with the help of a network of mothers and grandmothers.

Daughters are less differentiated from their mothers than are some. Born feminine, they remain so. In cultures which emphasize individuality and personal achievement, like ours, this sexual identity can make it difficult for them to define themselves as separate from their mothers, and the struggle to break away and be women in their own right results in a conflict in the mother-daughter relation which is expressed in adolescent crisis.

Mothers tend to identify with their own mothers. They also tend spontaneously to recreate patterns of child care which they may consciously reject, finding themselves, nevertheless, doing things in much the same way. Helene Deutsch said, 'In relation to her own child, each woman repeats her own mother-child history'.[11] In a traditional society young mothers are aware that they are participating in a flow of mothering behaviour similar to that of their own mothers.' In my own field work in Jamaica I asked adolescent girls and women having their first babies if they wanted to be 'the same kind of mother' as their own mothers were. Everyone wished to be 'the

[11] *Psychology of Women*, Vol. 1, Grune and Stratton, N.Y., 1944.

same' except that some of the schoolgirls said that they
wanted to 'have a job before getting a baby'. In contrast, Jamaican women who had emigrated to the UK and
were having babies in this country wanted to do things
differently, were deliberately adopting patterns of child
care they felt were superior to those they had received in
their own childhood, and contrasted 'the old-time way'
with techniques they had learned at the clinic or at
home economic classes in school.[12] In our own society
mothers may seek to refashion mothering behaviour in
deference to what they believe to be a more appropriate
model, but still find themselves acting as they remember
their own mothers behaving. They not only act like their
own mother, but in many ways they feel like her too, and
in our own society are sometimes able to appreciate and
begin to understand her for the first time. When the first
child is born, and after the difficult transition period of
learning to be a mother has been lived through successfully, there is often a reconciliation between mothers and
daughters who had been locked in conflict with each
other.

There is some evidence that women find it easier to
identify with girl babies, although boys are often given
more general social approval. In Southern India, for example, the Havik Brahmins are much more lenient in
their treatment of girls because mothers say that girls
have to leave their homes when they marry, so specially
cherish their daughters because they know that sooner or
later they must be separated from them. The boys are
going to be around all the time and will bring their
brides back to their mother's home. In many cultures

[12] Sheila Kitzinger, 'When Im Seem Bellyful Im Burps and Stops:
Breastfeeding contrasts' *Health Visitor*, Vol. 49, 1976, and 'Com-
municating with Immigrant Mothers' in *Caring for Children*,
edited N. L. Kellmer-Pringle, Longmans, 1969.

mothers stress the sexual difference between themselves and their sons, and between the boys and girls in the family. In our own society they comment on the child's strength, boisterousness, aggression and naughtiness. This is what it is to be a real boy! In peasant societies the size of a baby boy's genitals may be admired and mothers play with them.

In all cultures from the very moment of birth the mother helps to build the baby's gender identity. 'Is it a boy or a girl?' friends ask, as if it were the most important thing about a baby. The next task is naming the child, which will fix its sex usually unmistakably for everyone to realize. They look into the carrycot – 'He's a real boy!' they say, or 'Isn't she sweet? She's so pretty and feminine!' The mother may choose to dress her baby boy in blue, her girl in pink. In France flowers of the appropriate colour fill the mother's room. There can be no doubt! She talks to her boy and her girl in subtly different ways according to sex and later is explicit about what little girls do and how they dress and have their hair arranged as distinct from little boys. She buys toys and chooses dolls and miniature irons and cooking things for the girl and trains and Action Man and footballs for the boy. The result is that the child has a clear and irreversible sense of whether it is a boy or a girl by the age of three.[13]

The child's complete dependence on its mother who is usually the sole person to look after it can result in acute sensitivity to her approval. She represents love, and if this is withdrawn the child has no one else to love it. We tend to think of this as normal, but in most other societies the child does not need its mother's love so unconditionally. There are others who can love and rear

[13] Lawrence Kohlberg, 'A cognitive-developmental analysis of children's sex-role concepts and attitudes' in Eleanor E. Maccoby (Ed.), *The Development of Sex Differences*, Stanford, California.

W.A.M. – C

the child. Women in peasant societies may be deeply shocked when they learn that in the West a mother may reject, neglect or batter a child. In peasant societies there are always others watching over the care that a woman gives her baby, helping with chores, and sharing responsibility. Even in a social system like that of Jamaica, which has been fragmented by slavery, very few babies find their way to orphanages because there is always a grandmother, sister or cousin to take care of a child if the mother should be unable to look after it. Usually it is one of the grandmothers. In a *patrilocal* society, where the family is reared in or close to the dwelling of the father's parents, this is usually the father's mother.

Even in those societies where the young couple make a separate home, if the mother can get easy access to her own mother, as is often the case in tightly knit communities, for example London's East End, the maternal grandmother may take primary responsibility for guiding the new mother. Sometimes she actually takes over the children completely. This often happens when a toddler is weaned, and 'goes to granny', 'so as', the West African expression goes, 'to forget its mother'. In ex-slavery societies the maternal grandmother, or in her absence a maternal aunt, often rears the first-born children of her daughters because they have not yet settled down in stable relationships with men. So, in these societies a middle-aged woman expects to have a second family of small grandchildren to bring up.

When a small child is completely dependent on its mother and care is not shared, her threatened or actual withdrawal of love is often used to control its behaviour. Children compete to gain love, and as they grow older are encouraged by the mother, and increasingly by the father too, who now comes in to reinforce his wife's child-rearing techniques, to strive for success at school and in the world outside the home in order to gain more approval from their parents, which, it is implied, is 'contingent upon performance. For, although his parents are consciously committed to love their child regardless, they too have success needs that must be met partly through the child.'[14]

Mothers, nervously suspecting that their child may be falling below standard, and that their offspring are not fat or beautiful enough, have too few teeth, are not consuming as wide a variety of solid foods as the next baby, are not talking, sitting up or walking as soon, or are not potty-trained or reading as early as the infant next door, compare their children's performance and compete with other mothers.

It is part of the socialization process for living in an industrialized, capitalist society in which the success ethos is all important and where individual accomplishment is all. Some children never survive it, since nothing they do can ever live up to their parents' expectations or demands of them. Others succeed, and reinforce this system of child-rearing in their turn when they themselves have children, whom they encourage in the same way.

The parent achieves success through the child, and in a highly competitive society the parent who has little success in his or her own life may have a great incentive to live through the child, and see it as an extension of self. The mother who is restricted to the home but who longs to compete in the outside world is particularly likely to express herself through her children. She may try to do this in an inappropriate way, to the child's shame, because, not operating in the larger world in which the child is required to act, her modes and standards of behaviour are outdated and irrelevant. The father is more likely to have an occupation which gives him a sense of achievement outside the home and family unit.

Parenthood is not a static situation, of course. As the family grows and develops, and relationships within it

[14] Gerald R. Leslie, op. cit.

shift, so parenthood itself involves change. It is a process, not merely a role to be adopted. The type of mothering which works well with a newborn baby is unsuitable for a toddler, and that which is right for a toddler is wrong for the adolescent. Mothers need to be capable of continual adaptation to new challenges which come as their children pass from babyhood into childhood, and then grow up to become new adults. Many excel at one stage of development, but cope badly with other stages.

The stage during which the child needs to be enclosed and protected by a mother who envisages the baby as a part of herself is a kind of extension of pregnancy, and usually lasts for the first three to four months. If the mother remains purely enclosing as the baby begins to explore its world she can either stunt the child's psychic growth, or a battle royal can develop between mother and infant. Ann Dally[15] believes that in psychoanalytic terms there is a conflict in mothering between the fact that the child was a part of the mother, and is later a kind of physical extension of herself, but then must become separate and independent – and yet only when the right time has been reached :

> Growing up successfully depends on the resolution of this conflict and this means both love and distance. Yet love tends towards closeness, integration and belonging and so conflicts with distance. There is always a tendency to avoid the conflict by developing either love or distance at the expense of the other, or to deny the conflict by pretending that one is the other. If the conflict is avoided there may be love with insufficient distance or distance with insufficient love. Both situations are hazardous. If the conflict is denied there will be confusion in the mind of the child about the nature

[15] Ann Dally, *Mothers: their power and influence*, Weidenfeld and Nicolson, 1976.

of love and distance. He will lack the means to distinguish between them. Sometimes both love and distance are lacking and this is the worst of all. If the mother is totally centred on herself she is unable to love the child and any apparent love can only be self-enhancement: Yet she may be emotionally dependent on the child and unable to separate from him. The absence of both love and distance can lead to a stranglehold which can, and sometimes does, destroy the child.

Societies value and institutionalize different types of mothering, identifying mothering predominantly with enclosure, extension or separation. The traditional Jewish mother often emphasizes enclosure to the exclusion of other types of mothering. Perhaps it is because of the Jewish people's history of persecution. Young middle-class parents today are increasingly concerned to experience physical closeness and to feel spontaneous enveloping love for their babies, but many educated women are anxious that they will be unable to feel this unselfconscious enclosure love, and try to acquire it instead through studying books on child-rearing.

In most of the developing countries parents try to maintain rigid control over their children as if they were extensions of themselves, and it is thought right that children's activities and thinking should be dominated by unchanging parental values. Problems can arise in the parent-child relationship when Arab sons come to the West to study, for example, and are no longer willing to accept parental authority. This type of parenting was typical of that of Victorian middle-class England, when rigid parental values and the ideas that children must be moulded if they are to grow up to be good adults were accepted as normal. It is implicit in Freud's psychoanalytic teaching, since he was reflecting the Viennese world he knew and from which his patients came.

When the mother has no experience of the child

either as enclosed in her love, or later as an extension of herself and her own body, but treats the baby as separate from the beginning, both she and the child suffer emotional deprivation. This must often have happened in the middle- and upper-class nursery when a nanny took over the baby from the very early days, and when contact between mother and baby was restricted to the mothering time assigned to the early evening. It also occurs with mothers who cannot trust their feelings, who try to make child-rearing an intellectual exercise rather than a spontaneous relationship.

It is when motherhood is at its most spontaneous that it best serves as the channel of the cultural process. It is the first agency of acculturation to which each new individual is introduced. For many individuals it remains throughout life by far the most effective.

It starts with the way the mother feeds her baby. I do not mean by this only the difference between breast or bottle, but the mood in which she feeds. Some mothers relax, forget time and enjoy talking to and watching the baby during feeds. Others are tense, watch the clock and treat the baby a bit like a car which has to be filled with petrol, jiggling the baby up and down when it stops for a few seconds or starts to play.

In the way that the mother presents milk to her baby and responds to its need for nourishment, she is presenting her sense of the nature of the ties that bind human beings together and what life is all about. This is the baby's first introduction to the value system of the society into which it is born. But of course it must go on from there.

Our mental images of motherhood tend to be linked with the initial stages of that relationship. The image of maternity is personified in the enveloping, protecting, encircling arms of the mother. We forget that the mother is also the person who encourages her child to go away from her to explore, but who is waiting ready to safeguard and guide when the need arises. We may forget, too, that the mother has to let her adolescent child go away from her completely and become a separate personality, a confident man or woman able to enjoy satisfying adult relationships.

4
Getting and Not Getting Pregnant

Bring forth and multiply, and replenish the earth. O
Sun Moon! Oh Ponomosor! May this woman bea
twelve sons and twelve daughters! . . .[1]

You son of a clear-eyed mother, you far-sighted one
how you will see game one day, you who have strong
arms and legs, you strong-limbed one, how surely you
will shoot, plunder the Herreros, and bring your mothe
their fat cattle to eat, you child of a strong-thighed
father, how you will subdue strong oxen between your
thighs one day. You who have a mighty penis, how
many and what mighty children you will beget![2]

O son, you will have a warrior's name and be a leade
of men. And your sons and your sons' sons will remem
ber you long after you have slipped into the darkness.

There is pride in having borne the number they have
yet almost never is there expressed desire for more

[1] A Kharia chant quoted by Verrier Elwin, *Folk Songs of Chat
tisgarh*, OUP, 1946.
[2] A Hottentot song translated by Willard R. Trask, and quote
in *The Unwritten Song: Poetry of the traditional and primitiv
peoples of the world*, Vol. 1, Macmillan, N.Y., 1966.
[3] A Didinga mother's song, translated by Jack Driberg and quote
in *Initiation: translations from the poems of the Didinga an
Lango tribes*, Golden Cockerel Press, 1932.

The most common example of the first is the ever present suggestion of self-esteem in both words and intonation of answers to the question of **how** many children the mother of a large family has – 'Eleven. I done my share, didn't I?' or 'Ten and all a-living.' The pride becomes even more exaggerated when the larger sized families of the previous generation are being reported – 'My mammy raised and married thirteen', 'I was one of seventeen', or, and this was the largest number reported and that by a husband glowing with vicarious elation over the achievement, 'I was next to the youngest of twenty-two'. The bearing, 'raising', and 'marrying off' of children are everywhere recognized as being a positive achievement, a contribution to the world as well as to the immediate family.[4]

'He can't stand me like this, and to tell the truth I can't stand myself,' a pregnant woman in an English antenatal class said.

For thousands of years and all over the world fertility has been sought after and barrenness shunned. How else could a man provide for himself in his old age? How else could his name be carried on? How could the flocks be tended, the earth tilled, or the battles fought? The home was, or aimed at being, an economic unit in which more hands meant not only that food had to be shared out further, but also lighter work, and each child started to contribute to the household economy as soon as it could hold a tool or care for others smaller than itself. And a woman's pride was in her fertility, the fruits of her womb. 'These,' said the Roman matron . . ., 'are my jewels.'

So great was the emphasis on fertility that in certain African tribes (the Dahomey, for example) an impotent

Margaret Jarman Hagood, *Mothers Of The South: portraiture of the white tenant farm woman*, Univ, of N. Carolina Press, 1939.

husband urged his wife to sleep with a friend or relative, or if a wife could not bear children another woman was brought in to bear them 'to his name'. In some societies barrenness or impotence are sufficient grounds for divorce. In Tikopia, a small island in the Western Pacific, for instance, couples may separate on grounds of childlessness without any formal annulling of the marriage. In Sudanese Africa the Nuer bride does not even go to her husband's home until the first baby is weaned. There is no point in the relationship continuing unless the child survives.

Traditionally the prospective parents depended on the good wishes and correct actions of the whole society. They depended also on the spirits who represented the tribe, and linked present with past and future, and the natural with the supernatural world. Human beings, alive and dead, and supernatural beings were all ritually united in promoting fertility. Fertility was not just a personal, private matter, but involved the cosmos.

In most of these societies maternal and infant mortality was high. Where life was hard, as among the Eskimos, and wherever there was barely enough to eat during some seasons of the year or after periods of drought, as in large parts of Africa, only those supremely fit would survive to childbearing age. The others died in childhood, or occasionally survived but remained barren. Disease also picked off young people in their prime: malaria, the Black Death, smallpox, measles, tuberculosis, leprosy and venereal diseases. In Europe, too, there were periods when death was an everyday fact of life. It has been estimated that in two years, between 1348 and 1350, a quarter of the population of Europe died from plague, and Boccaccio described the plague in Italy as killing 40,000 in Genoa, 60,000 in Naples, and 96,000 in Florence.[5]

[5] F. N. Clive Wood and Beryl Suiters, *The Fight for Acceptance: a history of contraception*, Med. & Technical Publishing Co. 1970.

In the twentieth century too infant mortality in many peasant societies is high. Of 80 women studied in one South African tribe, the Kgatla, in the years 1929–35, there were 206 babies born alive, and 21 miscarriages or stillbirths (9 per cent). Of 206 babies born, 57 did not survive to maturity (28 per cent). Three out of every 100 died within two months of birth, eight died later, but while they were still being suckled, and 16 died later in childhood.[6]

Birth Control

Yet with all the emphasis on fertility, the charms, prayers and rites, parents have often been aware that they had too many mouths to feed, and that the children they have brought into the world, although a long-term investment and security for their old age, are in the present a liability. Even though one might anger the gods and 'go against Nature' by putting a curb on fertility, sometimes it is an urgent necessity. So societies evolved ways of limiting the number of children a woman bore, sometimes effectively, but often involving magic practices, potions and signs which could have had little practical result.

Egyptian papyrii describe three contraceptive pastes, a kind of glue, a mixture of honey and sodium carbonate, and crocodile dung, which were inserted into the vagina to provide a spermicidal barrier over the cervix, or neck of the uterus. Papyrii of 1550 B C tell how to make lint tampons soaked in honey and fermented acacia leaves. This was probably a good method; lactic acid, which would be produced from the fermentation, is still used in spermicides today. Both male and female sterilization was also known, but was rarely used.

The Talmud permitted Jewish women to use contraceptives. A cotton tampon was used and an oral contraceptive consisting among other things of pounded crocuses.

[6] Isaac Schapera, *Married Life in an African Tribe*, Pelican, 1971.

A woman who did not want to conceive might also try jumping around after intercourse, in a vain attempt to dislodge the semen.

The Greeks may have invented an intra-uterine device, since a hollow lead tube filled with mutton fat was sometimes inserted into the cervix to hold it open, but we are not told why. A vinegar douche was also used by women in ancient Greece. Aristotle advised smearing the cervix and vagina with oil. Dioscorides's *Herbal*,[7] written in the first or second century after Christ, recommends eating the fruit of the 'Chaste tree', whatever that may be, and pounding willow leaves and taking them in water. Dioscorides also advised using pessaries made from pepper, herbs, sickle wort and peppermint juice, mixing the whole lot up with honey and putting it over the cervix. Soranus believed that a woman could avoid conception if she did not have an orgasm, and that she could make matters surer if she leaped around, sneezed, drank a cold liquid and wiped out the vagina after intercourse. But he also recommended wool tampons soaked in oil, honey, resin and the juice of the balsam tree. One possible ingredient was pomegranate pulp, which, like other acid fruits, would have had a spermicidal action. When I was working in Latin America I discovered that peasant women in Colombia today sometimes use a hollowed out half orange as a cervical cap.

Islamic authorities recommend withdrawal, pessaries made of cabbage, pitch, ox-gall and elephant dung in various mixtures, and oral contraceptive potions, and the physician Rhases went into great detail about how to procure abortion by a method of curettage. He also added, rather hopefully, 'Joking, too, is useful'.

In the Middle Ages the witches and wise women were

---

[7] This and other material on contraception is derived from Clive Wood and Beryl Suiters, op. cit., and Jean Medawar and David Pyke (Editors) *Family Planning*, Pelican, 1971.

experts on birth control and abortion, and just as women would go to them for a love potion, a charm to prevent a baby from falling ill or simple herbal medicines, so they sought their help to prevent conception or to get rid of an unwanted pregnancy. The Catholic Church saw this as a powerful threat to its authority, and in 1484 a Papal Bull was issued which stated: 'By their sorceries and by their incantations, charms and conjurations, they suffocate, extinguish and cause to perish the births of women . . . so that men beget not nor women conceive.' We shall explore the subject of witchcraft later.

Most of the information that comes down to us about contraception in the Renaissance and in both France and England in the seventeenth and eighteenth centuries concerns the lives of courtiers and men of letters, and it is difficult to get any idea of how peasant families lived, or what they used to avoid unwanted births.

We know that complete breast-feeding, that is, without the addition of any solid foods or other milk, at any rate when the mother herself is not having a good diet, makes it unlikely that a women will ovulate, and every peasant woman breast-fed as a matter of course. In contemporary peasant communities prolonged lactation, for two or three years or even longer, is used deliberately to reduce fertility, and is especially effective because there is often an unwritten rule that complete intercourse should not take place while a mother is still breast-feeding her child. The Koran specifically praises those women who breast-feed for two years and avoid intercourse during this time.

Withdrawal is the most commonly used birth control technique in the world. But perhaps most significant of all, throughout pre-industrial Europe, was that marriage was delayed until years after women had attained reproductive maturity, coupled with religious sanctions against illegitimacy. By the middle of the sixteenth century, if not before, the average age at marriage for women was the middle or late twenties. By the end of the seventeenth century it was nearer thirty.[8]

The condom – made from the caecum of a sheep – appears to have been widely used in the seventeenth and eighteenth centuries by the middle and upper classes, and many verses were written praising its use. One described a woman who amassed a fortune by collecting used ones, laundering them and re-selling them. Casanova referred to the condom as 'the English overcoat'. In the seventeenth century also there are references to vaginal sponges, as well as to potions. Ben Johnson asked, 'Have you those excellent recipes, Madame, to keep yourselves from bearing children?', and the lady replied, 'How should we maintain our beauty else? Many births of a woman make her old, as many crops make the earth barren.'

When the vulcanization of rubber was invented in 1843 for the first time a safe contraceptive device could be mass-produced, and this heralded a revolution in birth control. The very first Family Planning Clinic was established in Holland in 1882, and also acted as an infant welfare centre, although the only technique it advised in the early days was a soap pessary. Later it developed the diaphragm, which hence became known as 'the Dutch cap'. But where effective contraceptives were unknown women still had recourse to older methods.

In the *Columbus Medical Journal* of 1883 a doctor wrote about 'the abuses of carbolic acid' which was used as a contraceptive douche, and described 'the little dark closets' where married women kept 'bottles of ergot, cotton root, savin, oil of tansy, etc. to produce as they call it "accidental miscarriage".' It was not until 1927 that Marie Stopes first went on the road with a mobile birth control clinic in England, parking her caravan outside the Bethnal Green public library, and later journeying into the country areas of England and Wales. Birth control then

[8] E. A. Wrigley 'Family Limitation in the Past', in *Family Planning* Edited by Jean Medawar and David Pyke, op. cit.

became a public issue of major importance, and the use of mechanical contraceptives which were fairly efficient became widespread. But even this must be qualified, and in a study of contraceptive practices in the United Kingdom in 1970, Ann Cartwright discovered that as many as 29 per cent of women studied stated that they were using a method of birth control when they last became pregnant.[9] Some of those who were using a cap (which must be fitted to the nearest 5 millimetres) had not had it fitted by a doctor, but had simply bought it at the chemist's and hoped it would do. In that study too, less than half of the women who had seven or more children had ever discussed birth with their Health Visitor. The implications must be that still in the 1970s some women who thought they were using modern contraceptives were adopting methods which were ineffective, and that even though the Social Services were designed to ensure home visits to provide for the health care needs of all the family, the mothers who most needed help found it difficult to get information from a knowledgeable person, and relied instead upon neighbours, family members (usually sisters-in-law and sisters) and friends.

Even where parents have wanted 'a full quiver' and where fertility has been greatly valued, in situations of dire poverty or of famine infanticide has always been practised. Babies have been 'accidentally' lain on in bed or, as I discovered when tracing my own paternal ancestors among Scottish crofters, records tell of babies who were 'dropped on the head' and died shortly after birth.

Infanticide was practised in ancient Rome, where an excess of children was considered inconvenient. In other societies abnormal babies or those who do not conform to a certain standard are drowned, buried, stifled or exposed, and in parts of Africa one of twins traditionally

[9] *Parents and Family Planning Services*, Institute of Community Studies, Routledge, 1970.

has always been killed.

The great migrations that have occurred throughout African history and prehistory necessitated some method of controlling births, since it was difficult to take pregnant women and small babies on long, exhausting journeys into the interior. The Zulu people have regularly moved towards the Zambesi at times of economic and political crisis, and later have flowed back towards the south of the continent again. When I was in South Africa a Zulu chief who is also a senior witchdoctor explained to me the ceremony of 'stopping the wombs of the women'. The use of contraception was a political, not a personal decision. The Elders met and discussed the situation, and before further action could be taken had to offer sacrifices and prayers seeking forgiveness of the ancestors. Small pebbles were then collected from a special sacred river and in the ceremony one was slipped into the uterus of each woman of childbearing age. It has been known for some time that Arab traders who did not want their camels to become pregnant during long treks across the Sahara used stones in this way, so providing the first evidence of the utilization of intra-uterine devices, but this Zulu practice is a unique example of it being used for many centuries on human beings, and as a matter of public policy.

Those working in the epidemiology of fertility control attribute the dramatic drop in the birth rate of those African tribes which went on these long migrations to starvation. Perhaps it was also a deliberate consequence of sophisticated population policies, the result not of chance but of planning.

In all societies, throughout history, mothers are not merely women happy with fertile wombs. They also worry about controlling inappropriate fertility, and about spacing their babies.

Pregnancy as a force for social cohesion

In many societies it is when a baby is on the way that the relationship between a couple, formerly only half recognized and provisional, becomes established as really a marriage. The Kgatla of South Africa have a system whereby parents change their name with the birth of the first child, and acquire a new dignity and status. They become known by the child's name, with the prefix 'rra' – father, or 'mma' – mother.[10] Divorce is often very easy before the first child is born, but once the woman is pregnant it becomes difficult, and involves long drawn out and bitter disputes between the families.

Among the Mbuti pygmies of the African Congo, after her first menstruation a girl lives temporarily with her future husband in a band consisting of other members of her age group, in a special '*elima*' house, where couples are expected to join in enthusiastic lovemaking and sexual experimentation as a preparation for marriage. The girls are able to invite in any boys they fancy, and summon them by whipping them with saplings. What starts as a series of wide-ranging flirtations finishes after a period of one or two months as a serious search for a suitable husband.

When the *elima* festival is over, a boy who has become betrothed goes to the girl's parents for permission to marry her. He sets the seal on the betrothal by proving himself a good hunter, kills an antelope, and offers it to the girl's parents along with other gifts such as a bow and arrows, a *machete*, or a piece of bark cloth. It is at this stage in the unfolding of the marriage that either the girl goes to live with him or he goes to live in her band. She builds a hut for them and they live in it without further ceremony. But when she becomes pregnant the marriage itself comes into existence. The union is afforded social recognition

[10] Isaac Schapera, *Married Life in an African Tribe*, Penguin, 1971.

and is formally incorporated as a unit of the social structure, and although separation would have been simple and straightforward prior to pregnancy, it is rare once they are expecting a baby. Pregnancy provides evidence that the marriage is 'working'.

Although attitudes to conception before marriage vary throughout the world, in some societies pregnancy being welcomed as evidence of fertility, and in others condemned, the important thing everywhere is that each child has someone who will take on the social responsibility of being a father, and one of the first tasks in pregnancy is to ensure that the coming child is accepted by a man as his, whether or not he is its biological father.

Many societies have means of giving a child conceived outside marriage a place in the structure, although one who is conceived before its mother has passed through initiation ceremonies and become a recognized adult may be a matter of great shame and disgust.

The most striking example of this is provided by the Kipsigis of Kenya, where bearing a child before a girl has been blessed as a potential mother is the unpardonable sin against the spirits, and contaminates the whole of the community. Such a baby must be born in the bush, where its pollution can harm no one, and be immediately suffocated. It is then thought of as never having lived. The girl goes through a process of ritual purification and, once clean, can later become a mother without further shame. The Christian missions tried to end this infanticide, and adopted the babies. But their mothers, utterly disgraced, then became social outcasts and were never able to marry.

Among the same people it is considered all right for an unmarried girl to become pregnant *provided* she has been initiated, and this is accepted as happy evidence of fertility by the man who hopes to marry her. He immediately makes the child his own by paying *bride-wealth*

– that is, he makes a gift of cows to the woman's family, and often to certain other of her relatives as well, in exchange for her fertility. He has claimed his rights as a father.

But in some African cultures unmarried mothers are harshly treated. A Kgatla girl is ostracized and the neighbours may collect outside her house and sing obscene songs. In the past the baby was probably killed at birth. In South Africa the Xhosa of the Transkei do not approve of premarital pregnancy, and once a girl is pregnant outside marriage she knows she has no hope of marrying.

During pregnancy the identity of the father is further emphasized, and publicly proclaimed by rituals and other duties to be performed and things to be avoided. If he commits adultery, for example, the child will get ill. The relationship of a mother to her child is immediately obvious for biological reasons. But that of the father is altogether more vague, so societies everywhere have ways of marking and identifying the father. Many otherwise incomprehensible practices have meaning when seen in this light.

When pregnancy is confirmed two social groups, that of the mother and the father, become more firmly linked. It is because these new links are being forged that during pregnancy the expectant mother's mother-in-law really comes into her own, and in most societies with a patrilineal descent system she is the person whose duty it is to give advice, see that the girl is looking after herself and makes preparations for the coming baby in a culturally appropriate way. In a traditional society she usually tells the pregnant woman about customs designed to ensure a safe path through pregnancy and childbirth. Older women among the Arapesh of New Guinea, for example, tell the pregnant woman to be careful not to eat the bandicoot or she may die in difficult labour, nor frogs, or the labour will be too quick, nor eels, lest the baby be premature. They remind her not to cut anything in half if she hopes for a boy.

In Guatemala pregnant women are warned by older women that if they spend too long at the lake enjoying themselves bathing, gossiping and combing their long black hair, the Lake Goddess will rise up from its depths, and she will make their mouths swell up and their teeth fall out.[11] The Guatemalan mother-in-law controls and conducts the pregnancy and the expectant mother herself is not even supposed to know she is pregnant. The mother-in-law arranges for the midwife to call regularly, to 'cure her sickness' and make her periods return, and this fiction is maintained by all. Moreover, if the pregnant woman does not obey her mother-in-law and fulfil her obligations as a good wife and daughter she puts the fetus in peril, and the baby may die. The mother-in-law warns the girl to listen to the midwife, and together they strive to keep her from feeling any violent emotions and to satisfy any cravings she may have. She must not go out of the house when the sun is high, or look at the full moon or the moon in eclipse, or point at the rainbow, or her baby will be malformed; nor must she get caught in a thunderstorm or the child will have clubfeet.

When the mother-in-law's role is to instruct and guide the pregnant woman in this way she is not merely handing down family or local traditions. Her function is wider and far more significant in terms of social continuity. She acts as the ritual agent between past, present and future.

Pregnancy as a ritual state
In many societies there is a whole medico-religious system catering for the needs of women, often existing alongside the established system, and operating surreptitiously against it. The control of fertility is largely in the hands

[11] Lois Paul, 'Work and Sex in a Guatemalan Village', *Women, Culture and Society*, op. cit.

of community witch-midwives or 'grannies' who deliver
babies and promote or curb fertility. This area is one of
feminine mysteries, and men have always held it in great
suspicion and have often been very frightened of it. This
is partly because witchcraft not only controls conception
and childbearing, but also a man's potency and virility.
One of the major denunciations of witches has always
been that they can make a man's penis wither, become
invisible or even drop off, and the *Malleus*[12] refers to the
witches' 'glamour' which is cast over the penis to make it
disappear, and to 'the impotence of the member to perform the act'. The secret arts of witchcraft are closely
linked with the worship of the Earth Mother. This control
over fertility corresponds to the man's control over
nature in agriculture, sowing and harvesting, and is no less
important.

Pregnancy is in most societies a *ritual* state. The expectant mother is in a special ritual relationship with
society, including the father of the child, both their kin
groups, the past in the persons of the ancestors, and the
cosmic environment represented by the Gods.

In Sumatra, for example, the expectant mother's mother
and the baby's father perform rituals to proclaim pregnancy. These start in the fifth month and serve to link the
two families more closely. The woman's mother takes a
gift of rice cake to the man's mother, and gives him or his
mother a present of money. Next month the man's mother
returns the call, taking rice to the woman's mother, and
later rice cakes to the pregnant woman. In the seventh
month she takes rice, spices, soap, talcum powder and a
new sarong to her, and is accompanied by a specialist in
Islamic lore who makes a salad of fruit and burns incense
to invite the souls of the ancestors and other spirits to
eat it[13].

[12] See Wood and Suiters, op. cit.
[13] Nancy Towner, 'Matrifocality in Indonesia & Africa and among
Black Americans' in *Woman, Culture & Society*, edited Michelle

So the ceremonies of pregnancy have an important integrative function in the social system. But they do more than this. They link present with past and the human with the divine.

Birth is significant not only because of its effect on the marriage and on the immediate family, but also because it occurs at the linkage point of the generations. Above and beyond its emotional significance for all the individuals involved is a spiritual significance – and perhaps childbirth derives at least a part of its personal emotional significance because of this wider social meaning.

Where ancestor veneration is at the root of religion, the ancestors are intimately involved with conception and pregnancy. The Mossi of the Sudan pray to them for large families at earth shrines where there are landmarks such as trees, mountains, rocks or rivers. The priests of the shrines intercede for the people, and when this is correctly done the spiritual agents of the ancestors pass into the wombs of women and are born as children.[14]

The pregnant woman is in *ritual danger*. That is, she is thought of as being exposed to risk herself because she is in an 'in between' state, not yet a mother and yet no longer a virgin or simply a bride. She has left one status behind but has not yet been accepted in another. So she is in a *marginal* state of existence. And here the French use an adjective, 'liminaire' – 'of the threshold', to describe the rituals which help her through this difficult process, and enable others to protect themselves, in turn, from the dangers she presents, for there is very often an additional element of *contagion*. As she is passing through this transitional phase of identity she is then also a threat to others.

Zimbalist Rosaldo and Louise Lampierre, Stanford Univ. Press, 1974.
[14] Elliott P. Skinner, 'Christianity and Islam among the Mossi', in *Gods & Rituals*, ed. John Middleton, University of Texas Press, 1976.

The unborn baby is in ritual danger too. It has no place in society. No one even knows what sex it will be, what it will be like, or whether it will survive. So it, too, is in a marginal state. Hence it is treated as not only at risk itself, but also as vaguely threatening.

The Lele of Central Africa consider the child in the womb as vulnerable, just as its mother is constantly in danger too, but they believe also that the baby is likely to be malicious. The Lele expectant mother avoids going near sick people, who might be affected by her baby and would become worse. Among the Nyakyusa a pregnant woman should not go near grain growing in the fields, since her unborn baby may take it and the harvest be poor. If she speaks to those who are reaping or brewing beer she can affect the quality of their products unless she first makes a ritual gesture of goodwill to cancel the threat. The unborn child has 'jaws agape', they say, and is continually snatching at food because it is so hungry. Food is spoiled; plants will not grow; the smith's iron cannot be worked; the milk goes bad. And the father of the child is at special risk in hunting and if he goes into battle.

The significance of taboo

In peasant societies young women are inclined to do very much what their mothers did before them, and there are no great innovations in baby care or in conduct during pregnancy. In preliterate societies the continuity is even more pronounced. But in Western, industrialized society, in a situation of rapid social change, there is almost inevitable discord between the generations on such matters, and the rules and avoidance which were previously part of a logical and cohesive pattern become 'old wives' tales'.

Ideas like not lifting your arms above your head lest the cord gets twisted round the baby's neck, and that if you are frightened by a mouse the baby may be born with a mouse-shaped birth mark, or that if you do not get the food you crave – strawberries for instance – it will be born with a strawberry birth mark, are all remnants of a once co-ordinated system of prohibitions and instructions about conduct.

In pregnancy prohibitions and instructions of this kind frequently have the force of *taboo*, a term derived from a Polynesian word which means 'to forbid' or 'forbidden'. This concept exists in one form or another all over the world. It is 'touda' among the Ila of Rhodesia, 'bwanga' among the Bemba, and 'haram' in Arabic countries. Neglect of a taboo results in some dreadful change affecting the person who flouts it, a change which can contaminate other people too, so that the offender becomes a danger to others. The consequences of breaking a taboo are quite different from human punishment, for the result is *automatic* punishment from spiritual forces or gods.

The concept of taboo operates around a core idea of pollution and cleanliness. Pollution has been described as 'matter out of place'.[15] In many cultures the human body is perceived as a vessel, the exits and entrances of which must normally be kept closed, and which must not be contaminated. All body products, matter issuing from the interior of the body, whether it be blood, pus, saliva, semen, faeces, urine, or nasal mucus – even breath and body heat – must not be allowed to invade other people's body boundaries. For some societies, including those within Judaeo-Christian culture, the essence of all these forms of pollution is represented by the mixing of the male and female principles of on the one hand, semen, and on the other, menstrual blood.

Not only should the menstruating woman keep away from men and all important activities (in agricultural communities it was thought that if she churned the butter or cured the bacon, for example, the butter would go sour and the bacon go bad), but in some cultures anybody in an

[15] Mary Douglas, *Purity and Danger*, Penguin, 1970.

especially vulnerable condition must carefully avoid the menstruating or pregnant woman. If the Guatemalan expectant mother stares at a baby, animal or even a plant, her 'hot', 'strong' blood will make it die.[16]

The pregnant woman's body is in a category of phenomena which are quintessentially feminine and dangerous, and which must be kept apart from other phenomena which represent the male principle. If life is to be orderly, if society is to function, if values are to be maintained, the male and female principles must be kept separate from each other except under specified conditions.

Expectant mothers in our own society who hope for natural childbirth sometimes think that everything about pregnancy and birth in simpler societies is inevitably better than in industrialized societies. This is far from the truth. Instead of passing the days of pregnancy ripe with fulfilment, a woman in a pre-industrial society may live in a culture in which pregnancy involves rules and regulations about behaviour which make normal life impossible for both parents. This evidently occurs with the Mundugumor.[17] In this New Guinea cannibal tribe pregnancy is not welcomed, and the effect of taboos in which the father must share when a baby is on the way is merely to make him more irritated with his wife. If he walks amongst men who are making a gong they will scrupulously brush away the chips lest he tread on them and harm the gong, and in case the bits of the gong harm the unborn child. He cannot even put a fence around his garden unless some other man comes and puts in the posts. If he goes into the forest to gather ratan he must be careful to collect only green ratan or the baby will be stuck in the uterus. He must not have intercourse with his wife or they may have twins, and that would be even worse

[16] Lois Paul, in *Women, Culture and Society*, op. cit.
[17] Margaret Mead, *Sex and Temperament*, W. W. Morrow, New York, 1935.

than one baby. So in Mundumugor society the hostility that a man feels towards his own sons is already established long before the baby is born. All the same, the Mundugumor are exceptional. In most societies ritual in pregnancy is supportive rather than merely an extra irritation.

In my own anthropological field work in Jamaica I recorded a wide range of rules which guide the pregnant woman and regulate her daily life. She is not to step over a donkey's tethering rope lest the birth be overdue, or put corks in bottles in case she has a difficult prolonged labour and does not 'open up'. She must not see a corpse lest her blood becomes chilled and the baby turn cold inside her and die, for in pregnancy the blood is hot, and ritual separation must be kept between categories of objects which are 'hot' and others which are 'cold'. Pregnant women must drink with discretion because too much water drowns the baby. They must not make too much preparation ahead of time or the child may be stillborn, a belief that corresponds to the English superstition that if an expectant mother buys the pram before the birth her baby may not survive.

The Jamaican pregnant woman must not drink soursop juice or she will have great pain in labour, drink out of bottles or coconuts lest the baby be cross-eyed, or walk over soapy water when someone is scrubbing the floor, or she will have abdominal pain. She must not lift her arms above her head, or the baby's neck is stretched, and on returning to its place when she lowers her arms again will be scorched, so that it is born with a birth mark on the neck. She must not eat coconuts or the baby grows too quickly. If she sees anything shocking or ugly, or becomes upset about something, the baby may be marked. If she notices a person without a leg, for example, her baby may be born like that, or if she wrings a chicken's neck and feels sorry for the bird the baby can be born resembling a chicken. She must also be very careful how she moves, and it is thought particularly dangerous to double a foot under her when sitting.

Jamaican pregnant women are exposed to the activities of the spirits of the dead, the *duppies*. When women suffer from eclampsia (fits) it is thought to be spirit possession. In Hindu India eclampsia is also seen as spirit possession, and since it is much more common in the rainy season, and is associated with a general deterioration in health during that season, it is believed that spirits seeking reincarnation wander abroad at that time and inhabit the bodies of pregnant women.

Positive instructions in Jamaica include taking 'bitters' in the form of bush teas. This is to stop the blood becoming overheated and so endangering the child. The expectant mother eats callalu which is like spinach, to make her blood 'rich'. She is also supposed to eat okra, a vegetable which has a very slippery interior, to make the baby slip out easily.

Taboos can be very powerful. In the Andaman Islands a name is given to the baby before birth, and from that moment on until it is born and is several weeks old, no one may speak the name of the mother or father. They can say only 'the father of' and name the child. The parents also abstain from eating certain foods or they will become ill and the baby may die. It is significant that the Andamanese observe identical taboos when mourning the dead. They never use the name of a dead person, and the relatives must not eat pork or turtle. The parents of the child being born have, like the person who has died, an abnormal *ritual status*, and therefore run the risk of misfortunes.

Although sexual intercourse may be encouraged during pregnancy in order to 'feed the womb' or 'nourish the baby', in some societies it is taboo. Among the Mbuti of the Congo, intercourse is taboo during pregnancy. It is also taboo before hunting.[18] The Mbuti depend on hunting for food, so prohibition of intercourse before birth and before going out on a hunt stresses the importance of these two activities. Moreover, pregnant women are not allowed to accompany a hunt. For these hunters and gatherers the forest is not just an environment but a living thing, naural and supernatural, which they depend on, obey, and love, but of which they are also in awe.

Taboos like these provide public recognition in a symbolic way of the importance of pregnancy and child-birth to the parents and to the wider community of which they are a part. This is the basis of all ritual, of whatever kind: *ritual value* is given to occasions and natural and supernatural, which they depend on, obey, and love, but of which they are also in awe.

Whilst pregnancy in most societies is considered a special ritual condition, and one which links the woman, and the coming baby as well, to the earth and to the gods, it is rarely an illness. Peasant women continue their normal activities and remain active until contractions start, and frequently during a large part of the first stage of labour. Keneba women of the Gambia continue to carry loads of clay or salt on the head weighing up to forty pounds. They also pound grain, cook, wash, clean, draw water from wells sometimes sixty feet deep, gather firewood, collect edible leaves and snails, look after hens and goats, extract salt a mile from the village, dig clay for pottery, make soap, beat earth floors of huts that are being built, and work on the rice farms up to eight miles from the village.[19] Throughout the world activities of this kind are considered suitable for pregnancy provided the woman is careful to observe taboos which guard the health of herself and the baby.

[18] Colin Turnbull, *Wayward Servants*, Eyre and Spottiswoode, 1966.
[19] Barbara Thompson, 'Infant feeding and Child Care in a West African Village', *J. of Tropical Pediatrics*, Vol. 13, 3, 1967.

Being pregnant today

Our own society lacks ritual activity of this kind, or anything which really *celebrates* the unfolding process of pregnancy, drawing together the future parents and the families in glad preparation for the birth of the baby, and linking this one baby's birth with universal powers. We offer a very inadequate structure of emotional support for prospective parents as people who have to turn into mothers and fathers, and still less which serves to create any wider social cohesion.

The pregnant woman becomes a 'patient' in the same way that anyone who is ill or who suffers a handicap becomes the object of medical attention. The recording and monitoring of the pregnancy is taken over by professionals who are not themselves part of the community in which the mother lives, and family and friends are powerless to affect it one way or another. Although pregnancy in a primitive society may have been a time in which alarming warnings were given to the expectant mother about what she must and must not do, our own society may have made the journey through pregnancy equally or more anxiety-arousing by making its progress one of continuous obstetric investigation, assessment and intervention.

For many women, especially first time mothers who are twenty-eight or more and so classed as 'elderly primigravidae', pregnancy is like walking across a minefield of hidden dangers. Too much weight gain and medical brows are furrowed; too little and doctors are concerned about placental malfunction. In a study I did of women's subjective experiences of induction of labour[20] it transpired that women were told they were being induced because they had put on too much or had not gained enough, and

[20] Sheila Kitzinger, *Some Women's Experiences of Induced Labour*, National Childbirth Trust, London, 2nd ed., 1978.

that what was considered 'normal' weight gain was defined so narrowly by some obstetricians that only a small proportion of women could hope to qualify for a labour that was not started artificially. Blood pressure must stay within carefully defined limits, but no studies have been done to determine if there are any socially created stresses in the life of a pregnant woman today which may make it likely that she should become hypertensive. In discussion in antenatal classes expectant mothers themselves have suggested that just going to the hospital makes their blood pressure go up. Some comment that their blood pressure is lower when they are examined in the surgery of a general practitioner whom they know well, and may be lower still when the midwife visits the home and checks blood pressure in familiar surroundings. Although a steep rise in blood pressure is certainly dangerous, hypertension is used as the great argument for induction and also as a reason for going into hospital for the birth, sometimes for what appear to be inadequate reasons. One midwife remarked that she had been told by an obstetrician, about a woman who wanted to give birth at home, 'That's all right. Just string her along, and in the last week or so I'll tell her her blood pressure is up and she must come into hospital.'

Abdominal girth, position of the fetus, haemoglobin counts and other blood tests, urine tests for sugar protein, other tests of blood or urine for oestriol production from the placenta, pelvic assessment, abdominal and vaginal examinations, sonar scans and perhaps an amniocentesis to detect whether or not the fetus has a chromosome abnormality or spina bifida or microcephaly or . . . there seems to be no end to the fascinating investigations which can be made. Used with discretion when there is indication of the need for them, such tests are of undoubted value. Used wholesale, just because the apparatus is there, or the team is doing research, with inadequate explanation, and without reference to the woman as a *person*, they cause confusion and distress.

One result is that probably the majority of expectant mothers have very little confidence that they are capable of giving birth to a live healthy baby *without medical help*. They no longer trust their own bodies. This has not occurred by accident, but as a direct consequence of the development of male-oriented obstetrics. In Suzanne Arms's words,

> The history of childbirth can be viewed as a gradual attempt by man to extricate the process of birth from woman and call it his own . . . Man placed woman on her back in labour, then devised metal tools to pull her baby out, then knocked her senseless with anaesthesia. And it was man who, throughout history, did it all in the name of 'saving woman from her own body' . . .[21]

Grateful as most women are for all this care and awed by the advanced technology, it is not difficult to understand how a woman can feel that she is merely a container for a fetus, the development and safe delivery of which is under the control of obstetric personnel and machinery, and that her body is an inconvenient barrier to easy access and the probing of all those rubber-gloved fingers and the gleaming equipment, and even – ridiculous, but we are talking about *feelings* – that if she were not around the pregnancy could progress with more efficiency. The expectant mother has become the *object* of obstetric skills. Her experience of care in pregnancy is all too often one of being 'processed' through the antenatal clinic, 'herded' with other women holding their little bottles of urine, and their tights and knickers in plastic bags, with no one of whom they can ask questions in an unhurried atmosphere or discuss the things that are on their minds. Sometimes the system works efficiently : 'We

[21] *The Immaculate Deception*, Houghton Mifflin, Boston, 1975.

all smoothly slid through the machine . . . One is only a number on a card. I saw a different doctor at most visits.' Sometimes the machine creaks and comes to a standstill: 'Waiting time was anything up to three hours, and was usually at least an hour and a half.' Often the procedures actually cause acute anxiety in the mother: 'There was a muddle over dates because too many doctors were involved and skimmed through the notes, and I got very worried' . . . 'The obstetrician stood between me and the sonar scan picture – then said, "Strange." When I asked what was the matter he said, "Nothing. Nothing," so I presumed the fetus had the wrong number of arms and legs.'[22]

Each woman who receives her antenatal care in a large modern hospital is at risk of no longer feeling herself actively the creator, the 'I' who in her unique way makes her unique baby. In terms of human values that is a loss which it is difficult or impossible to estimate.

Pregnancy in our society can also be a very lonely time. The woman gives up work as the time approaches and must fall back on her own resources. Grete Bibring[23] has pointed out that she may turn for support and understanding to her husband because she does not get the support she needs from society. Yet he may be less able to give help than normally because their relationship is also affected by the pregnancy and is going through a process of transformation. They started off as Jane and Bill and now have to become 'Mummy and Daddy'. The future grandparents may be hundreds of miles away, and even if they are near they have no defined roles, and may worry about interfering. It is true, too, that many expectant mothers want to show that they can be in

[22] From a study of women's experiences in maternity hospital, Sheila Kitzinger, *The Good Birth Guide*, Fontana, 1979.
[23] 'Some considerations of the psychological processes in pregnancy', in *The Psychoanalytic Study of the Child*, ed. R. Eissler, S. Freud, et al. Vol. 16, Int. Univ. Press, New York.

dependent and can cope with pregnancy and a baby without seeking help from their mothers, so there is often an emotional barrier to getting help from them.

Expectant fathers

The Arapesh of New Guinea[24] rely on the prospective father to contribute towards the health and welfare of the unborn baby by his own careful conduct, both in the way that he has intercourse deliberately and thoughtfully in the early weeks of pregnancy and in the emotionally supportive stress-free environment he should aim to create for the pregnant woman. In fact, the verb 'to bear a child' applies equally to women and men, and childbearing is believed to be as much a strain for the father as it may be for the mother. He is involved from the very beginning of pregnancy because the Arapesh believe that a man must really work at sexual intercourse in order for a child to be conceived, and that he must continue doing this until the menstrual periods cease. But once the woman's breasts begin to enlarge the child is complete in miniature and from then on intercourse is forbidden.

Shared taboos and responsibilities, which are accepted as normal and inevitable throughout the culture, whether they entail the prohibition of intercourse during pregnancy, or mean that the couple have to make love to 'feed the womb', can have the effect of drawing in the man on preparation for the baby, who in this way affirms his paternity. He is intimately bound up with the baby's life even before it is born.

However much he is 'allowed' or even encouraged to be present in labour, in our own society the expectant father fills a role subsidiary to those of the doctor and other personnel, and one which is perceived as considerably less important. It is a brave man indeed who summons up the courage to attend the antenatal clinic

[24] Margaret Mead, op. cit.

W.A.M. — D

with his wife, and after having got there, to penetrate the holy of holies of the examination cubicle, and talk with the doctor. If the husband is invited to a 'fathers' evening' at the hospital it may be to give him rudimentary information about what is being done to his wife so that he does not intrude disruptively on the institutional 'management' (and this is the term used) of the pregnancy and labour. Nothing he does is thought necessary for the safe outcome of the pregnancy. There are no taboos for him to observe, no family ceremonies he should conduct. When it is a first baby he is in especially uncharted territory, and because of the speed of social change he knows it is pointless to seek advice from his own father.

There must be as many expectant father jokes as there are mother-in-law jokes in our culture. Even when the ridicule begins to fade it is perpetuated in midwives' and doctors' stories about fainting husbands: 'We don't want to have to pick you up off the floor', 'I've never lost a father yet!' Thus the man is denigrated and deprived of the ability to support his wife just when she may most need him.

Studies have been done of 'the couvade syndrome',[25] a term derived from the custom of *the couvade*, which as we shall see in chapter 6 involves participation by the father in childbirth sometimes to such an extent that he pretends that it is he who is having the baby and not his wife. In Western culture the 'couvade syndrome', which usually takes the form of psychosomatic illness, expresses the father's identification with the experience through which his wife is passing and an attempt to share in it – whether through anxiety about the possible outcome of labour or envy of the female reproductive function.

[25] W. H. Trethowan and M. F. Counlon, 'The Couvade Syndrome' *Br. J. of Psychiatry*, Vol. III, 470, 1965.

Perhaps it is because the man's emotions are so often forgotten and his transition into fatherhood neglected, that expectant fathers have been found to suffer from a wide range of psychomatic illnesses which they, and their doctors, often do not realize are associated with the pregnancy. They include backache, toothache, abdominal swelling, an odd feeling that the baby is moving inside them, and loss of appetite. In one English city 57 per cent of a group of 221 men whose wives were pregnant developed symptoms which cleared up once the baby was born. The significant thing is that these men were not psychiatric cases, but an ordinary cross-section of the population of prospective fathers. Perhaps psychosomatic symptoms like these substitute for the rituals and taboos observed by expectant parents in many other societies. For many couples they may, apart from the equipping of the nursery, be almost the only way in which they can be sympathetically united in preparation for the child.

Anxiety in pregnancy

Even though a woman's social function may revolve entirely around her role as a childbearer and rearer, most cultures make provision for anxiety, and it is accepted, too, that expectant mothers are often in two minds about a particular pregnancy. However much a woman wants to be a mother, pregnancy does frequently involve discomforts and weariness and a feeling of being taken over by an unknown and even hostile stranger. Dakota Indians express this ambivalence by anticipating that pregnant women may experience great changes in character, and that formerly mild tempered women may suddenly become aggressive, argumentative, or even violent. Although mothers never strike their children normally, it is considered understandable for a pregnant woman to smack her child. Our own society tends to devalue women's anxieties, and doctors and midwives often try to give reassurance when what is needed is acceptance of the reality of anxiety. Pain may be referred to as 'discomfort', a complicated delivery called 'giving you a bit of help' and women are told to 'try not to think' unpleasant thoughts or 'to forget about' worries. Sometimes in antenatal classes and clinics reassurance is so consistently well organized that a woman who is anxious or emotionally unstable believes that she must be the only one who is feeling like this.

Some of women's hopes and fears about pregnancy, labour and motherhood may be expressed in dreams and many both dream more often and more vividly than usual in pregnancy. In many societies dreams, especially those experienced during transitional phases of life such as pregnancy, are considered especially significant. In Jamaica a woman expects to have a fertility dream when she becomes pregnant, and it is this rather than the obstetrician's examination which confirms pregnancy. The symbols of pregnancy consist of ripe fruit, such as pumpkin, pawpaw or melons bursting with seed, and shoals of fish. In contrast to the dreams of English expectant mothers which I recorded, those which Jamaican peasant women told me about were often very pleasurable and almost sensuous; 'good spirits' appeared who often, like the peasant midwife, or *nana*, whose role is essentially to mother the mother, anointed or massaged the dreamer with oil. Both the Jamaican and English women dreamed of small furry animals – kittens or puppies for example – and sometimes that they actually gave birth to them. Although Jamaican women had anxiety dreams too, in which they stood on the edge of, or fell from, a precipice, or were consumed by fire, the English women's dreams were much more likely than the Jamaican to be disturbing and to involve danger. There were often situations in which they found themselves exposed, humiliated and at the mercy of forces beyond their control: there were dreams of physical injury, often involving amputation of a limb or an operation in which a tooth was extracted. The birth of a baby often seemed to be a loss of a part of the self, and not just a loss but a surgical removal.

In contrast with Jamaican women the anxiety dreams of the English mothers were usually connected with the hospital. A frequent dream was that they were tied down on a delivery table or anaesthetized against their will. Some women experienced repeated nightmares of this kind. There were other dreams in which they had to pass through very tight, narrow passages, apparently symbolic representations of the unyielding birth canal. The English women were also more likely to dream that they had given birth to a fully grown child of three or four or thereabouts, which usually seems to be an unconscious attempt to make the whole process of childbearing and coming to terms with the new baby so simple that it is no longer daunting. Women often have this kind of dream before or just as they start antenatal classes, and as they find an opportunity to express themselves in discussion and to hear about other women's anxieties, the more frank dreams of threat and danger take their place, to be followed very often in their turn by positive and vivid dreams of the labour as a fulfilling and deeply rewarding experience.

Expectant mothers in peasant cultures may be apprehensive about labour, but although birth is more dangerous in these societies, feel that it is basically unthreatening and a fulfilling feminine activity and that pregnancy is a normal state of the feminine organism. An ancient Chinese term for an expectant mother is 'the woman with happiness inside her'. Pregnancy is as much a part of the rhythm of female life as the rhythm of the seasons, springtime and harvest, is unfolding of the year.

Pregnant women often dream of their mothers. The Jamaican pregnant woman may believe that a mother or grandmother who has died is visiting her in spirit and is protecting and guiding her, and welcomes the advice that comes to her in the dream and tries to follow it. An American, Jean Lazarre[26], whose mother died when she was a child, refers to the same kind of experience when she writes: 'I got pregnant and she returned to me, but in a new way. When my first baby was still a tadpole inside me, she came into my dreams. She came as a wise priestess offering love and encouragement.' It seems as if the pregnant woman, in widely different cultures, identifies with her own mother and comes much closer to her emotionally. In our own culture women who have been in intense conflict with their mothers often say in discussion in my antenatal classes that they have a new understanding and sense of partnership with them. Pregnancy links the generations as the expectant mother starts to relive through her body an experience which is universal and shared by most women, and the older woman lives through the recollected emotions of childbearing.

Women sharing

Just as members of the extended family and neighbours together form a work force in the fields, to fish, hunt or cook, or to dance to make the rains fall, so the successful outcome of pregnancy depends on the combined good wishes and right actions of everyone, including dead as well as living members of the society. There is collective responsibility to support the pregnant woman and the child that is coming to birth. The Chinese date life from the beginning of pregnancy rather than the moment of delivery. Pregnancy is not merely a waiting time, but one of preparation.

In our own culture we have almost forgotten the part which other women can play in sharing with the mother the experiences through which she is passing and helping her to feel safe and cherished. One newly delivered woman described her midwife as 'the shepherdess' of birth. In

26 *The Mother Knot*, McGraw-Hill, 1976.

the past the domiciliary midwife filled this important role of shepherding mother and baby through birth and the early post-partum days. She was not concerned with the uterus only but with the expectant mother as a person in her family, and when she helped a woman she did not act as a labour technician, but as someone who had the skills to support her emotionally through the experience of birth. In the United States today women are trying to recreate this kind of loving care by helping each other through pregnancy and in childbirth, and in the absence of sufficient trained midwives lay birth attendants are helping during pregnancy and in labour.

Birth is a keypoint in the social system. When a baby is expected the pregnant woman is one of the major protagonists in a process of social integration which unites previously disparate elements and reinforces weak links in the chain of interaction. The bringing of a child to life is not just a personal, private act, but one which actively promotes social cohesion.

In most cultures women in their protective and supporting roles are at the centre of this network of people working, feeling and acting together to help towards a safe coming to birth of a new member of society. It may be just as important a contribution to society as the more commonly recognized political functions usually performed by men.

5
Childbirth — a Social Act

Instinct, Culture and Society

Labour itself is not only a biological act but also a social process. We have seen already how in some societies it is the birth of a child that is the consummation of a marriage, rather than sexual intercourse, and how in many parts of the world a girl does not achieve adult status until she has given birth. The birth is a social process because it affects the interrelationship not only of husband and wife but of the members of the kinship and descent groups with which both are aligned. It is social too because it defines the woman's identity in a new way; she is now a mother. In highly segmented societies, like India or South Africa, or any country where there are extremes of poverty and wealth as in Latin America, knowing how childbirth is conducted at different socioeconomic or caste levels can also tell us a good deal about the relative status of everyone concerned.

Part of what happens in childbirth is purely instinctive and physiological, of course. A woman does not have to read a book about it or have lessons before she knows approximately what to do to get the baby born. There are elements in birth, too, which the human mother shares with other mammalian mothers, especially the higher primates. Human behaviour often ignores certain of these biological elements, and culture frequently remodels them so that the resulting actions are maladaptive. This happens in simple societies just as in advanced ones, but the more that childbirth is taken over by experts, whether they are obstetricians, shamans or witchdoctors, the more likely it is that the mother's behaviour will be affected by external and social cues rather than internal ones coming from inside her own body.

Childbirth, like many other physiological processes, is never simply 'natural'. Just as eating, drinking, excreting waste products from the body, physical movement, sexual intercourse, puberty, maturity, old age and dying are culturally defined, so birth reflects social values and varies with each society.

A woman in labour seems to be engaged in a purely physiological and in many ways solitary activity. If things are going well she probably feels that what she is doing is entirely instinctive. But even though she may bear her child completely alone and unaided, society expresses its values about pregnancy and childbirth, its importance, its risks, and its meaning, through her.

Human childbirth is a cultural act in which spontaneous physiological processes operate within a context of customs, the performance of which is considered essential or desirable for a safe outcome.

Anthropologists do not write much about birth – possibly because they are usually men and are not permitted to take part in the rituals surrounding labour. They have, however, written so extensively about the disposal of the placenta that one might be forgiven for believing that this must be one of the most important rites in primitive and peasant childbirth. One suspects that the male anthropologist, not allowed to witness the birth, waits outside the birth hut for the moment when someone emerges bearing the placenta and he can at last make some useful addition to his notes.

From the evidence available from female anthropologists, it is clear that birth is rarely the casual 'dropping of a baby' it is popularly believed to be in simpler societies. Instead it is surrounded and shaped by ritual and myth, injunctions, prohibitions and taboos.

Just as table manners and defecation, for example, are closely regulated by society, so that people eat and empty their bowels in a certain way, in particular places and at special times, and there are unwritten rules, conventions and etiquette controlling their exercise, so are attitudes to and behaviour in childbirth socially controlled.

In every physiological activity which involves the exits and entries of the body the way in which we use our bodies is intimately bound up with ideas about their location, worth, and how they work. These ideas for the most part consist of fantasies about the body's inner geography – the position, size, structure and function of various organs which may be only vaguely related to fact. We have ideas, too, about our body boundaries which are an essential part of our sense of wholeness and identity.

In every society there are culturally approved ideas about how babies develop inside the uterus, how they are born, and how the mother and other people can help or hinder the process. When labour occurs the participants expect certain kinds of things to be done, often without even thinking consciously about what they are going to do, or why.

I recently visited a young Arab expectant mother whose husband wanted her to have private antenatal lessons in their home. The teaching was complicated by the presence of the husband and a senior wife, both of whom made it clear that they knew all about labour and that the purpose of the instruction was to make the girl strong to push the baby out. Every word I said had to be translated by the husband, and at last, impatient with my not getting to the point of it all, he grabbed her by the shoulders, directed her attention to himself, took an enormous breath in and started to bear down violently, straining and groaning and gasping and straining again as if his life depended on it. Even a male realized that labour was pushing, and pushing she must learn!

There is a very wide range of activity considered appropriate in labour, and whereas in some societies birth is made a matter of great drama, in others it is thought of as an ordinary and everyday process.

We must not imagine that childbirth is always easy in less advanced societies, or that women necessarily give birth without pain. Although many healthy women give birth casually in the fields or in between household tasks, and continue their work after, there is a high fetal wastage through miscarriage (one in eight pregnancies in one African village, for example).[1] Some girls who suffer from anaemia, protein malnutrition, or endemic diseases such as malaria, never attain childbearing age, or die before they safely deliver their first baby. So the healthy women are picked out, by natural and cultural circumstances, to survive and become mothers.

There may be strict rules about a woman's behaviour in labour which make her husband ashamed if she allows herself to cry out in pain. Her labour may be a testing time comparable to that of her initiation at puberty. In a West African village where Barbara Thompson[1] carefully observed women in labour it was clear that they were expected to have their babies without making a sound, and if a girl cried out she was called a coward and told that she was making her labour longer than it need be.

The after-effects of birth may also be traumatic for the mother. Injuries to the tissues surrounding the vagina may not be repaired, and in parts of South Africa the girl who has torn badly and who has lacerations extending into her anus becomes a social outcast who must live alone in a hut.

[1] Barbara Thompson, 'Infant Feeding and Child Care in a West African Village', *J. of Tropical Pediatrics*, Vol. 13, 3, 1967.

Body Fantasies in Childbirth
In my own research in the comparative sociology of childbirth I found that one of the commonest body fantasies
in peasant societies is that the baby can go up into the
mother's chest, so choking her. To avoid this the mother's
body may be stroked or massaged to direct the baby
down and long scarves or other pieces of cloth are
wound round her to apply pressure to the top of the
uterus and make sure the baby descends. In Colonial days
in America, and still today among peasants in Latin
America, a strip of cloth was wrapped around the upper
abdomen and back, and women on either side pulled it
alternately, thus effecting pressure above the uterus and
massaging the woman's abdomen and back. The main
idea behind it seems to be to make the baby go down
rather than up. In societies where no medical help is
available a long, obstructed labour may be terminated
by rupture of the uterus and death of the baby and
mother, and to those helping it must look really as if
the baby has burst up out of the womb.

The fantasy about the body which corresponds to such
ideas is that there is one long tube from the mouth, down
through the throat and chest into the stomach and uterus,
and then separating out into the passageways leading to
the orifices below. It is often believed, as among Jamaican
peasants, that anything introduced through the vagina
can emerge, possibly with dire results, in the throat and
mouth. This is one reason why mechanical contraceptives
may be unacceptable. When I was in Jamaica there were
myths about how a condom could come off and work its
way up inside the woman's body until it finally choked
her.

A main concern of the helping women who attend a
woman in labour is to reassure her and everyone around
her that the baby is moving down the birth canal as it

should. They do this not only through giving her comfort and companionship but often by magical practices and prayers which invoke supernatural powers to ensure a safe outcome.

Where there is little scientific control of childbearing, magic practices give some hope of controlling the physiological processes by harnessing the powers of ancestral spirits, gods or other spiritual forces. These practices have a logic of their own. There is contained within each system of magic in internal logical pattern and in all magic there are clues about the things which are important in that society.

In parts of East Africa, for example, a woman who is having a long and arduous labour may have her vagina packed with cow dung. It is an act which has significance in pastoral societies where the main economic value is cattle. The dung is meant to encourage the birth of the child by letting it smell how wealthy its father is.

In other pre-industrial societies dramatic myths may be recounted and re-enacted in front of the labouring woman in which basic ideas about the human body and the relation of its parts and functions are expressed and that particular act of giving birth is related to universal forces. The labour hut may be full of men banging drums and chanting and singing. What to the observer is a cacophonous pandemonium seems very different to all those engaged in the drama, including the mother. The saga symbolizes the encounter of the forces of good and evil and life and death in the woman's body. The goal of such dramatic myths is to achieve harmony between spirit and physical worlds, thus freeing the woman to deliver her baby normally.

Perhaps the most vivid example of this kind of thing is among the Cuna Indians of Panama, when a *shaman* (medicine man) intervenes at the request of the midwife in cases of difficult labour and sings the baby out of the labouring woman's body.[2] The woman lies in her hammock and the *shaman* squats underneath it. The song starts with a description of the problem the midwife is encountering, her request to the *shaman* to help, and his arrival on the scene. Then it goes on to describe the things he has done in the woman's hut in preparation for the song-drama: fumigating it with burning cocoa beans, praying, and making sacred wooden figures. The whole song represents a search, with the help of the sacred figures, for Muu, the god who created the baby. Muu dwells in the vagina and uterus, 'the dark deep whirlpool', of the woman in labour, and the battle to wrest from Muu the woman's vital essence which the god has stolen so that the baby can be born takes place inside the mother's body. Each organ possesses its own soul, and everyone's vital essence consists of the harmonious co-operation of all the different souls in the body.

The *shaman* summons the spirits of alcoholic drinks, of the winds, the waters and the woods, and even the spirit of 'the silver steamer of the white man', and the woman's body is described in terms which relate it to the whole earth and all the forces of nature. Then the *shaman* tells how the medicine men are penetrating her body to do battle with Muu, and lighting up the way. He traces the journey along the inner path in a sort of emotional geography of the internal organs, inhabited by monsters and fierce animals, and tangled by fibres intertwining and netting the uterus. The *shaman* calls the lords of the woodboring insects to come and cut the threads. This is followed by a tournament, which the *shaman* and his helpers ultimately win. Then he must make his difficult descent with the aid of the lords of the burrowing animals. Although when they went into her body he and

[2] Lèvi-Strauss, *Structural Anthropology*, New York, Anchor Books, 1967.

his assistants had to go 'in single file', on coming out they can travel 'four abreast'. The cervix (the mouth of the uterus) is dilating as it should.

Through the psychodrama of myth the *shaman* gives to the labouring woman a metaphoric language in which her ordeal can be expressed and given meaning. This is a highly sophisticated form of psychotherapy, and no other treatment is involved. The Sia of New Mexico give another kind of ritual expression to the processes of dilatation and delivery. The labouring woman's father dips eagle feathers in ashes and throws the ashes to the four points of the compass. He then draws the ashy plumes down either side of the woman, and down the centre of her body, as he prays for the safe delivery of the baby. The midwife does the same with a prayer that the child may pass down the road of life safely and quickly. The woman's sister-in-law then places an ear of sweet corn near her head and blows on it during the next contraction. The prayer blown on the corn blows through the passageway of life.

In India it is the custom for a grain jar to be burst to let all the grain pour out, just as the child will be quickly and easily born. The imagery can have a vivid effect on the mind of the labouring woman. Or a tight furled flower is put near the mother which she watches, and as the petals open so her cervix will dilate. Both images provide a focus for the mother's awareness. But they do more than that. There is unity between the body of the mother and the changing form of the flower, between her body and the rest of the natural world. When culturally significant symbols, such as the eagle's feather and the corn, the grain jar and the flower, are used like this the experience of the moment is linked to permanent values and the labour is given pattern and meaning.

In many non-Western societies the psychological element in some childbirth difficulties is understood and techniques exist for encouraging better psychosomatic coordination. In some African societies a woman having a difficult labour is urged to confess her sins so that the birth may proceed. The psychological impact of getting rid of guilt may allow her to get on with her labour. These techniques are based not only on ideas about the body, about health and sickness and dirt and cleanliness, but also on concepts of good and evil. If the most disgusting thing that a woman can do is to break an incest taboo or to commit adultery, such acts committed during pregnancy may endanger the life of the coming child, and so have to be confessed and expiated. Among the Manus of New Guinea, the husband and wife are exhorted to confess any hidden anger they may feel against each other so that the labour can proceed normally.[3] In Hawaii the midwife may be called in to use magic and give the pain to an animal or someone else who lacks moral fibre. (A lazy brother-in-law is said to be the favourite choice.)

In the civilizations of the past the goddesses of reproduction were often invoked to protect the mother and baby, and religion provided its own framework of emotional support. In the Mesopotamian invocation to Ishtar, the Sun God, birth attendants placed the labouring woman under divine protection:

> May this woman give birth happily!
> May she give birth,
> May she stay alive,
> May she walk in health before thy divinity!
> May she give birth happily and worship thee![4]

When labour is prolonged for a Zuni Indian woman a member of the Great Fire Fraternity can help by singing

[3] Margaret Mead, *Male and Female*: A Study of the Sexes in a Changing World, New York, Morrow, 1949.
[4] Quoted in *Birth*, edited by Davil Meltzer, Ballantine Books, N.Y., 1973.

special songs to the Beast Gods to hasten delivery. Among Moslem peoples today the midwife may recite blessings from the Koran during labour.

We have seen that it is generally accepted that every child ought to have a father, although the man who is a baby's social father may be quite different from the biological father. In some societies, notably those disorganized by slavery, men who are willing to accept the social responsibilities of fatherhood are hard to come by.

In Jamaica delivery can be speeded by getting the mother to sniff the sweaty shirt of the father of the child. The point about this is that a large proportion of babies in Jamaica are born to women who are not in a stable union and the most usual time for a man to decide he has had enough and leave is just before or just after the birth of the baby. Having his sweaty shirt around is a fairly good sign that he is available to 'response for' the baby. Reminding the woman of her good fortune at a critical point in the labour probably has a valuable psychological effect and gives her fresh strength.

All the same, it is important to realize that in peasant societies, as in our own, many customs associated with birth are based on empirical reasoning. In any peasant society where older women deliver babies they must rely to a great extent upon the experience they gain as they go along and on the things they learn from other practitioners of the art which have been found to work. Most women in labour need only basic nursing, comfort, and encouragement. Peasant midwives have developed many techniques for giving this sort of help.

A wide variety of comfort techniques are used: hot towels wrapped around the body; massage of the abdomen, back and perineum; breathing techniques which the mother is encouraged to use during contractions; different adjustments of the woman's posture or movements she is urged to perform, (although these sometimes include marked physical exertion or even being shaken upside down to speed up labour); tranquillizing herbal teas or, as among the Manus, a sustaining hot coconut soup,[5] and other medicines to prevent bleeding; and in South America and the Caribbean techniques for assisting the expulsive reflex of the uterus by getting the mother to blow into a bottle, used when there is a delayed third stage.

The Zuni Indians give birth on a bed of hot sand, clean and comfortable and symbolic of the lap of mother earth. The woman's mother puts sand on the floor and pats it into a mound about 20 inches across and five inches high. She lays a sheepskin over it. After the delivery the sand is swept up and thrown away.

Posture for Labour and Delivery

Women in labour are not normally expected to lie down. They move about, changing position frequently and carrying on with normal tasks in the house or outdoors for as long as they feel able. Recent research by Caldeyro Barcia in Latin America, Professor Mendez-Bauer in Madrid and at the Queen Elizabeth Hospital, Birmingham and Southmead Hospital, Bristol, suggests that it is physiologically much better for the mother and baby when she keeps moving; the uterus contracts more effectively, although pain is reduced, the blood flow through the placenta to the baby is better and labour is shorter.[6] Mendez-Bauer found, for example, that when the woman was standing, contractions were 100 per cent more effective than when she lay down. Mothers in peasant cultures would probably be very surprised to learn that we have only just discovered this.

When I was doing research in a big Jamaican maternity

---

[5] Margaret Mead, op. cit.
[6] Peter M. Dunn, 'Obstetric Delivery Today', *Lancet* April 10, 1976.

hospital there was a constant battle between labouring women and midwives, the women wanting to get up and crouch down or rock their pelvises back and forward, with knees bent, and the midwives trying to get them on the bed, where they were expected to lie still and be good patients.

One middle-class labour ward sister, who was embarrassed that I, an outsider, should witness this, said, 'I don't know why you want to see them do this. They are just like animals!' The staff were acutely aware themselves that the urgent movements made by the labouring women did not fit a white middle-class code of behaviour, and they were ashamed for them.

The Sia Indian Woman sits on a low stool, wrapped in a blanket, with her back to the fire and gets up to walk around when she feels like it. As she starts bearing down she kneels on a bed of sand, her hands clasped round her father's neck and her back supported by the midwife's body, who sits with her arms around her and massages her abdomen. The labouring woman among the Siberian nomads leans against parallel rods, about one metre from each other, with a cross bar, during contractions, and hangs from her armpits, so that the whole lower part of her body is loose, supported by the crossbar. On Easter Island, which is exceptional in that the midwives are male, the woman chooses either to stand with her legs apart or to sit, and the midwife stands behind her, supporting her with his body, and massages her abdomen slowly and rhythmically.

The posture which women are expected to adopt during advanced labour varies, from the sitting posture used in European medieval labour chairs or stools (changed only in the reign of Louis XIV when obstetricians delivered his mistresses on a flat table so that he could hide behind a curtain to see everything),[7] to swinging from the rafters

* Described by Suzanne Arms in *Immaculate Deception*, op. cit.

of a hut. The most commonly adopted posture, which is also the most physiologically advantageous, involves a curved back, knees bent and the muscles running along the inner thighs relaxed. In this position the pelvis opens up by as much as 30 per cent. Dakota women used to give birth in a pile of sand, their feet supported against pegs, and their hands holding other pegs at the side in just such a position.

The Manus of New Guinea give birth in special houses where the old women of the tribe live, built on stilts over the sea.[8] The labouring woman lies on her side on a mat on the floor, with her feet against a board. Three midwives support her, one on each side and one holding her back. The woman hooks one leg over a midwife's leg, and changes sides frequently.

Among another New Guinea people, the Usiai, the woman sits between the legs of her sister.[8] Her husband's father's sister sits in front of her with her arms around her massaging her back, and the labouring woman rocks between the bodies of her two helpers.

In West Africa a labouring woman may kneel, with women holding her on either side. She may prefer to hang from the rafters, swinging backwards and forwards for part of her labour.[9] Or she may crouch between two house posts, pulling herself up and down with her arms during contractions. For delivery she squats with a helping woman on each side with their arms crossed with hers, another midwife exerting pressure against her back, a fourth massaging her abdomen and two other women supporting her legs. This rounded back, crouching position with firm support from a helper's body is used – with various modifications – in most peasant and primitive societies. It is only we who get women to lie flat on their backs with their legs in the air, like beetles on their

[8] Margaret Mead, op. cit.
[9] Barbara Thompson, op. cit.

backs, in a position which is convenient for the obstetrician but very often uncomfortable and difficult for the woman because it means that she has to push the baby 'up-hill'.

The squatting position is the one spontaneously adopted by human beings for defecation, and childbirth entails release of the same pelvic floor muscles that are used in emptying the bowels. So a modification of the squatting posture helps the woman to deliver more easily than if she were stretched flat. With modern methods of preparation for childbirth in the West mothers are again being allowed to adopt semi-squatting positions for delivery, or to get on all fours, kneel, sit right up or get into any other position which is comfortable.

Dirt, cleanliness and purification
Rituals of cleansing are almost invariably involved in childbirth. The mother often gives birth, as in parts of Africa or India, in a special birth hut which no one else may enter, except those attending her. This has the useful effect of isolating the mother and baby from possible infection. Both mother and baby need to be purified, and this is done with libations of oil, sacred signs or chants, purging, or bathing in water to which special herbs or colouring substances may be added.

A major threat to the life of babies born under unhygienic conditions is neonatal tetany, because the umbilical cord is often cut with a dirty and rusty knife, frequently one that has been used in the fields or for killing a chicken. In Keneba, a village in Gambia, more than half the babies die.[10] For ritual cleanliness and freedom from pollution overlaps with, but is often very different from, practical cleanliness, just as immersion in the polluted River Ganges is spiritually purifying but may result in disease.

[10] Barbara Thompson, op. cit.

Purification rituals mark the crisis through which both mother and child have passed, and also guard them against the threat of the unknown, the powers of outer darkness. Some of these involve actual physical cleansing, such as the customary squatting over a bucket of steaming water 'hot like nine days' love' adopted among Jamaican women, a good method of cleaning the perineum without needing actually to touch the area. The newborn child may be bathed immediately, as often in our own society. There is really no need for this, as apart from some blood stains, babies are born clean. They are often covered with vernix, a cold-cream-like substance which protects the baby's skin inside the uterus, but the removal of this at birth does more harm than good. Cleansing of the newborn has ritual significance rather than hygienic validity.

Purging is a drastic method of cleansing, popular in various forms throughout the world, and especially so in our own society, where regular bowel motions are considered essential for health and cleanliness, and where the sale of laxatives has reached astronomical proportions. These attitudes to bowel functions are carried over to childbirth. In technologically advanced societies the labouring woman is given an enema or suppository to empty the bowel. In other societies the woman may be given a dose of castor oil, a traditional way in our own society also of trying to start off labour when it is delayed.

The placenta, or afterbirth, has a special place in childbirth customs. It is the thing most intimately associated with the baby, which it brings with it from its other – intra-uterine or spirit – world. So it is often held in reverence, and may, for example, be buried under a tree which is thenceforward that child's tree throughout his life. In West Africa wise men are called in for placental divination. They examine it closely rather as we might look at tea leaves in a cup, to foretell the child's future.

The West Indian practice of counting the knots in the cord is closely connected with this; the number of knots is supposed to indicate the number of children the mother has still to bear. It may also be thought that anyone obtaining the placenta can get power over the child, so it must be disposed of carefully and secretly, either by burying or burning.

Men and childbirth

Childbirth, like menstruation, is in many societies something which is thought to bring danger to men who encroach too near. In Judaeo-Christian thought such ideas can be traced back to Leviticus. The seventh century Archbishop Theodore of Canterbury proclaimed that a newly delivered woman must be isolated for 40 days till clean, and that if any women went into a church while menstruating she had to fast for three weeks. The Penitential of Archbishop Egber (AD 735–66) states that 'every religious woman should keep her chastity for three months before childbirth and for 60 nights and days after'.[11] This is not for the woman's sake, but because a newly delivered woman is dangerous to men. Not only is the menstruating or parturient woman ritually unclean, but her body products, nail parings, hair clippings and, most important of all, her body secretions and blood, are also taboo to men, and can result in illness or even death. We shall have a closer look at ideas about women representing purity and pollution according to the functions they fill for men in chapter 12.

In the past attending women in labour has been largely the province of other women, and throughout the world it is the responsibility of women to help a friend, neighbour or relative in labour, except in those few societies

[11] A. W. O. Hassall, *How They lived 55 BC-1458*, Blackwell, 1962.

where a woman goes off into the bush alone to deliver her baby. Amongst the Keneba of Gambia for example, every mother is supposed to be a competent midwife.[12] You learn how to help other women have babies just as you learn how to cook. In Elizabethan times in England a woman laboured surrounded by her 'gossips', a great deal of strong drink was consumed by all, including the mother and 'there was often more merriment than at a feast'.[13]

Men who engaged in midwifery did so at their peril. In England the first male midwives were not recognized until the seventeenth century. Until then a physician who was requested by the midwife to assist at a difficult labour had to creep up on his hands and knees and hide under the furniture. The traditional English position for giving birth, on the left side, is supposed to derive from the woman's modesty at letting a man see her body, since in this position she has her back to the doctor and he need not see her face. Even when male midwives became accepted they were expected to grope under the bed-clothes, sometimes with the sheet tied round their necks for decency's sake, when delivering a baby, and to rely entirely upon the sense of touch.

Men would never have got involved as experts in childbirth in our own society had it not been for the barber surgeons' guilds which developed in the thirteenth century. By their rules only surgeons could use surgical instruments. They were called in when things got complicated, and in 1616 Dr Peter Chamberlen, a member of the Huguenot family who invented the forceps, wanting to control a proposed guild of midwives and planning to teach them himself, came in for such criticism on the grounds that he only did deliveries using instruments 'by extraordinary violence in desperate occasions' and that he

[12] Barbara Thompson, op. cit.
[13] Jean Donnison, *Midwives and Medical Men*, Heinemann, 1977.

knew nothing at all about natural labour[14], which was perfectly true. When men did do midwifery they charged more than women, and by the second half of the eighteenth century it had become fashionable to get a male physician : even small tradesmen whose wives were pregnant sought to show that they could afford to care for them in the best way by getting a doctor to do the delivery.

At the same time maternity hospitals were being built as places where very poor women could go to have their babies and simultaneously provide clinical material for the doctors and their students.

Midwifery became popular for aspiring doctors because it was a way into general practice. Once a baby had been delivered the whole family might come to a doctor to treat their ailments. It was in the interest of all male doctors to limit the power of midwives and to restrict their knowledge. The textbooks that were written for midwives by them omitted a great deal of important information on the grounds that only doctors should know certain things. In one book, *The Midwife Rightly Instructed*[15], midwives are told that they should not know how to treat haemorrhaging and are told not to aspire 'beyond the capacities of a woman'. Presumably if the midwife was in an isolated home and could not get the doctor her patient was to be allowed to bleed to death.

By the nineteenth century, the male doctors had won the battle. Midwifery had become subordinate to obstetrics. The midwife acted on the instructions of the doctor and as his helpmate. The ladies' Medical College and Florence Nightingale's attempt to establish a training for midwives of the same standard as that for doctors failed. There was to be no separate speciality. A woman either had to

---

[14] For a fascinating account of the history of midwifery read Jean Donnison, op. cit.
[15] Thomas Dawkes, 1736. Quoted in Donnison, op. cit.

try and get training as a doctor or be a midwife working under the authority of the male medical profession.

The presence of the father at childbirth is more complicated. There is a strict rule in many cultures that he should stay away from the place of birth. Male and female elements must be kept separate. But even when he is not supposed to be there it is often believed that the baby's health and life depend to a great extent on his actions. If he goes off with another woman, or polishes his spear, or goes fishing on the day of the labour, he is putting the baby's life at risk. He must watch his actions and in this way help the birth. So he actively participates in the birth though he is not physically present. The Koran states that a father should offer prayers at birth, and it is he who introduces the baby to the world by placing a piece of date in its mouth.

Where the husband delivers the baby himself, as he does among the Bang Chan of South East Asia, he must be specially protected from female forces. He takes in his hands incense, flowers and a lighted candle which allow him to cross over into the sacred world in which birth takes place. Then he prays for the help of the spirits to make the winds of birth strong in his body, for it is not he but the winds which deliver the baby, and he is there only to receive it.

In the custom of the *couvade* the husband shares in the birth by acting it out either at the same time or after his wife is in labour, or by sharing in the lying-in period. An Arapesh father, for example, waits to hear the sex of the baby.[16] Then he says 'wash it' or 'do not wash it' depending on whether he wishes it to live or not. If the child is to be saved he takes a bundle of soft leaves to his wife so that she can line the net bag in which the baby is suspended in a crouching position, a coconut shell of water for bathing the baby, and pungent leaves to keep

16 Margaret Mead, op. cit.

evil out of her hut. He also brings his wooden pillow and lies down beside his wife, and both have nothing to eat or drink for the first day after birth. They concentrate on performing magic rites for the welfare of the child. They remain in seclusion for five days. The father must not touch his own body nor touch tobacco. He must eat all food with a spoon until a ceremony of ritual cleansing is performed at a pool in a special leaf house built beside it. Even then his diet is still restricted, and he must not eat meat until after the child is a month old.

In this way many societies give the father a definite part to play in childbirth. At the same time they protect him by careful ritual from the emasculation which may be thought to result from taking on what is essentially a feminine activity. When the process of participation is over the man is reinitiated into manhood in rites similar to those used when the boy becomes a grown man. He is then a father who has successfully borne a child.

Although the child's father may be called upon to fill this role, and male magicians may be summoned when things seem to be going wrong, in primitive societies the man as childbirth technician is not usually involved in normal labour, and there is no male who corresponds to the obstetrician of Western society. This function rests entirely with midwives.

The Midwife-Witch
The history of midwifery goes back to and merges with that of witches. Midwives are often attributed with special magic powers in relation to fertility, the development of the baby, the labour, and the child's survival. So the midwife was frequently also a witch, and had power over the spirits of the newborn, and is still consulted for charms and love philtres in many peasant societies.

We have seen already that universally the maintenance of health has largely been the responsibility of women. The whole substratum of health care in peasant societies, involving the use of bush teas and herbal medicaments, massages and psychotherapeutic procedures, has been in the hands of women healers. Only when these measures fail is recourse made to the more dramatic methods of male experts, the *shamans*, witchdoctors and priests. The healing skill of these women is from one point of view an aspect of mothering. It grows out of the capacity to *nurture*, and is an extension of the ability to support inherent processes of growth, while at the same time mediating between the natural and the supernatural. These are really not two separate functions, but one, for the right balance which is the foundation of health is itself wholly dependent on an equilibrium between the natural and supernatural worlds. Because this is so, healers have usually also possessed magico-religious power. They have corrected not only the imbalance of physical but also of spiritual elements. This is why they are witches as well as being experts in the art of folk medicine.

In medieval Europe witches were said to kill and eat unbaptized children. A Swiss witch is reported to have confessed that she killed babies in their cradles, or when lying beside their mothers, in such a way that it looked as if the baby had been laid on or had died naturally. There was a popular belief that there was a special opportunity for midwives to kill babies at the moment of delivery by thrusting pins through the soft spot, or fontanelle, into the brain. When a baby was still-born the midwife who delivered a number of still-born babies or ones who died shortly after birth was especially vulnerable to attacks of this nature. It was the custom of medieval midwives to leave the nail of one finger to grow extra long, and to trim it till it was pointed, in order to rupture the bag of waters when necessary in labour. It is understandable that it might be with this weapon that the witch-midwife could be thought to kill the babies she delivered.

One Professor of Theology in the fourteenth century, instructed by Pope Innocent VIII to assist the inquisition in persecuting witches, declared that it was all the fault of the midwives, who were enemies of the Church: 'No one does more harm to the Catholic Faith than midwives.' It was these women who caused the death of, or allowed to die, unbaptized infants, hence lost to the Faith. The Pope announced that these witches had 'abandoned themselves to devils, incubi, and succubi, and by their incantations, spells, conjurations, and other accursed charms and crafts, enormities and horrid offences, have slain infants yet in the mother's womb.'

A similar pattern of black and white magic, indissolubly intertwined, consisting partly of spells, prayers and incantations, partly of medicines and bush teas, and partly of faith healing, psychotherapy and the laying on of hands, exists all over the world.

In peasant societies midwives are some of the most important people in the social group formed by women. For not only do they practise herbal medicine and healing, but preside over the forces of fertility and the coming into being of each new member of society. Thus they are important to the society as a whole, with high status and considerable power.

The real or apparent control of fertility has always been a central one in pre-industrial societies, as we saw in chapter 2, and one which is inextricably bound up with the welfare of society as a whole. Those with power over fertility control the society. Mary Douglas says of the Lele[17] of the Congo that she was struck by how childbearing and hunting were always coupled together, and that if there had been a series of bad hunts villagers soon started remarking how few pregnancies there had been recently. When diviners are called in to right matters,

[17] 'The Lele of the Kasai', in *African Worlds*, edited Daryll Forde, OUP, 1954.

failure in hunting is always linked with barrenness in women, and when all is well again the Lele say:

> Our village is soft and good now. Since the diviner went home we have killed three wild pigs and many antelopes, four women have conceived, we are all healthy and strong.

Perhaps this is why traditionally the power of midwives has extended far beyond their childbirth functions. The whole of social life has depended on them because they control the balance between male and female worlds.

From the vantage point of Western industrialized society peasant midwives are often seen as dirty and ignorant crones. From within the peasant society, however, it is evident that these 'wise women' of the community are exceptional and highly gifted. In countries where educational opportunities are few, it is the more intelligent who find means of canalizing their skills in dealing with people in this way. The Catholic Church always viewed midwife-healers with as much alarm as those who were thought to do evil, for the power of the woman healer was a dangerous counterweight to the male authority of the Church. They functioned alongside and in opposition to ecclesiastical power, and to male medicine which was itself regulated by the Church. Szasz says that:

> Because the Medieval Church, with the support of kings, princes and secular authorities, controlled medical education and practice, the Inquisition (witch-hunts) constitutes, among other things, an early instance of the 'professional' repudiating the skills and interfering with the rights of the 'nonprofessional' to minister to the poor.[18]

[18] Thomas Szasz, *The Manufacture of Madness*, Delta, USA, 1971.

A leading English witch hunter said:

> For this must always be remembered, as a conclusion, that by witches we understand not only those which kill and torment, but all Diviners, Charmers, Jugglers, all Wizards, commonly called wise men and wise women . . . and in the same number we reckon all good Witches, which do no hurt but good, which do not spoil and destroy, but save and deliver . . . It were a thousand times better for the land if all Witches, but especially the blessing Witch, might suffer death.[19]

So both male-controlled medicine and the Church were implacably opposed to female controlled healing and regulation of fertility, and created a conflict which persists to this day. Where peasant midwives have had the opportunity of learning basic techniques of cleanliness, it is sometimes possible to harness their skills in giving comfort, guidance and emotional support to women alongside a system of modern obstetrics in a developing country. Books have been published on the training of midwives in India, for example, which incorporate traditional methods and equipment, and which take into account the cultural context of birth. But in most countries there is a complete dichotomy between the old peasant way of having a baby and the new Westernized obstetrics, and the two systems co-exist, neither learning from the other.

A Peasant Birth in Jamaica

Nanas are the folk midwives who in the past delivered most Jamaican babies, and had to because there were too few trained midwives. Their activities are illegal, how-

---

[19] Quoted in Barbara Ehrenreich and Deirdre English, *Witches, Midwives and Nurses, A History of Women Healers*, Glass Mountain Pamphlets, N.Y.

ever, and when a *nana* helps at a birth it goes down as 'unattended' or 'her mother delivered' on the birth certificate. There are three highly respected positions in the Jamaican village, all of which are held by women: the school teacher, the postmistress and the midwife. They are the pivots of the social system and are links in all the relations between women in the community. And since traditionally it is women who maintain households and keep each family going, with the men often leaving, they are very important.

Midwifery practice in Jamaica is part of a system of folk medicine and healing in part derived from West African concepts of sickness and health, and in part from European methods. From Africa (but also from Europe) came some of the ideas about 'unblocking' the body from sickness, and removing lumps, clots of foreign objects which are stopping up the free flow of body liquids. From Europe, in the books of plantation owners of the eighteenth century, came ideas which had grown out of the medieval theory of 'humours'. A balance must be kept between hot and cold. All foods and drinks can be divided into 'hot' and 'cold', not literally hot and cold ones, but spicy, pungent ones which are supposed to heat the blood and mild ones which cool it down. The *nanas* combine both methods with great expertise.

I was able to interview some *nanas* and found them impressive women of strong personality. Many of them had daughters who were studying midwifery, some of them in Britain, and who sent them back textbooks which, they said, kept them up to date.

When the *nanas* talked about their work they emphasized that it was the art of 'freeing' the body so that the baby could be born. A basic method of helping childbirth is through touch. It is really a kind of laying on of hands. When oil is used, as it often is, it is called 'anointing'. This does not start only in labour, for the *nana* visits the woman in her own home from about the fourth month of pregnancy. There is a good deal of talking about local matters and how the pregnant woman is feeling, and the *nana* does an abdominal examination, following this with a massage with oil from the wild castor oil plant the purpose of which is to 'shape' the baby. She is helping the mother to 'grow it right'. She usually gives advice about diet in pregnancy and urges the woman to eat iron-rich foods, plenty of fruit, vegetables and fish, and to drink bush teas. These herbal teas are prescribed according to the woman's condition: cerasee 'to clean the blood' or for high blood pressure, 'fever grass' for headaches and mixed with rum for vomiting, cape gooseberry, sometimes called 'wild tomato', to prevent miscarriage, 'granny humpback' or ruthupstick for indigestion, 'king of the forest' or soursop for high blood pressure, convolvulus, called 'the love bush', as a laxative, 'strongback' for bladder infections and 'shame root' as a sedative. She may advise against certain foods, particularly eggs which are considered 'binding'.

By the time she goes into labour the woman and the *nana* attending her know each other well, even if they have not known each other and each other's families for years before. When labour starts she and the *nana* prepare the labour room by putting thick layers of old newspapers on the bed, and a clean cloth, which may be a cotton dress over it. Both tear up old, clean rags to make nappies for the baby. Water is collected in a pitcher from the nearest standpipe or spring. Paraffin lamps are filled and special wood which burns like a bright torch may be used if there is no money for paraffin. The *nana* puts the pot on to make more bush tea. If contractions are not good this may be 'spice tea', a mixture of different spices which according to a Jamaican medical practitioner has a proved oxytocic action.[20]

[20] James Waterman, 'The functions of the isthmus uteri' in *Caribbean Medical Journal*, Vol XIV, 3-4, 1952.

Any other children are sent out to neighbours, or if it is night they are bundled over to the side of the bed to give the labouring woman room to deliver, and a clothes line with a blanket over it may be suspended down the middle of the bed. The children lie listening to the progress of the labour and catch the first glimpse of the newborn baby as it is lifted up over the washline for them to see immediately.

The usual drinks for the first stage of labour are mint or thyme tea. Both are supposed to speed up labour. Thyme probably contains a cardiac glycocide which also has the effect of increasing the efficiency of contractions and of uterine muscle tone.[21] Doses of castor oil may also be given if labour is slow. The *nana* uses wild castor oil, which is a good deal less strong than the commercial variety.

When the woman is ready to lie on the bed the *nana* starts massaging her abdomen with oil or the slimy scraping from 'toona' leaves. She reckons that she helps get the baby into the right position by doing this. As contractions get stronger she tells the woman to breathe lightly and rather quickly, or there will be 'too much hackling'. (She is probably suggesting that if the breathing becomes too strenuous there will be hyperventilation). 'Do not take deep breaths in, or the baby will go up out of the belly,' she tells the mother.

If the mother is getting tired or if contractions are weak and ineffective, the *nana* may wrap her round in hot towels 'giving the whole body a souse down', following this by massaging her lightly with olive oil all over. If she has backache she uses a strip of cotton cloth about one foot wide which she pulls from one side to another, producing friction in the small of her back. As the woman

[21] Dennis Adams, Kenneth Magnus and Compton Seaforth, *Poisonous Plants in Jamaica*, UWI, 1963 and personal communication by Dr Magnus.

approaches full dilatation she also uses hot compresses —
sometimes a heated stone, over her lower abdomen, or may
make quick, light patting movements with a rag soaked in
hot water over the place where there is pain, all the time
speaking to and soothing the mother. 'You have to coax
them,' one *nana* told me. 'Give them good words and cheer
them up.' She encourages the woman to 'blow out' until
she can see the top of the baby's head in the vagina,
meanwhile 'bussing' the perineum with oily hands to help
it relax. If the baby's father is present the *nana* asks
him to get up on the bed behind the mother to support
her back. 'You push gentle,' said one *nana*, 'and you give
a little rest and you push again. Pushing hard brings in
weakness. Let it open gradually.' The mother usually
delivers the baby sitting up in bed, her feet on the bed
and her hands on her thighs. If it does not cry immediately
the *nana* lights a cigarette and blows the smoke on to the
fontanelle, 'for the spirits', one expression of her ritual
function in interceding between the human world and
that of the ghosts of *duppies*. The baby is immediately
handed to the mother. *Nanas* are very wary of taking
any active part in the third stage, because they know that
if the woman has a post-partum haemorrhage they will
be thought to have caused it.

So they usually give the woman thyme tea and let her
deliver the placenta herself, cutting the cord only after
the third stage is completed. If the third stage is delayed,
they get the mother to squat over a bucket and blow into
a bottle. This causes the diaphragm to press down on the
top of the uterus and the abdominal wall to press in on
it, and is an effective way of encouraging separation.

Once the placenta is delivered the perineum is cleaned
by the woman crouching over a bucket of steaming water
'hot like nine days' love'. The *nana* washes the baby in
cold water, which is thought to make it hardy, rubs
asafoetida into the baby's fontanelle to protect it from
duppies, treats the cord stump with finely ground nutmeg

(which is slightly antiseptic) mixed with talcum powder and gives it a prelacteal feed of 'Jack-in-the-Bush' or mint tea which helps to clear out mucus. The baby lies on the bed beside its mother, close against her body, and suckles at will. The *nana* makes cornmeal porridge for the mother and perhaps for the other children, and clears up the room. Before she leaves she tells the mother that she must stay indoors with the baby for a week, lest the *duppies* come for the child, and must bind her hair in a turban and not wash it so that she does not get 'baby chill'. Neighbours come bringing food for the family and boys and girls are sent off on errands. If they can afford it there will be some rum drinking to celebrate.

The *nana* cares for mother and baby in the first few days after delivery and may also look after the other children and do cooking and washing if the woman's own mother or an aunt is not available. She simply takes over and mothers the new mother.

The Jamaican *nana* gives a good deal of emotional support to women in pregnancy, labour and the puerperium. She provides for the mother a continuing personal relationship and herself fills the role of a mother who accepts responsibility from early pregnancy on, who is known in the community, and who meets the expectant mother at the grocery store and the market, in church, washing clothes down by the river, and gossiping with other women under the shade of a tree outside her homestead. She may give advice casually during pregnancy as they pass the time of day. She knows exactly what sort of life the pregnant woman is leading, what her worries are, any family difficulties and money problems, housing and ill-health. The result is a prototype of family and home-centred maternity care.

Birth in South Africa
In segmented societies where there is a cultural clash between forces representing the old and the new, the

peasant way and the technological method, different modes of childbirth reflect positions in the social system. This is strikingly the case in South Africa.

The Bantu ideal of childbirth is represented by the traditional Zulu way of giving birth, which is rarely possible today in the townships, but it is still there as an ideal. According to Zulu custom a witchdoctor should be present to bless the ground on which the firstborn is to be delivered, and to help in case of need, but is not necessary with second and subsequent births.[22] Maidens smear cow dung on the floor of the grandmother's dwelling where the labour usually takes place. 'When the child is born it must look on something beautiful, for this will affect its life.'[23] So coloured beads and special childbirth carvings decorate the room. 'The first minute of life is the most important.' If the woman bleeds too much, the witchdoctor orders a red calf to be sacrificed and she is made to drink some of its blood. After delivery, the woman is always given a special dish of spinach to make the blood strong. A retained placenta is delivered by getting the woman to blow into a bottle (an almost universal practice in peasant societies for dealing with a delayed third stage). It used to be the custom for a male witchdoctor to deliver his own child, so that it might inherit his spirit, but a witchdoctor informant told me that the hospitals make this impossible, for doctors and nurses 'do not realize that the forces that activate the birth are much older than humanity itself. They turn birth into a spiritual nightmare.' But still wherever possible Zulu children are taken to see a birth 'to instil in them respect for human life' and so that they learn 'to regard birth and death as part of life'. This is considered an important part of their education.

[22] Vasamazulu Credo Mutwa, a Zulu witchdoctor, personal communication.
[23] Vasamazulu Credo Mutwa, op. cit.

In the third month of pregnancy, the Zulu woman is taught how to breathe 'to give life and strength to the child'. Each morning she goes outside the hut, and, facing the east, takes three deep breaths, followed by a long breath out, to breathe out all evil. In labour the woman concentrates all her energy on breathing alternately through her mouth and her nose 'to lessen her consciousness of pain'. Traditionally there is an opening through to the sky in the central point of the roof of all Zulu dwellings, and it is on this that the labouring woman focuses: 'She must kneel, concentrating on this space, through the hole where she can see the stars. We say of a woman who is in labour: "She is counting the stars with pain." '

The Changaans and the Bechuanas, like the Zulus in labour, kneel. But the Bushmen woman makes a space in the bush, like a nest of grass, and tying a rope to the branch of a tree, bears down while holding the rope.

A great number of home deliveries in the Bantu townships are reported as 'unattended'. These babies are usually delivery by folk midwives. In the customs they adopt can be seen an area of culture contact between traditional Bantu practices common to all the tribes and Western style methods. One of the folk midwives who served as my informants had been a nurse in a large American-style hospital for seven years before she had gone into midwifery among her own people and had also started training as a witchdoctor. She combined Western skills she had acquired as a professional nurse, but with which she had been dissatisfied because of their isolation from traditional social values, Zulu tribal healing and the cult of spirit possession.

She described to me the importance of asepsis, but was also convinced that it was important for the mother to drink herbal teas in pregnancy 'to make the baby play free inside'. She knew about modern methods of obstetric intervention, but explained that if labour is prolonged one should deliver a child by smearing one's hand with bone marrow and helping the baby 'get through the road that is closed'. Both mother and midwife 'must follow the pain, keep quiet, and listen'. The mother should handle the baby and kiss it at delivery, for 'the child must know who is the mother'.

Within several miles of the homestead where I talked with these folk midwives there exists the enormous modern hospital for Bantu patients. The delivery ward was full of groaning, writhing women – the majority of them labouring alone. Oxytocin drips and pumps were in widespread use. This was the meeting place of the old Africa and the new technology of the West. Pools of blood lay on the floor like sacrificial outpourings, and Bantu nurses were happy to leave them there as a witness of the blessings of the earth, while they busied themselves with technologically sophisticated modern equipment and ignored the labouring women as far as possible, which it was not so difficult to do as they did not speak the same languages anyway.

All the straightforward cases were delivered at home or in the Soweto clinics: these hospital mothers fighting to give birth were selected from the township as possibly complicated cases. Birth was very far from normal here, and it was conducted in a way I had seen before in American hospitals catering for black 'clinic patients' from large urban ghettos: impersonal, conveyor-belt obstetrics accompanied by a plethora of technical innovations and machinery.

In South Africa childbirth for white women is very different from that for Bantu women. An obstetrician who delivered his upper-class patients in the most luxurious private maternity home of the city said, 'There's the woman, varnishing her nails, a box of chocolates at her side, the radio blaring and the baby hanging at one breast, and she is supposed to be trying to feed it . . . they're spoiled little rich girls in here!' This clinic was designed to provide private rooms for mother and baby, but now, according to doctors, is losing money because the patients cannot stand having their babies with them, and prefer nursing homes where the newborn are lined up in central nurseries to be looked after by the staff. Sister told me: 'Lots of mummies are silly. They handle their babas as if they were little china dolls. They go home with a sister, and often two sisters, one for the day and one for the night; and when they leave, an African nanny takes over.'

I asked what education was provided for women (and fathers, too, perhaps) in caring for and relating to their own babies, and she said, 'Mummies like to cuddle too much. They spoil the babas.' Indicating the glass doors leading from each mother's bed through to the small nursery for three or four cribs, she said, 'Of course we lock the hatches when the daddies come. They are not allowed to touch the babies.' I wondered who was colluding with whom, since it was not surprising that parents who were not encouraged to explore and handle their babies failed to develop confidence. 'But,' protested the obstetrician, 'we can't have women molly-coddling their babies!' At night, according to the paediatrician, the mothers are fed several sleeping pills and the babies are removed to the central nursery. The women wake up 'with breasts like footballs'.

At another maternity home for whites only, the nuns sat in a circle with beaming faces and fresh white habits, offering tea and cakes. This is the private clinic where Grantly Dick-Read introduced what were then his revolutionary ideas of birth without fear. But here babies were not with their mothers at all, but in solid masses of plastic cribs in rows like cemeteries for the war dead. 'Oh it's rarely that a mother asks for her baby,' Matron said. 'We believe mothers need a rest.' The nuns glowed as they tended 'their' babies. Fathers were taboo, and although some were present at delivery, most were sent to the fathers' waiting room downstairs where they smoked and worried together and – latest development of modern technology – viewed the deliveries on a television screen. The mothers and mothers-in-law turned up too, and sat watching their daughters deliver with vicarious pleasure or suffering. All the mothers were white: 'We have to get permission from Community Development when perhaps an Indian doctor's wife wants to have her baby here, and she has to be kept separate. We have a room downstairs where we can keep her.'

In the next maternity hospital outside Pretoria, German nuns of the Holy Cross were delivering the babies of African women. There were six midwife-nuns, with twelve African staff midwives and, they said, 'It feels like a family.' Although many patients came in with severe post-partum haemorrhage or protracted labours, there had been no maternal deaths over the last two years, and there was little cross-infection. The maternity home was in an area recently proclaimed by the government as European. Some 80,000 Africans had already been moved from it, and the nuns lived from year to year, with an annual permit to continue their work – but never knowing whether African nurses would be able to complete their training, or even whether it was worth painting the walls. 'We are hung between heaven and earth,' Matron said. She took me for a moment to the stillness of the chapel – 'our powerhouse'.

In South Africa Bantu and coloured women have no choice about maternity care, and even white women have little choice. All mothers, white as well as black, are effectively denied the opportunity to decide how they want to have their babies and the kind of post-partum care they prefer. It is a maternity system where the consultant obstetrician is king, and where midwives are undervalued, have no association of their own, and have few links of any kind with midwifery associations outside South Africa. The mother is subservient to the direc-

tion of her obstetrician, and later of her paediatrician –
both of whom follow the fashions of their American
counterparts, since they often have at least part of their
professional training in the United States.

Having a baby in East Germany

European cultures of childbirth incorporate a mythology
and system of rituals no less pervasive than that in any
primitive society. With us, too, childbirth is above all
a social act. In East Germany gynaecology and obstetrics
are harnessed to the services of a Communist state. (My
research in East Germany was undertaken in 1965, so that
the material presented here is largely historical.)

Education for childbirth is available for all East German
pregnant women. This takes the form of 'pregnancy
gymnastics' (dating from the Nazi period), and Russian
and French-based psychoprophylaxis, together with instruction about the Pavlovian psychology of conditioned
reflexes and the rudimentary anatomy and physiology of
reproduction. Classes are split into theory and exercises
in a highly systematized and rigid way. The exercises are
rarely linked to what is actually going to happen in
labour, and consist of keep-fit exercises which include
many movements which British obstetric physiotherapists
consider potentially dangerous, because they encourage
the stretching of pelvic ligaments and may result in
strain.

The psychoprophylaxis taught here – in the last six
weeks of pregnancy, when the women are exempted
from work – is similar in many ways to that first taught in
France after Lamaze returned from the USSR, having
developed the initial techniques. Formal lectures,
authoritarian and dogmatic, take place round an enormous boardroom-style table or with the women sitting
in rows, often presided over by the portrait of a bearded
Marx gazing sternly on the scene of twenty or thirty
hugely pregnant women. Exercise classes take place in a

gymnasium, however, and are led by a gymnast. The emphasis is upon muscle training and athleticism: 'Breathe in 1 2 3 4. Breath OUT 1 2 3 4 5 6. Breathe in Breathe out. Relax.' The commands are rapped out like a drill sergeant. The instructress is not concerned with the mother's subjective sensations – only with her *correct behaviour.*

The discipline of psychoprophylaxis is used as a means by which the pregnant and labouring woman is assimilated to Communist values and her behaviour regulated. This last bastion of free enterprise and individuality – the intimacies of psychosexual life, the inter-relationship between mother and baby, and between husband, wife and child – is made to conform to norms which each woman fulfils, fails to fulfil, or over-fulfils.

The inculcation of socially approved attitudes to and training in techniques for coping with labour has little to do with any personal decision on the part of the expectant mother herself. It is something that is done to her, rather than something she sets out to do herself. When in a large university hospital I asked what women were taught about awareness and conscious control of the pelvic floor muscles, I was led downstairs to the clinic basement, where I saw women sitting in rows, their white hospital gowns drawn to their waists, knees spread, while opposite them men in rubber suits aimed hoses of ice-cold water between their legs!

At the same time there co-exists with this a great deal of the old German view of Mother Nature. One teacher introduced the subject of foetal development with, 'Nature said, let not the eagle lay her egg in the nest which is blown away or from which it can fall. Let us keep the egg within and make a nest within the body. And so there developed – a uterus.' This view of a kindly, bosomy Nature exists side by side with theories of conditioned reflexes and diagrams of Pavlov's salivating dogs, their maws gaping and saliva dripping into test tubes screwed into their cheeks.

In the labour wards the women lay like sandbags, quiet and still, breathing correctly, then softly moaning; the ones I touched were extremely tense, although the gymnastic teachers around did not seem to realize this. They were acquiescent, obedient.

Birth is considered a subject unsuitable for men, and although expectant fathers may be taught how to bath a baby, they are *never* allowed to be present with their wives in labour or at delivery. This was a shocking idea to them, and they rationalized their refusal to consider it by references to germs, explaining bacterial attack on the human body in a way similar to that in which undesirable influences can endanger the body politic. The mother's emotional asepsis was protected not by allowing her her husband's loving care, but by training in psycho-prophylaxis and by the provision of tanks of oriental fish in the labour wards.

All placentas were sent to the state cosmetics factory to be used in face creams. The birth rate was steadily dropping, however, and this may explain why the scarlet star soaring in mammoth splendour above the hospital roof was not lit up that day. It shines whenever they over-fulfil their norm, although what this meant in terms of a hospital I never discovered.

I shocked doctors and nurses when I talked about feeding a baby when it cries. This was a new idea to them, but apart from being disgusted at the laxity and indulgence implied in this method of infant feeding, they were neither interested nor curious. They smiled kindly and said that *their* way was better: 'The child will become undisciplined. He will grow up a little tyrant,' they said, as we looked at tiny newborn babies in their cribs. (Much later, in a completely different context, I happened to remark that my children ran in from school ravenously hungry for their tea, and was told, 'Ah, that is because they were not disciplined as babies.')

When a child is born the father is instructed to 'use severe words to stop the soft-hearted mother from rushing to the basket at the first shriek of its occupant'.[24] This belief about discipline is such an essential tenet of their faith that when I asked in one hospital what the nurses did when the newborn babies cried between scheduled four-hourly feeds, I was confidently told, 'There *is* no crying here', information which I found it difficult to accept at face value.

Such an attitude is not uncommon in hospitals generally, but in Britain and the United States there is a growing awareness of the interdependence of mother and child and the need for family-centred medicine and admission of mothers to hospital with their sick children. There is conflict between this concern with human relations and the routines and traditions of institutions, but at least we are *aware* of that conflict, and from the discordance is born social change. This was not so in East Germany in the sixties.

The social context of childbirth and the expression of political values in preparing for it and the care of the mother are evident in the modern Communist state. What may not be so clear however, is the more subtle way in which values are expressed and behaviour ritualized in the institutions catering for childbirth in Western democratic societies. For in any society the way a woman gives birth and the kind of care given to her and the baby point as sharply as an arrowhead to the key values in the culture.

[24] From a booklet written for expectant parents.

6

Ritual and Technology in Contemporary Hospital Childbirth

The modern hospital, no less than a peasant community, evolves its own culture. Some practices are technologically and empirically based. Others are enshrined in the mystique of hospital practice. These are linked with social expectations and medical assumptions about what a patient is and how she should behave, and with concepts of purity, pollution and contamination. In this chapter I want to look at some of the customs of the modern Western maternity hospital and to see what social functions they may fill.

Most obstetricians in the West are men, which is odd to start with. When a woman goes to her obstetrician she encounters his ideas about attitudes and behaviour appropriate to a female patient. The relation between doctor and patient is basically an asymmetrical one, and he is the dominant partner. So his view of her role, both as patient and as mother, forms the basis of their interaction. Her preconceptions about what doctors are like and how they behave operate in the transaction too, but are expressed less often.

The woman who attends the antenatal clinic or who is in labour is supposed to be a 'good patient'; that is, she is meant to be quiet, placid, polite, appreciative of what is being done to help her, quick to respond to instructions, able to comprehend and remember what she is told without requiring the information a second time, clean, neat and self-contained and should not disturb other patients, or the staff, by emotional instability of any kind. The word 'patient' itself derives from 'passivity'; the patient is someone to whom something is done.

As I observed interaction in a labour ward in a British maternity hospital I noticed that midwives were most satisfied with the management of a case when they could write on the record sheet 'patient resting peacefully' whether the labouring woman was in fact relaxing well, or whether under the influence of narcotic drugs she was quietly moaning and groaning, but *without disturbing anyone else.* The ideal of the case sheet was a woman who was tucked up in bed, more or less inert. In writing 'patient resting' on the card the midwives were offering to the obstetrician an assessment of which he would approve, for this was his aim too.

The male obstetrician tends to make assumptions about female psychology which derive perhaps from his view of his own mother, sister and wife. He may assume, or be taught as part of his medical training, that the act of coming to him puts the patient in 'a parent-child' relationship. As one text book puts it:

. . . by the patient's dress, walk, makeup and attitudes in answering questions, a judgment of her personality begins . . . The physician notices whether the patient is reacting to the interview in a feminine way or whether she is domineering, demanding, masculine, aggressive.[1]

Obstetricians can feel perplexed and threatened when patients do not behave according to this stereotype of the good patient. In answer to the woman's questions about obstetric procedures or hospital routines this finds expression in phrases like 'Just leave it to us'; 'don't worry, we know what we are doing'; 'it's a very good hospital'; 'the midwives will make you as comfortable as possible';

[1] *Obstetrics and Gynaecology*. J. R. Willson, C. T. Beecham and E. R. Carrington, 4th edition. Mosby, St Louis, 1971.

'I'm sure you will like it here', the American beneficent 'don't bother your pretty little head about that', or a definitive and authoritative statement that the less the mother knows the better.'

On the other hand the doctor's anxiety may be expressed in verbal attack on the patient who questions his judgment with threats that unless she relies on him she is endangering her baby's life: 'You don't want to harm your baby, do you?' or even 'Do you want to kill your baby?'

The husbands of maternity patients who want to be involved in the birth can also increase the doctor's anxiety. In one discussion in a group of expectant parents a father asked, 'Can husbands share in the decision-making about whether to have Pethidine or not?' and the obstetrician, who was very concerned to establish good communication replied, 'We always like husbands to be there' and seemed unaware that he had evaded the question. Frequently reassurance is offered instead of information to both man and woman, the effect of which is to *raise* the level of their anxiety. Questions are also sometimes answered in technical terms which the woman cannot understand, and then although it appears to the doctor that he has given information, nothing, or even misleading information, has been conveyed.

So there are three psychological factors which profoundly affect patient-doctor interaction in the antenatal clinic and maternity ward: assumptions about each other's roles, the doctor's and the woman's anxiety, and poor communication between them. Obstetricians are now aware that there are frequent breakdowns in communications, and have probably always been sensitive to the patient's anxiety. What they may understand less well is their *own* anxiety and how can it permeate the patient-doctor relationship.

The doctor's whole training prepares him or her for a protective barrier against the patient. This process starts when as a medical student he begins to dissect a body and has to forget that there was once a person inside it, and it is reinforced by special medical humour much of which focuses on the subjects of death or the female body. The ward round, with the big chief progressing from bed to bed trailed by a small crowd of doctors and students, to whom he turns to ask questions about 'interesting cases', further refines the skill of talking about people as if they were not really there and of evading personal contact. Moreover the career structure of medicine is such that the doctor depends on superiors' and colleagues' approval and trust. He dare not step too far out of line, whatever his own feelings.

In hospital he also enters a total institution which dictates his own behaviour rigidly – how long he can reasonably spend with each patient, for example, or whether Sister will disapprove of him sitting on a patient's bed, and sometimes more subtly and pervasively, whether it is acceptable to touch a patient other than when examining her and, if it is, but only sometimes, what conditions must be met (for example, is it all right to console a patient who has had a stillbirth?)

The organization of many antenatal clinics incorporates procedures which many patients find humiliating. We have seen already that the antenatal clinic can be an ordeal for any woman. Patients wait, with their specimens, in rows, and dressed in white hospital smocks, as they are slowly processed through the clinic system. After the tests on blood, urine, blood pressure and general health, the summit is attained and the woman goes into a small cupboard to await the summons to emerge into the open clinic through the other door, where she is told to get up on the examination table. Her vision is restricted at either side by cubicle walls which screen her from other patients, but not from nurses, students and doctors. Naked from the waist down, she lies flat while a group of men form round her lower end and her abdomen and vagina is uncomfortably and sometimes painfully prodded and ex-plored. Comments she does not understand are made about her body and its contents, and her private parts are re-ferred to as 'the vulva' 'the bladder' 'the perineum' 'the uterus', thus depersonalizing them. Sometimes no word passes between the doctor and the woman; she is simply the body on the table. If he has instructions to give her he may pronounce them while she is still supine and ex-posed, or if he has time, may ask her to sit up so that he can explain something. Only occasionally does he let her get dressed so that she can sit talking to him face to face clothed and herself once again, while he explains that all is well, or that she must lose weight, have more rest or be admitted to hospital.

In the modern hospital this is our own ceremonial *rite de passage* into motherhood. It involves separation from 'normal' people going about their everyday lives; taking over by agencies outside the woman's own control; investigation and assessment involving exposure of the most intimate parts of the body to men and strangers; and subjection to alarming and sometimes painful procedures at which she must not flinch because 'it is for the sake of the baby'. Only after these rites of separation and humilia-tion does society remake her as a mother.

The labour
It is not only the action in the antenatal clinic that is ritualized, but entry to hospital for childbirth itself involves further ritual. The first ceremonial is that of the admission procedure. Husband and wife are separated while the labouring woman undergoes 'prepping', consist-ing of both medically useful recording of data about the condition of the mother and the fetus, together with other predominantly ceremonial rites: shaving the pubic hair, enema, bath, dressing in impersonal hospital nightwear and putting to bed.

While this is being done by uniformed strangers, verbal

exchanges may take place which serve to further define the woman's role as patient. These at first sight may seem the stuff of normal conversation between equals, but in fact entail forms of what Goffman calls 'presentational deference'.[2]

The midwife makes a complimentary remark about a patient's hair or the pattern of her sponge bag, or asks, 'What do you want, a boy or a girl?' These appear to be simple expressions of sympathetic concern and friendly interest, but in effect, because of their context, they invade the individual's personal reserve:

> which becomes clear if it is the patient who pays the member of the staff these compliments or asks the midwife or doctor about their families. Taken together, these rituals provide a continuous symbolic tracing of the extent to which the recipient's ego has not been bounded and barricaded in regard to others.[3]

It is all part of the making of a compliant patient.

Let us look more closely at exactly what is done when the patient is 'prepared' and at subsequent events in labour. There is not only no evidence that shaving of the perineum reduces the amount of bacteria on the skin, but indications that, in fact, chances of minor infection are increased because the razor has scraped the surface cells and so allowed the introduction of bacteria.[4] We may see perineal shaving, therefore, as a way in which the labouring woman is de-sexed, the area around anus and vagina being ritually returned to its pre-pubertal state.

The purging of the expectant mother with an enema is often done not only when the woman's lower bowel is

[2] Erving Goffman, *Interaction Ritual — essays on face-to-face behaviour*, Penguin, 1972.
[3] Goffman, op. cit.
[4] See H. Kantor et al. 'Value of shaving the pudendal-perineal area in delivery preparation', *Obstet & Gynec.* 25, 509-512, 1965.

obviously full, but when it is almost empty. That is, it is done, not because it needs to be done, but because it is an act of ritual cleansing and purification. Moreover, it involves taking over personal body processes by an external institution, and thus the control of that which is most intimate. The regulation of bowel functions is maintained throughout the hospital stay, and midwives make regular rounds with laxatives asking who has 'been', and continuing institutional control over elimination.

There is rarely any medical reason why the father should not be present and participate in the birth, nor why labour cannot be family-centred as in many peasant communities. Yet still in some hospitals fathers are told to wait outside during the admission procedures, whenever the doctor or midwife examines the mother, or throughout the whole of the second stage of labour and the delivery. The woman's body has been appropriated by medical personnel. To permit his presence is to confuse two categories of social identity, that in which the woman is wife, sexual being and mother, and that in which she becomes the patient whose actions are under the control of the doctor. In order to avoid confusion between these two social categories modern obstetrics takes labouring women out of their own homes, separates them from other members of the family, and often, too, from the father of the child they are bearing, and puts them through what amounts to an initiation process on entry to hospital which has the effect of a ritual subjugation.

The donning of special clothing – gown, head cover, mask, overshoes – is a device familiar in religious ceremonial by which the ritual act of birth is dramatized. But it is also one which has the effect of segregating the labouring woman from her everyday existence and isolating her from her normal social relations, and also depersonalizing the birth attendants.

Studies of ritual aspects of the use of masks and other uniforms in hospital show that the higher up in the hospital hierarchy an individual is, the less important is the special clothing and the more often is it discarded.[5] The consultant obstetrician may approach his patient in his ordinary suit, only donning special clothing for an obstetric manoeuvre. Conversely, the lower an individual is in the hierarchy the more special clothing he or she is required to put on, and the more consistent its use. The husband comes at the bottom of this hierarchy, and is often required to wear special clothing at all times, including a mask throughout the labour, although a mask kept on longer than fifteen minutes at the most no longer has any protective function.

The labouring woman is often covered from the waist down with sheeting. When an obstetrician isolates with drapes the lower half of a woman's body, it becomes *his* sterile field. But it is clearly neither his, nor, because of the juxtaposition of vagina and anus, sterile. It is a convenient fiction however, by which he asserts his rights and insists that the woman keeps hands off her own body, which becomes out of bounds. This is another way in which the genital area is depersonalized.

This depersonalization provides protection for the gynaecologist. The woman is no longer a sexual object. This is not a man looking at a woman's naked body, but a doctor confronting 'a case'. It provides an armour against his own feelings and against the introduction of human emotions, not only disruptive sexual emotions, but very often also those of tenderness, compassion, sympathy and friendship, in the doctor-patient relationship. It may be only in the presence of another man who *is* allowed to have these feelings, the woman's husband, that the gynaecologist can allow himself to relax and let some of the barriers come down. Now that men are more and more frequently with their wives in labour the armour no

[5] J. Roth, 'Ritual and magic in the control of contagion', *Amer. Social Review* 22, 1957.

longer serves its purpose of creating a protective barrier between doctor and patient. Obstetricians often say that they enjoy working with husbands because their presence permits a more 'normal', easy atmosphere. It is unfortunate that still in many hospitals the husband is sent out whenever the doctor comes in to examine his patient, when both the woman and her obstetrician might benefit from his presence,[6] and that antenatal care still takes place, for the most part, in the absence of the husband. Women complain about depersonalization even more in the antenatal clinic than they do in labour. Perhaps this is one reason why. There is a case for at least some antenatal clinics being held in the evenings and for the partner to be invited too.

It is sometimes remarked by doctors that women in labour are vulnerable, fearful and easily upset by minor occurrences, attaching too great a significance to casual remarks or ordinary routine procedures. They therefore see their main role in psychological terms as being one of 'reassurance'. Everything will be all right as long as the patient will 'trust' the doctor. But this vulnerability is imposed by the social situation and is not an isolated product of the fearful woman's mind. It results in large part from the 'show of normalcy'[7] which all hospital staff are concerned to maintain and which is part of their professional demeanour.

If it is the case that the subject is attempting to conceal all signs of being alarmed and the others are attempting to conceal all signs that would give alarm, then any minor sign can be taken as evidence that these shows are being strenuously attempted but have not been

[6] S. Kitzinger, *The Good Birth Guide*, Fontana, 1979.
[7] Erving Goffman, *Relations in Public: microstudies of the public order*, Penguin, 1971.

totally effective. This means that one sign can be as upsetting as a thousand and warrantably so.

It is fortunate, however, that one sign, one signal, from a doctor or nurse that they recognize the person in the patient can be equally effective in turning a negative experience into a positive one, and permits spontaneous emotional processes in mothering to unfold. A woman who had a long series of obstetric interventions starting in early pregnancy, each of which necessitated the next, and then an emergency Caesarean section, found herself unable to relate to her baby. She felt, she wrote, 'an incongruous emotional numbness. I had no real awareness of motherhood . . . I sat holding the baby awkwardly, trying to feel something.' But there was one Sister who gave emotional support to the mother-child relationship and who helped the mother to start breast-feeding. She led both the parents 'into a room with a low chair, made me comfortable with pillows', removed their masks 'and showed me how to hold the baby and – the miracle occurred! He was my baby – he sucked! . . . and then, tact upon tact, she left us! John touched his son for the first time . . . He was ours.'

The room in which a woman has her baby in a modern hospital in the West is very different from the dwelling or forest clearing in which a woman gives birth in a pre-industrial society. Whereas the traditional mode of childbirth places the woman in the centre of the unfolding drama, modern childbirth involves advanced and sophisticated technology and cumbersome equipment compared to which the labouring woman seems dwarfed and insignificant. The signals which the obstetricians and midwives receive and interpret come not directly from her body but from the monitors and other machines which fill the labour room. It is on the screens and the unwinding paper chart that all eyes are fixed. 'An eventual aim,' said one Professor of Obstetrics, 'must be for every woman to have her baby in an intensive care situation.'[8]   Another obstetrician remarked to colleagues:

> Labour wards now look like some scientific hell-holes with instruments everywhere, wires everywhere . . . If we used telemetry and got rid of the wires (we can monitor a man's heart on the moon) surely we could monitor a baby without having to have a wire attached.[9]

Not only have the machines taken over the centre of attention, but they have also immobilized the woman in labour, who cannot get up and walk about, or even change position freely in bed. In no peasant societies are women completely immobilized in childbirth; in contrast, helping-women encourage her to adopt various postures and to move around in order to help the descent of the baby's head. In our own society modifications in behaviour during childbirth have been accepted as necessary because of the new machinery, without any research into the possible effects of these changes. It is likely that iatrogenic factors (i.e. caused by medical interference) are giving rise to conditions which in their turn have to be treated by still further new obstetric techniques. Inserting an electrode through the woman's vagina and cervix and slipping it on to the baby's scalp allows monitoring of the fetal heart, for example, but also introduces an additional risk of infection so that intramuscular injections may have to be given too.

The actual posture which the woman is required to adopt in the delivery room is also symptomatic of the

[8] C. R. Whitfield, in *The Management of Labour*, edited by Richard Beard, Michael Brudenell, Peter Dunn, Denys Fairweather, Royal College of Obstetricians and Gynaecologists, 1975.
[9] S. Simmons, 'Induction of Labour', *The Management of Labour*, op. cit.

elation between obstetrician and patient. It is only in our
Western technological culture that the woman having a
baby has to lie flat on her back with her legs in the air
in a psychologically disadvantageous position for pushing.

It is easier for the obstetrician to examine and to inter-
vene in labour when the patient is supine. The position
adopted as routine for deliveries conducted by an obste-
rician (as opposed to a midwife) in which the woman,
often without sensation from the waist down, lies flat with
her legs raised in lithotomy stirrups, and in the USA, with
her wrists and ankles tied or clamped, sometimes with a
shoulder restrainer holding her firmly in position as well,
indicates that the function of the expert is that of
'deliverer', and that the woman herself is not perceived
as the active birth-giver.

An integral part of the obstetric delivery is an incision
of the mother's perineum to enlarge the birth opening –
an episiotomy. This turns every birth into a surgical
operation and produces a wound which must be sutured.
It is a ritual mutilation through which the majority of
women in our society pass in order to be mothers. Although clearly some women require the birth canal en-
larged, and some babies need to be born quickly, routine
episiotomy for virtually 100 per cent of all women, as is
done in the United States today, is necessary because the
obstetrician is in command of the birth and wants to get
the task over and done with as quickly and efficiently as
possible, without wasting his time or relying on the
vagaries of nature, or on biological rhythms which do
not readily accommodate themselves to hospital schedules.

But this may not be the only reason why obstetricians
take charge of women's bodies. Almost universally woman
is seen as having a threatening power which can weaken
and emasculate men, and as we shall see in chapter 10, her
sexuality and the products of her body are considered
potent and dangerous. She is like a bomb which can be

defused only by denial of her sensuality, by carefully circumscribed behaviour on her part, by meticulous avoidance during those critical periods when her body opens up and its fluids and other substances emerge, or at any time when a man is engaged on some task which involves special skills and concentration. The shame which women feel in Eastern Mediterranean countries, the rituals offered by husband and wife during her unclean time in Judaism and Hinduism, and the taboo on sexual intercourse before going into battle or on an important hunt, engaging in a community activity of great significance or making sacrifice to the ancestors, which is typical of tribal societies, all indicate that everywhere woman is at once the creator and the destroyer, the terrible goddess Kali, who bears life in her hands. Perhaps this is how all children feel at some time about their apparently omnipotent mothers. Girls grow up and start to menstruate themselves and develop the power to bear babies in their own bodies. But boys can never do this. Some psychoanalysts have explained frequently encountered male attitudes in terms of 'uterine envy'.[10]

The obstetrician, as distinct from the midwife who is traditionally far less interventionist, seeks to take control of childbirth. It is then almost as if he, and not the woman, gives birth to the baby. The intricate technology has defused the bomb, childbirth has been de-sexed. The previously mysterious power has been analysed, and he has harnessed it to a masculine purpose and according to a masculine design.

This may be one explanation, at least, for the fact that rates of induction of labour rose to 50 per cent or more in British hospitals in the late sixties and early seventies, in spite of the fact that obstetricians themselves state that, 'most of the figures have shown that increasing the induction rate has not resulted in any appreciable improvement in the perinatal mortality figures', the

[10] Ian Suttie, *The Origins of Love and Hate*, Kegan Paul, 1935.

xtent to which perinatal mortality can be improved by
.arting labour is extremely small',[11] and even that 'the
eterminants of perinatal mortality remain unknown and
ay not primarily be medical'.[12]

It is not a new idea for doctors to start off labour
rtificially. Looking at the history of induction and speed-
ıg up of labour can give us some idea of what women
ave suffered at the hands of those obstetricians who treat
e uterus as a fascinating thing to play with rather than
art of a woman. *Accouchement forcé* was practised in
e nineteenth century. In the early twentieth century an
bstetrician tried used children's balloons to open the
ervix. He pushed them inside; then poured water into
em, and pulled. Another method was to use castor oil,
rge soapsud enemas, repeated doses of quinine, and
jections of pituitary extract. One advocate of this
ethod said that if the woman did not go into labour
ter doing this repeatedly for three days, it was safe for
e obstetrician to go away for the weekend. It was
timated that quinine killed 5 per cent of the babies.[13]

Acceleration of labour with ergot was introduced in
3o8, and the doctor who did so commented, 'Rarely have
been detained more than three hours.' But within a few
ears it was found that the stillbirth rate had increased
armingly as a result of this practice, and ergot, which
ad been called the '*pulvis ad partum*' became known as
e '*pulvis ad mortem*'.

Then sparteine was tried, but that led to the uterus
ontracting strongly in an uncoordinated and acutely
ainful way, even hours after the last dose was given, and
was found that it could also slow or even stop the
eart.

Modern methods of induction have become possible be-

Richard Beard, *The Management of Labour*, op. cit.

A. Turnbull, *The Management of Labour*, op. cit.

G. W. Theobald, 'The Induction of Labour', in *Obstetric Thera-
eutics*, D. F. Hawkins, ed., Baillière-Tindall, 1974.

cause very few mothers have a seriously malformed pelvi
nowadays, and because of the discovery of penicillin an
the invention of the oxytocin drip in 1947.

One problem with the modern method of induction o
labour by ultravenous infusion of oxytocin is that unles
the dosage is very carefully regulated the woman's uteru
can go into a state of hypertonic spasm. This spasm result
in a reduction of blood flow to the placenta, and the bab
may become distressed, or even die. The uterus of
woman who has had a previous Caesarean section, an
which is therefore scarred, and that of a woman who ha
already had a number of babies, may rupture in a
induction unless the contractions are monitored meticu
lously, and the drip turned down or switched off if the
get too powerful. This is why women having induced o
accelerated labour should always be connected to machine
which provide continuous monitoring of the strength o
the contractions and the baby's heartbeat.

Induction rates vary greatly between different hospital
and even between different consultants in the same hos
pital. Whereas some obstetricians reckon to do no mor
than 15 per cent inductions, others select anything up t
75 per cent of women for induction. It has not bee
shown that high rates of induction save any more babie
Cardiff was one centre where in the early seventies ther
was a high induction rate. One conclusion drawn fror
lengthy research carried out in Wales, however, was tha
'there is no evidence that a woman in Cardiff having
baby in 1973 was any more likely to end up with a liv
child than in 1965'.[14]

As women told others about their experiences of i
duced labour, and further information was published i
medical journals, there was reaction on the part of son
consumers who saw the high induction rates as evidenc
of unnecessary interference in labour. Some obstetricia

[14] J. F. Pearson *The Management of Labour*, op. cit.

explained this as a phenomenon engineered by press and television and even by research into the subject. It was not, they thought, 'real':

> I do not believe that . . . we are seeing other than the response of a relatively vocal minority of the patient population. If the vast majority of patients were not encouraged by the media, and by questionnaires, to express disappointment and frustration, and discontent, they could be effectively dealt with.[15]

Nevertheless, after public disquiet was expressed the high induction rates of 1971–4 were dramatically reduced over a short period, and in at least one large teaching hospital an induction rate of over 40 per cent was in a few months reduced to one of 25 per cent without any rise in perinatal mortality. It looks as if public attitudes and many women's wishes to experience labour as naturally as possible has had an effect.

While all this has been happening, the drop in perinatal mortality, in spite of a world-wide steady reduction, is still in Britain behind many of the developed countries of Western Europe, and noticeably behind the Netherlands, Switzerland and the Scandinavian countries (See table over).

The availability of pharmacological pain relief in the modern hospital also means that labour is very different from that in a peasant society. The most commonly used analgesic agent in Britain is Pethidine ('Demerol' in the USA), which is a narcotic, first introduced to take the place of morphine, since it was claimed by the manufacturers that only very small doses were needed (25 or 50 milligrams) and that it was non-addictive. In fact it is an addictive drug (but not if taken only in childbirth) and the doses now given start at 100 mgs and go up to 200 mgs.

[15] J. Selwyn-Crawford, *The Management of Labour*, op. cit.

Perinatal mortality in the countries of Europe

	Perinatal mortality per 1000 births (to the nearest decimal point)	
	1968[16] (or nearest year)	1972[17]
United Kingdom	26	22
Finland	19	17
France	25	21
W. Germany	25	24
Italy	32	30
Netherlands	20	17
Norway	21	17
Sweden	16	14
Switzerland	19	16

Since it is injected several times in many labours some women are getting as much as 500 mgs of Pethidine, which is a knock-out dose. Pethidine is often combined with other drugs. Pethilorfan is a combination of Pethidine with Lorfan and is used so that the baby is less likely to have breathing difficulties at birth than with Pethidine alone. Unfortunately the Lorfan reduces the analgesic effect of Pethidine. Sparine (added to reduce nausea) results in a decrease of the activity of the uterus for up to two hours, so prolongs labour. Although in some hospitals mothers control their own pain relief, asking for it as and if necessary, in many Pethidine is given as routine, and the

16 Adapted from R. Maxwell, *Health Care*, McKinsey, New York, 1974.
17 I am grateful to the DHSS for obtaining for me and making available these figures.

patient does not share in the decision-making.[18]

In the West we are alert to the deleterious effects of some of the practices in pre-industrial societies: the exhortations and ceremonies in the name of religion or the consequences of meddlesome midwifery. To us, these practices may appear cruel in the extreme. We may be less aware of the cruelty that can be involved in our own culture of childbirth because we take it for granted. We may accept medication for pain relief, for example, as necessary in childbirth and not recognize its disadvantages. In the case of Pethidine these are many. It sends women into a drowsy stupor in which labour can take on a nightmare quality, reducing the ability to cope with pain, and making it impossible to control breathing and relaxation.

On the other hand ours is a drug-orientated culture. We start some babies on Merbentyl (an anti-spasmodic) which is handed out with orange juice at the health clinic, and then put them on to junior aspirin. Pharmacological pain relief, tranquillizers, nicotine and alcohol are a part of normal life and for many are props to get through the business of living each day. Whenever we have a pain we expect to be able to remove it with yet another miracle drug.

It is not surprising that the dramatic events of labour are anticipated as producing sensations which every woman has a *right* to have removed. To feel pain is to go back to the Dark Ages. To have no sensations is the modern way of giving birth.

Regional anaesthetics, of which the most well known is the lumbar epidural, have been hailed as the answer to pain in childbirth. An epidural can certainly give pain-free and even sensation-free labour, and is safer than

[18] Sheila Kitzinger, *Some Women's Experiences of Induced Labour*, National Childbirth Trust, 2nd ed., 1978.

general anaesthetic. It should be used with discretion however. Some women experience a swift and dramatic drop in blood pressure which can be bad for them and the baby. Some have an allergy to the local anaesthetic used. The possibilities of the mother having difficulty in breathing, becoming unconscious or remaining paralysed are exceedingly remote, but are there nevertheless. A much more likely problem is that the baby will have to be delivered by forceps, and in most maternity units where elective epidurals are available the forceps rate has shot up.

In one London teaching hospital epidurals have increased from around 16 per cent of deliveries in 1971 to 60 per cent in 1975, and over the same period the forceps delivery rate has increased from 15 per cent to 29 per cent.

An epidural also usually means that urine must be drawn off from the bladder by a catheter, since the woman has no sensations which make her want to empty her bladder. This lack of sensation may remain for the first day or two after the delivery, so during this time too she may need to be catheterized. Infection is far more likely when a catheter is used. One study indicates that 29 per cent of women who have catheters passed have 'significant bacteriuria' as compared with 3 per cent of those who have not. A forceps delivery also makes urinary tract infection five times more likely.[19] Obstetricians sometimes say that an additional disadvantage of epidural anaesthesia is, in the words of one, 'the need for constant observation of the patient',[20] an objection which should perhaps be discounted if we think that all women should be watched and cared for in labour.

[19] See M. G. Elder and C. A. Hakim, 'The Puerperium', in D. F. Hawkins, op. cit.
[20] D. D. Moir, 'Drugs used in labour: analgesics, anaesthetics and sedatives'. in D. F. Hawkins, op. cit.

An article describing the advantages of epidural anaesthesia published in a midwifery journal[21] was illustrated with a photograph of a laughing mother sitting up in bed, oblivious of her labour, while watching television, and explained that this patient delivered shortly after the photograph was taken. (Although it was strange that the testcard seemed to be giving her such pleasure, the claim that the woman need have none of the sensations of labour holds true.) Obstetricians often pride themselves on having a patient who is 'talking, laughing and joking' while delivering a baby, and engaged in what, for the woman who has not had regional anaesthesia, is a major psychosexual experience in which talking and joking would be only a distraction, just as it would be at the height of lovemaking.

Ultimately, however, there is no drug which solves the problems of being alive, no pill which can eradicate the stress of living. Moreover, while easing stress, medication has at the same time produced new problems for our society. In childbirth it has, for example, reduced the significance of an act in which the woman still participates, but passively. This is associated with a wider impoverishment, for the images which grow out of actual life experiences, and particularly from universal life crises such as those of giving birth, initiation into adulthood, marriage and dying, are increasingly lost.

In pre-industrial societies the unfolding script of the individual's life cycle, with its transformations, becomings and peak experiences, provided the scenario for the ritual representation of change in social status and modifications role. The physiological and biological processes created the images in which the individual's relation to society conceptualized. Central to these rituals was a complicated metaphor which used the great experiences of being

[21] D. H. Jones, 'Epidural analgesia in obstetrics', *Midwives Chronicle*, November 1975.

born and dying as archetypes which occur again and again in dramatized form, to symbolize acts of creation and renewal on the one hand and destruction and departure on the other. In the majority of these rituals both are involved, since each person must die to the old before he or she can be born into the new social state. Rites of rebirth from the mother form major themes in many religions from East to West. Having a baby is not just a biologically, not even simply a socially, significant process. It has many layers of meaning and provides one of the most important and richest themes of all ritual.

We have 'emptied the notions of death and birth of everything not corresponding to mere physiological processes and rendered them unsuitable to convey other meanings'.[22]

In achieving the depersonalization of childbirth and at the same time solving the problem of pain, our society may have lost more than it has gained. We are left with the physical husk; the transcending significance has been drained away. In doing so, we have reached the goal which perhaps is implicit in all highly developed technological cultures, mechanized control of the human body and the complete obliteration of all disturbing sensation.

[22] Claude Lèvi-Strauss, *The Savage Mind*, Weidenfeld and Nicolson, 1966.

7

Bonding, Loving and Learning

The Passage from Nature to Culture

Babies, unlike tadpoles or tortoises, survive only because there are mothers, or others able to take their place who can respond to them in a nurturing way. Part of this maternal response is purely instinctual. Much of it is learned, and is acquired from the culture, for even instinctual responses need an appropriate setting in which they can unfold. The apparent dichotomy between 'nature' and 'nurture', and the old argument as to which is most important, is, in fact, a highly artificial one. All behaviour depends on *both* organic *and* environmental factors.

In this chapter I want to focus on learning how to be a mother, and to draw on evidence from the study of animal behaviour as well as from social anthropology. This learning takes place in two significant phases. The first occurs during the female's own infancy and youth, and develops out of her own experience of being mothered and her inter-relationships with others; the second intensive learning phase is triggered off by pregnancy, birth, and the presence of the newborn young and interaction with them. It is in this period particularly that endocrinological and social factors combine to produce mothering behaviour.

At the beginning of life the human baby's appearance and behaviour provide very effective signals for the mother to respond by caring for the child. The rounded shape of the newborn's head, the short face and large forehead, its plump cheeks, the smell of the skin, the fixed attention which comes from the eyes of a vigorous (and undrugged) baby, rooting for the nipple, the hunger cry, exploring hands and mouth and uncoordinated movements of the limbs are all evocative signals for maternal attention. In the baby, too, there is a special kind of intensive learning during the first minutes and hours after birth, which is a sensitive period for the development of attachment between mother and neonate.[1] It bears some resemblance to, but is a good deal more complicated than, the *imprinting* or object fixation, described by Lorenz,[2] who watched geese and found that when the chicks hatched out they followed the first large moving object, whether it was their mother, another animal, or even the investigator himself. A similar imprinting phenomenon has been observed in insects and fish as well as in mammals, including sheep, dogs, deer, zebra, cows and buffalo. If these attachment mechanisms are interrupted the young develop abnormally.[3] Even so, it is, of course, very different with a human baby, or newborn babies would be emotionally attached to the midwives and doctors who delivered them!

It used to be thought that if a baby was born healthy and was physically well cared for there was no reason why it should not grow into a normal adult. The primary function of parents was believed to be to protect the newborn from harm, provide food, keep it warm and to remove waste products.

When the Emperor Frederick the Great unwisely decided to discover what language babies would speak when they grew up if no one spoke to them as children, he did not realize that the orphanage children in his experiment

[1] John Bowlby, *Attachment*, Penguin, 1965.
[2] Konrad Lorenz, *Methods of Approach to the Problems of Behaviour*, Academic Press, N.Y.
[3] Konrad Lorenz, op. cit.

would die, 'for they could not live without the petting and joyful faces and loving words of their foster mothers'.[4]

So little was the baby's need for loving, tender care understood as late as the 1920s, that in spite of all the attention given to providing a hygienic environment for babies in foundling homes in the United States many of them died, and in some there was a death rate of almost 100 per cent.[5] Such attitudes changed slowly, and even in the 1950s Gesell,[6] in his work on the development of children, implied that the unfolding of a child's abilities took place in an environmental vacuum. Nothing could be farther from the truth. For although there are for each species pre-existing genetically determined patterns of development, they unfold only if environmental conditions are right. Just as the relationship of the fetus to its uterine 'nest' dictates the development of the baby while still in the uterus, so the relationship of the newborn baby with those who care for it affects its development as a human being, not only in the first year of life, but probably far beyond.

One important element in the environment is stimulation. Special kinds of stimulation are necessary for optimal social and emotional development. Babies need the stimulus of things to see, moving objects and people to follow with their eyes, patterns to explore, voices and other sounds to hear, and hands to hold them. Ethology (the study of animal behaviour) has increased our understanding of human development. Although one cannot infer that because a particular stimulus is right for a rat, human infants need similar treatment, ethological research raises questions about human mothering. When

[4] Ashley Montagu, *Touching*: the human significance of the skin, Harper and Row, 1972.
[5] Ashley Montagu, op. cit.
[6] Arnold Gesell, 'The ontogenesis of infant behaviour', *Manual of Child Psychology*, edited by L. Carmichael, Wiley, New York, 1954.

chimpanzees are reared in the dark they are very slow at learning later, and are unable to discriminate between friends and strangers. When puppies are reared in small cages, unable to see either human beings or other dogs, and are let out when eight to ten months old, after which they are treated normally, they are over-active and nervous, of low intelligence, are easily dominated by other dogs, and suffer mental and social retardation for years after.[7] Deprivation in infancy for any species seems to have long term consequences.

It has been discovered that baby rats develop and actually grow faster when they are handled frequently. This seems to be because they utilize their food better and have a higher output of growth hormone when they are handled.[8] The work of Harry Harlow with baby rhesus monkeys is well known.[9] When reared without a mother, they much prefer a surrogate mechanical mother which is soft and which rocks to one which is hard or stationary, even if the latter supplies milk. Soft body contact and rocking seem to generate a feeling of security, resulting in 'well-balanced' adult monkeys.

From the earliest moments of life the human baby's development, too, is affected by and grows out of his relationship with his mother. The stimuli which the baby receives from his mother, and those which she gets from her baby, play a significant part in his development.

Newborn babies are most alert when they are well propped up or upright. Heinz Prechtl discovered that when you put babies under two weeks down on their backs they tend to get drowsy.[10] The way the baby is handled from birth may have a lot to do with its alertness

[7] Anthony Ambrose, 'The Comparative Approach to Early Child Development: the data of ethology', in *Foundations of Child Psychiatry*, edited by Emanuel Miller, Pergamon, 1968.
[8] Ambrose, op. cit.
[9] H. F. Harlow, 'Development of affection in primates', in *Roots of Behavior*, edited by E. L. Bliss, Harper, New York, 1962.
[10] 'Problems of behavioural studies in the newborn', *Advances in*

and therefore the amount of learning that takes place in the first weeks of life. In most cultures the baby is carried around close to its mother in a semi-upright position against her body.

Babies can smell their mothers too, and can soon distinguish their own mother from anyone else. Aiden Macfarlane did an experiment with pads soaked in breast milk and found that by the time a baby was five days old he preferred a pad soaked with his mother's milk to a clean one, and usually by six days turned his head more towards one soaked with his own mother's milk than another mother's.[11]

But more than biology is involved, even from the very earliest moments of life. The relationship between the mother and her baby reflects the interaction between the parents, and between them and other members of the family and society. The baby's behaviour is part of an *interactive system*.[12]

This is so with animals too. When a mother monkey has never herself been adequately mothered as a baby, and especially when as a motherless baby she has not been able to play with other monkeys, she does not respond correctly to the baby's cues, and either neglects it or becomes hostile. Her ability to mother well depends on her having been mothered herself, and having learned the give and take of living with her peers. For normal social relations in adulthood, including mothering, grow out of social contacts in infancy.

Immediately following birth the mother begins to learn, if she is given the opportunity of uninterrupted contact

the *Study of Behaviour*, D. S. Lehoman, R. A. Hinde and E. Shaw, eds., Academic Press, 1965.
[11] Aidan Macfarlane, *The Psychology of Childbirth*, Fontana/Open Books, 1977.
[12] Ambrose, op. cit.
Mary Ainsworth, 'Patterns of attachment' in *Early Human Development*, edited by S. J. Hutt and Corinne Hutt, OUP, 1973.

with the baby, the signs by which she is soon able to recognize her baby as distinct from any other. For this to happen the infant must, of course, be with her, to be watched, heard and touched.

During this period the animal mother maintains contact with her young. When a mother cat has given birth she immediately starts to lick her young all over, and then nudges them in the direction of the nipples so that they can suckle. A goat first licks the amniotic fluid from her newborn, hears its bleating, and then responds to this by further nuzzling, tasting, smelling and exploring of the kid's body. Stimulation of face and anus seem to be particularly important in some mammals, and what looks like cleaning the newborn is also an important factor in the bonding of mother and baby. If the animal mother is anaesthetized at delivery, or immediately following it before she has started to lick her young, or they are removed at this time, she never recognizes them as her own. If a kid is taken away from the mother goat, for instance, for two hours after birth, she does not accept the kid as her own when it is brought back.

A human mother, too, responds to her baby's cry and this response is not only 'mental' ('I ought to attend to the baby') but also *physical*. Studies in Stockholm[13] have shown that her baby's cry, heard on tape on the third post-partum day, immediately increases the temperature of the mother's breasts as shown on thermograms of the chest wall, and this is followed by a sudden heavy dripping of milk. This suggests that communication between mother and baby during the time when lactation is getting established is very important, that the two ought to be together, and that feed times should relate to the baby's crying rather than to the clock.

[13] J. Lind, V. Vuorenkoski and O. Wasz-Hockert, 'The effect of cry stimulus on the temperature of the lactating breast primipara', in *Psychosomatic Medicine in Obstetrics and Gynaecology*, ed. N Morris, Karger, 1972.

But this kind of interaction does not occur in a vacuum. The mother is partially prepared for it by endocrinological changes which occur in her body at the end of pregnancy, and also by her emotional readiness for labour and expectation of the baby. Even being in labour may help this readiness. Perhaps this is why women who have had Caesarean sections sometimes face more difficulty in breast-feeding. It is not just that they are uncomfortable if they hold the baby in their arms or are recovering from the effects of anaesthesia, but very often the baby is presented to them like a package, a kind of gift provided by the hospital, and they may find it hard to link the child with which they are confronted with the process of pregnancy; it seems as if it cannot have been born from their own bodies. The continuity is broken. The phrases they often use in describing their experience are 'It was a shock . . .' and 'I couldn't believe he was mine.' The result is that they may not yet be emotionally ready for interaction with the baby. It can be very important that they have time alone with the baby to discover and get to know it and to begin to feel themselves mothers. The same thing can happen when a labour is induced, perhaps for pressing medical reasons, before term, or at any rate before the expectant mother has reached the stage, so common in the last two weeks of pregnancy, of feeling that she has had enough of waiting, wants to get on with the birth, and longs to push her baby out into the world and have it in her arms.

When labour is able to start naturally the woman is not only physiologically ready, with a soft and partially dilated cervix, but is also emotionally 'ripe' to become a mother and to respond to her baby in an appropriate manner, partly because of hormonal modifications which are associated with the start of labour and with subsequent lactation.

When a woman cannot start labour naturally, or when she must have a Caesarean section, the environment in which she gives birth and meets her baby can often make up for the physiological and emotional lack of readiness. If she is able to be with her baby on the third or fourth day after delivery she experiences the extraordinary sensation of the 'let down' reflex, which precedes the rush of milk down to the nipples, a spontaneous and uncontrollable response to the stimulus of her baby crying or actually sucking.

Human mothers share in a pattern which is typical of interaction between mothers and their newborn young in many other species. It is an intensely powerful biological bond which impels the mother to action to protect and cherish and feed her baby. Often it is a further development of mating behaviour and of relations between the mother and father, and is an integral part of the bond between them too.

The work of Hinde[14] has demonstrated that changes in the environment cause changes in the endocrine state in female canaries, and that when light or temperature or both are increased the female begins to stay close to the male. Her production of oestrogen is then further stimulated by contact with the male, and she starts to build a nest. The male canary has been stimulated to peck out the female's breast feathers because of her endocrinological changes, and her whole breast area has become more vascular. This means that it is more sensitive to touch, and she receives stimulation from the side of the nest as she sits in it. She seeks this stimulation and visits the nest more frequently. This in turn triggers off further endocrinological changes which lead to her laying eggs. Thus the endocrine level in the canary is to a large extent the consequence of environmental stimulus, and the stimuli themselves result from increased sensitivity initially produced by the endocrine activity.

Mother mice and rats are very sensitive to any dis-

14 Referred to in Bowlby's *Attachment*, op. cit.

turbance in their environment. If the nest is disarrayed the mother mouse rushes to rebuild it, or if the pups are removed seeks to retrieve them.[15] But the mothers only do this because they are already in a 'maternal state', which is partly the result of endocrine changes, but also of stimulation from the pups (in pregnancy females do not retrieve pups). In the three or four days after birth the mother initiates all interaction with her pups, and has to do so, because they do not yet have their eyes open and have little hearing, so that they depend on stimulation through physical contact. If the pups are removed in this period the maternal state quickly fades. We can therefore conclude that during this time stimulation from the pups is important in keeping the mother in a maternal state. At the end of the second week the pups begin to walk and start to leave the nest, and at this stage they initiate suckling and interact with each other. If the pups are removed during this time the mother's maternal state does not wane so quickly. It is rather less dependent on stimulation from the pups. Finally there is a stage starting at four weeks when the pups become independent and then the mother is less likely to retrieve and suckle them, and the 'maternal state' gets weaker, even if the mother's own pups are replaced by other younger pups.

Recent research has also focused on the effect on human mothering of this combination of hormone changes and stimuli from the baby. Research of this kind has become very important because of the light that it may be able to throw on women who are unable to be adequate mothers, or who actually physically harm their babies.

When I examined 86 of the labour reports I had received from mothers who had attended my own antenatal

---

[15] Niles Newton, D. Peeler, and C. Rawlins, 'Effect of lactation on maternal behaviour in mice with comparative data on humans', *Lying-in, J. of Reproductive Med.* 1, 1968.

classes and who had described in detail their first encounter with the baby, I found that many used words descriptive of touch. They commented on the delightful feeling of the infant kicking against the inner thighs as it was being born, or lying across their legs or bodies immediately following delivery. Many talked about the baby's appearance, and a few of them felt rather negative about it at first, but the predominant theme in the majority of accounts was the excitement resulting from *touch*, including the pleasure of holding the baby in their arms. Even if they had thought before that the baby looked odd or ugly there then occurred a sudden flood of feeling, which often led to laughter, tears or kisses, in which the husbands who were present at delivery were also involved.

We know that when a newborn baby is handed to the mother and she is allowed to get to know it in her way, there is a definite sequence of events in the process of which there is evidence of an emotional 'unfolding', sometimes slowly and gently, sometimes in a passionate rush.[16] The mother starts by touching the baby hesitantly with her finger-tips, and then, four to eight minutes after, she starts stroking the baby, with her whole palm caressing the infant's body (or at least she does this if the baby's body is left uncovered). The sequence of types of touch has been described by Rubin[17] as starting with exploration with slightly stiff finger-tips. She tends to run a finger-tip over the baby's hair and finds that it is silky. She traces the contours of the baby's face and profile with a finger. But she holds the baby rather stiffly as if it were a bouquet of flowers. It is only later that the whole hand is in maximal contact with the baby's trunk and still later

16 M. H. Klaus, J. H. Kennell, N. Plumb and S. Zuehlke, 'Human maternal behaviour at the first contact with her young,' *Pediatrics* Vol. 46, 1970.
17 Reva Rubin, 'Basic maternal behaviour', *Nursing Outlook* Vol. 9, 1961, 'Maternal touch', *Child and Family* Vol. 4, 1965.

that the entire arm is involved in handling it. Rubin thought that it took about three months for this stage to be reached.

But the mother is not acting in an environmental vacuum, and the management of labour (including the drugs given) together with the setting within which she meets her baby, whether she feels at ease, and surrounded by friends, for example, can affect the way in which she begins to get to know it. Research by Aidan Macfarlane in Oxford[18] has demonstrated that the way the delivery is conducted and the people present have a powerful influence on the manner in which the mother greets her baby. He has recorded the meetings with videotape, and there is wide variation in the degree to which mothers relate to the baby and feel free to touch and explore it. When certain midwives did the deliveries there was more expression of emotion and more flesh to flesh contact between mother and baby, not because the midwife told the mother that this should be the case, but because she provided an environment in which the woman was able to express spontaneously whatever she felt and do whatever she wanted to do.

Marshall Klaus and John Kennell[19] did an experiment in which they left babies for one hour with their mothers within three hours of birth, turning on special heat lamps so that the infant did not need to be clothed and the mother could enjoy flesh to flesh contact. The staff went out so that this time could be intimate. They discovered that these mothers found it noticeably easier to relate to their babies afterwards than did mothers whose babies were put in a nursery, that they touched them more and apparently actually enjoyed them more, and that a year

[18] Aidan Macfarlane, *The Psychology of Childbirth*, Fontana/Open Books, 1977.
[19] Marshall Klaus and John Kennell, *Maternal-Infant Interaction*, Mosby, St Louis, 1977.

later the differences between the two groups were still significant. When they watched the mothers who had their babies with them they found that they started touching by gently poking their arms and legs with their fingertips, but in four or five minutes were already stroking the baby's trunk with the palm of the hand, and at this point became excited saying: 'I can't believe he's mine', 'He's gorgeous', or something similar.

Harry Harlow's work with monkeys[20] has demonstrated that the fact that the baby clings to the front of the mother's body, and is face to face with her, plays an important part in the attachment which grows between them. In this position there can be eye contact, another significant element in the development of attachment between the human mother and baby. Eye contact between mother and baby can be a major 'social releaser'[21]. Wolff[22] found that human mothers who did not play much with their babies suddenly began to do so as they appeared to focus their eyes during the fourth week of life. The mothers themselves had no idea why they found their babies more interesting at this stage. Robson[23] conducted postnatal interviews with mothers many of whom said that their babies seemed strangers to them until they felt that they were recognized and eye contact was established.

As the baby grows he develops other social releasers signals which trigger off response in his mother, and which increase the interaction between them. The initial response is often described as 'undiscriminating'. But such

[20] H. F. Harlow. 'The maternal affectional system' in *Determinant of Infant Behaviour*, edited by B. F. Foss, Methuen, 1963.
[21] N. Tinbergen, 'Social releasers and the experimental method required for their study', *Wilson Bull*. 60, 1948.
[22] P. H. Wolff, 'Observations on the early development of smiling' in *Determinants of Infant Behaviour*, op. cit.
[23] K. S. Robson, 'The role of eye contact in attachment', in *Early Human Development*, op. cit.

a description takes no account of the searching gaze of a healthy newborn infant when placed in its mother's arms immediately after delivery. Although the baby cannot yet 'know' the mother, he is clearly intent on finding her out.

His 'social smile' starts at about the fifth week of life. The mother may have been watching for it for some time and at last she is rewarded. It is like a gift from the baby: 'She smiled today. She recognized me.' Ambrose[24] has shown that the baby's smile leads the mother to smile back, talk more to the baby, and cuddle him. They are now really involved in a conversation. Ainsworth[25] demonstrated that a baby can differentiate between his mother and other people at eight weeks. Since most babies smile earlier than this, however, it is not surprising that mothers feel that they are recognized when this occurs. In fact many assume that the baby knows them long before this, but are apologetic because they think that this cannot really be the case. Evidence is now emerging which suggests that they are right, and Carpenter has shown how babies react to their mothers' and strangers' voices and faces as early as two weeks.[26] Especially if they can hear the mother's voice at the same time as seeing her face, babies stare at their mother much longer than they look at strangers. When the mother's face is accompanied by a stranger's voice babies become confused and turn away.

Aidan Macfarlane, writing on the significance of the baby's smile,[27] remarks that many of the baby's abilities are more of a surprise to psychologists than to mothers. When he was testing babies' visual fields mothers often observed that their babies could follow their faces 'but then went on to say that of course babies could not see'.

[24] op. cit.
[25] op. cit.
[26] Genevieve Carpenter, *New Scientist*, March 21st, 1974.
[27] 'If a smile is so important', *New Scientist*, April 25th, 1974.

He asked them when they thought their babies knew them, and they said 'in a couple of weeks, but of course that is not possible'. The mothers were right, and the books wrong.

What actually happens in the first weeks after childbirth is subject to wide cultural variation. Because the time immediately following delivery of the baby is important for both mother and child as one during which they first respond to and begin to know and learn from each other, the manner in which the culture controls and shapes this time is particularly significant.

The human baby has to be born at the end of about nine months, or its head, containing a brain which has a volume of between 375 and 400 cubic centimetres, as compared with that of a chimpanzee or gorilla whose brain is only about 200 cubic centimetres, would be too large to pass without difficulty through the mother's pelvic cavity.[28] This is one of the penalties we pay for our upright stance, which has tilted the pelvis, and greater intelligence. As a result the baby is born in a much more immature state than are many other animal babies. It takes eight months or more for the infants even to be able to crawl, and another six months or so before it can walk. It is not just a question, then, of the human baby being born immature but of developing only very slowly as compared with other animals. Montagu compares the length of pregnancy with the average age at onset of menstruation, the eruption of the milk and permanent teeth, the completion of growth and the total life span of primates and human beings. He uses the terms 'uterogestation' and 'exterogestation' to describe on the one hand, the baby's growth in the uterus, and on the other, the second half of gestation leading to adulthood which takes place outside the uterus.

[28] Ashley Montagu, *Touching: the human significance of the skin* Harper and Row, 1972.

'Birth no more constitutes the beginning of the life of the individual than it does the end of gestation. Birth represents a highly complex and highly important series of functional changes which serve to prepare the new-born for the passage over the bridge between gestation within the womb and gestation continued outside the womb.'[29]

These changes also serve to prepare the woman for passing over the bridge into motherhood, and where she does not experience them, where for example the birth is something that happens *to* her, an act which is performed by professionals on her passive body, rather than something in which she is actively involved herself, it may be much more difficult for her to cross over that bridge, as we shall see later.

Montagu goes on to say that

'with all modifications initiated by the birth process, the infant is still continuing its gestation period, passing, by the avenue of birth, from uterogestation to exterogestation in a continuing and ever more complex relationship with the mother, who is best equipped to meet its needs'.[30]

Symbiosis or separation

We cannot assume that every society permits extended contact between mother and baby during this period of exterogestation, and in some so many things are happening, and such complex rituals of one kind or another being conducted over either the mother or the baby separately, that contact is severely restricted. In some societies the baby is immediately taken over by

[29] Ashley Montagu, op. cit.
[30] Ashley Montagu, op. cit.

witch doctors or priests. This is especially likely to happen when there has been a difficult or protracted labour. We shall see later how handing the baby over to professionals rather than to the mother is one of the primary characteristics in neonatal care in many hospital deliveries.

The general pattern in pre-industrial societies is for the baby to be with and close to the mother, and to remain with her, day and night, for the post-partum weeks. He is often fixed to her body in one way or another, bound by shawls, slung in a net or special carrier, or wound into a strip of cloth which may actually also be her own dress, apart from the time when he is lying beside her, and frequently he is in flesh to flesh contact. Life outside the uterus is often thought of as a continuation of life inside it. The Ndembu of Zambia call the cloth which attaches the baby to its mother's back 'the placenta'. Because the baby is believed to be at special risk of the 'evil eye' or exposed to the malevolence of other jealous women, he is shielded from danger under the mother's clothing; in Mexico he is completely covered (face too, lest his spirit escapes from his mouth).

When interviewing in peasant societies I have often found it difficult to explain to mothers that this is not done everywhere in the world, for they say that of course babies must be with their mothers, for how else can they survive, and who else can the baby possibly belong to? And in South Africa I saw reactions of disbelief on the part of mothers deeply shocked to hear that in our own society babies are sometimes separated from their mothers and put in communal nurseries where they are looked after by women who are not even related to the mother. For this pattern of conduct in the West seems to be an aberration from a universally accepted norm. Everywhere else there are the loving hands of women in the family to greet the newborn, and a grandmother, aunt or older sisters and brothers to cherish and help tend it.

In many cultures acts performed on the baby by the

mother and those assisting her involve close observation of
and contact with him, including a great deal of touching.
In some cultures the baby is immediately massaged and his
head or limbs are 'shaped' by patting, kneading or pressing,
lest he grow up 'crooked'. In others he is anointed with
oil, bathed or rubbed with ashes, as in the Philippines, or
has patterns painted on his face and body.

In many societies the mother and baby are segregated
from the rest of society, not for their own good, but
because they are in a marginal state of existence, and
so are 'unclean', and therefore believed to have a dangerous, contaminating influence. This means that they are left
alone together, with food for the mother passed under
the door or through an opening. In Southern India the
Adivi mother stayed with her baby in a hut made of
leaves and mats for ninety days. If anyone touched her
they themselves became outcast and were expelled from
the village for three months. But the woman was not completely isolated; her husband made a hut fifty yards away
and stayed to watch over her. In India the old ritual
seclusion of mother and baby after delivery is giving way
to modern practices learned from the maternity hospital.
One result is that both mother and baby are exposed to
infection as they never were before. The Acholi woman
in Uganda keeps to her house for three days if she has
delivered a boy, and four if it was a girl, and is looked
after by either her mother or her husband's mother. Nobody is allowed to enter, for it is thought that should anyone else cross the threshold the baby may get ill or become blind, or the mother will become infertile. The
Dusun of North Borneo segregate mother and baby for
eight to ten days and nobody except the mother may
touch the infant.[31] This pattern of seclusion of mother
and baby together during the immediate post-partum

[31] T. R. Williams, 'Cultural Structuring of tactile experience in a
Borneo society', *American Anthropologist* Vol. 68, 1966.

period is found all over the world, and probably is an important factor both for survival of the newborn and for their 'tuning on' to each other and emotional banding.

It may be useful at this stage to look in more detail at what happens between a mother and baby in the time immediately after birth in a peasant society, and to see how this has the effect of helping the woman get to know her baby and feel herself into the role of a mother. I will take as my example the first twenty-four hours or so after the birth of a baby in Jamaica, because this is one area where I have done intensive field work myself.

A peasant way

The Jamaican baby who is born at home is delivered by the local trained midwife or by the *nana*. Even if the delivery is conducted by the trained midwife a *nana* may be called in to give guidance during pregnancy, and again afterwards to care for the mother and baby, as well as the other children. We have seen already that there is continuity in care which lasts throughout the pregnancy and the first post-partum week or two. Since the *nana* is almost invariably a neighbour, the contact is in fact a good deal more prolonged even than this, and the *nana*, as did the district nurse in rural areas of England, lives surrounded by 'her' babies who have grown up and whose babies she has delivered in their turn. So there is a secure and familiar environment for birth both in terms of the actual setting and the people involved.

After birth the *nana* puts the baby in bed beside its mother. Ideally, birth is followed by nine days ritual seclusion for both mother and baby in which they are cared for by the mother's mother – the 'Grandy' – or by the *nana*. They remain together within the darkness of the dwelling, windows or jalousies tight shut, the child because it needs peace, darkness and rest, and so that the

duppies or ancestor spirts may not know of its presence,
and to protect the mother against the dangers of 'baby
chill' (puerperal fever) and in order to allow her back 'to
mend', or 'knit up'.

Devout mothers often also use incense or 'holy water'
(which represents 'the spirit' in the local revivalist church).
They concentrate on making the setting ritually right for
the baby. Loleta, for example, had a baby a few hours old
when I visited her. The room was heavy with perfume and
she explained, 'I burn some sweet-smelling incense. With
the sweet smell it keep good spirits.' The *duppies* represent
the old pagan religion which has been swept away and
replaced by Christianity, but like the agents of any other
underground religion, their subterranean power remains
and they are never quite vanquished by the Christian
angels. Another newly delivered woman asked me for
advice on keeping *duppies* away and attracting the good
angels. I told her that a wise mother kept the house
clean and that way she could make the angels welcome.
Her eyes lit up, and she exclaimed, 'Yes! Keep the angels
manifesting by cleanliness!'

Maternal behaviour in these nine days is ringed round
with dietary and other taboos. Above all the mother
must avoid catching a cold, and since her head is particularly vulnerable, the hair is covered by a turban
made out of a kerchief. She must keep her hair from
getting damp at all costs, and must not allow rain to get
on to it – which keeps her indoors for an especially lengthy
time if it is the rainy season – nor wash it for as long
as three months. She must be careful to avoid backache from over-exertion and must not 'hackle' – become
exhausted from work or get emotionally overwrought.
The result is that mother and baby are secluded together
in a darkened, familiar environment removed from the
everyday worries of the peasant woman's existence. Often
what actually occurs is far from this ideal, and women

have to cope without anyone to care for them, and may immediately return to looking after a large family. But this is how Jamaican peasant women believe that it *should* be.

The baby only gradually emerges from ritual seclusion, and if the *duppies* should cause it to become ill, it is withdrawn into the dwelling hut again. It is normally kept in the shelter of the home for anything from six to twelve weeks, athough it may be brought out into the swept mud patch in front of the hut whilst the sun is up towards the end of this period. When the mother leaves the baby even for only a short time, the separation is ritually safeguarded by leaving a bible open at the twenty-third Psalm by its head, and often, too, a tape measure to catch the *duppy* (we can speculate that this is to 'take its measure'), and a pair of open scissors to cut off its retreat.

The shared seclusion of mother and infant means that the very important first days and weeks of the baby's life are normally passed within the dark and shadowy world of the household dwelling together with his mother, whose primary concern is to satisfy his needs. The two are islanded in an exclusive and special relationship. One of the most significant rules for early mothering is that the baby should not be allowed to cry. No Jamaican women would think it right to leave a baby to wait for a feed. One of the main reasons given for this is that if the baby cries the *duppies* will hear it and will come and fetch it; the baby will sicken and may die. Babies must be immediately 'hushed', and their mouths plugged with the always available breast. At night the mother lies with the baby beside her in the bed, and this continues to be the case so long as she is lactating, and often after she has officially weaned the child. Thus night feeds continue long after breast-feeds in the day have been dropped.

For three months the baby must be protected not only

from the other world but also from other women. No
menstruating woman may hold it or it will get constipated,
nor may any pregnant woman handle another's child.
Consequently the number of other people able to care for
the child is severely restricted, and the result is that the
mother-baby relationship is reinforced. Thus the initial
learning time in which mother and baby become attached
to each other is safeguarded and given special ritual
significance by the culture.

Mother and baby and the new technology

There is a noticeable difference between the first few
hours of life in a peasant culture such as that of the
West Indies and the beginning of life in any modern
maternity hospital. The woman having the baby is required to move out of her home, the equivalent of the
mother animal's nest, and to give birth among virtual
strangers. This may have the effect of making him the
hospital's property and not the mother's. This may be one
reason why there is often a crisis at home-coming, when
for the first time the woman has to accept responsibility
for her baby, respond to its cues appropriately, and take
on her new role of 'mother'. Moreover, the woman's
own body may in a sense no longer 'belong' to her in a
modern hospital, but functions because of things done to
it, and not spontaneously of its own accord. This raises
questions about the possible inhibition of maternal responses to the baby, and the even larger question of the suit-
ability of hospital as an environment for normal birth.

Although the hospital-delivered baby is more likely to
survive, especially if premature or otherwise at risk, the
human quality of the environment into which he is born
is often inferior, and he may suffer emotional deprivation
from the moment of delivery. Far from being a learning
time for the mother, the experience of the immediate
post-partum days frequently involves segregation not only

from society, but from her own baby.

In the United States, for example, babies are often automatically removed to a nursery immediately following delivery for six to twelve hours, and frequently are not allowed to be with their mothers except at scheduled feed times. Some hospitals do not permit the mother even to hold the baby after delivery, or if they do allow it, may insist that she holds it the other side of a sheet, so that no germs on her hand or body can be conveyed to the baby, and hence to the communal nursery.

It may take a long time for a woman to love her child when the beginning of her relationship with it has been interfered with by outsiders. When the baby needs special care and is taken to a nursery to be looked after, the estrangement may be complete, so that it may be difficult for the mother to feel that he really is her child, and sometimes she even rejects the baby when at last she is supposed to care for him.

Marshall Klaus and John Kennell[32] whose research I described earlier, also worked with mothers who were not allowed to handle their premature babies for a full three weeks, and remarked that when at last they were permitted to touch them they 'looked as if they were picking fleas off their babies'.

Medical intervention in labour, especially induction with oxytocin, is associated with a high degree of separation of mother and newborn baby. This is obviously sometimes because the induction occurred to save a high risk baby; but induction may be done for less compelling reasons, and in some hospitals babies are induced as a matter of policy at or within a few days of term, on the principle of 'better out than in after 38 weeks' when the mother's blood pressure is slightly raised, or for social and administrative reasons. A study in Aberdeen showed that there was significantly more fetal distress and that babies were

[32] Klaus & Kennell, op. cit.

more likely to have low Apgar scares after delivery and
to be admitted to special care baby units if oxytocin had
been used to induce labour.[33] Even if all is well at delivery
induced babies have a greater tendency to develop jaun-
dice[33] and this usually means that they are separated from
their mothers for phototherapy when a few days old.

Probably about 10 per cent of women really *need* to
have labour induced. Richard Beard, in whose hospital 22–
26 per cent of mothers were induced in 1971, got the proportion down to 11 per cent by 1977 associated with
a drop in the perinatal mortality rate.[34] Where more
women than this are being induced (and in some hospitals
the rate is up to 70 per cent) we can take it that this is
being done for very minor medical reasons and for
social and administrative reasons, and that the babies
of these mothers would not normally need to go to the
special care baby unit. If more than 10 per cent or so
have to be parted from their mothers we can infer that
something in the process of induction has harmed the
babies and that they have been subjected to iatrogenic
risk.

I examined the subjective experience of labour and
the post-partum period of 249 women who were pharma-
cologically induced or accelerated,[35] all of whom had
attended classes in preparation for childbirth, and had
reported on their labours to their antenatal teachers (that
is, they were not answering a questionnaire or being required to adopt attitudes to induction), and compared their
experiences with the reports of 206 women from the same
antenatal classes whose labours were not induced.

Induction of labour was more likely to be followed by

[33] W. H. Liston, H. J. Campbell, Dangers of oxytocin-induced
labour to fetuses', *British Medical Journal* Vol. 3, 606-7, 1974.
[34] 'Mother's wishes vs. doctor's duties', *Patient Care* Vol. II, 19,
1977.
[35] Sheila Kitzinger, *Some Women's Experiences of Induced Labour*,
National Childbirth Trust, 2nd ed., 1978.

separation of mother and baby for at least a few hours and to lead to him being what Martin Richards[36] has described as a 'one-day-old deprived child' isolated in an intensive care unit. Of the 249 women who were induced or accelerated 24 per cent were separated from their new born babies in this way, as compared with only 6 per cent of 206 women who were not induced. These intensive care units were often on different floors of the hospital and sometimes they were in other hospitals from that in which the mother remained. Forty-six of those whose babies were in intensive care units described their first sight of the baby but did not mention holding it immediately after delivery, and the phrase which they used again and again was that the baby was 'whisked away'.

Ninety-two per cent of those who were induced said they had drugs for pain relief. This compared with 50 per cent of women whose labours were not induced who did not have pain-relieving drugs. Many of those who were induced had Pethidine and said that they became 'woozy' or were 'knocked out' or 'unconscious'. We have already seen the effect that this drug can have on the experience of labour, but it can also affect the way in which a mother reacts to her baby, for if the drug-induced somnolent state persists throughout the second stage and delivery the woman may be a passive partner in the meeting with her baby. Even so, occasionally it is clear that the mother had held the infant but only knew she had because her husband told her about it later. Not only did she not remember having the baby in her arms, but she often could not remember him at all, and her next meeting with the child was, in effect, a first encounter. Thus in 105 cases out of 249 induced labours (42 per cent) the normal mechanisms by which attachment is initiated be

[36] Martin Richards, 'The one-day-old deprived child', *New Scientist* 61/891, 1974.

tween mother and baby were delayed.

Women often described vividly their reactions to their first sight of the baby, the experience of separation from it, and the anxiety which frequently accompanied the separation. One woman said: 'I was absolutely shattered and exhausted. I wasn't at all interested in seeing the baby. All I wanted to do was to go to sleep.' Another, who felt that the labour was taking place without and in spite of her, remarked: 'If I had not woken as the baby was being born I would never have believed him mine.' This feeling persisted with one woman and merged with depression: 'I find myself going to pieces. Withdrawn into myself.' In a letter written when the baby was several months old she described how she found herself hitting him 'without reason' and was very frightened. Fortunately she had enough awareness of what was happening to seek help. Some of these mothers asked not to hold the baby after delivery because they felt 'too tired', 'exhausted', or 'drugged', because they were vomiting, or were 'afraid I might drop the baby'.

There are many accounts in which the mother reports on her feelings after the birth and says things much as: 'The Sister took her away. I did not really mind. I was completely exhausted'; 'I was utterly exhausted. I heard a baby cry. Unfortunately I was still drowsy, so the memory is hazy'.

Sometimes it was the husband who woke his wife up or somehow got a response from her to acknowledge the baby's birth, as did the man who shook and slapped his wife, who was 'hopelessly muddled with Pethidine', so that she should be 'conscious enough to be aware of the birth itself'. Other women came out of 'a haze' to see the baby hanging upside down in front of them, and described how they were 'stunned' by this sight or sometimes 'coolly disinterested'.

The husband of a woman whose baby was cot-nursed for 36 hours reminded the staff that the mother had not seen him at all, and the mother said: 'The baby appeared to react violently against me when he met me eventually (the only one who'd never held a baby before) and against breast-feeding attempts. The staff were annoyed by my messing up hospital routine by taking so long to try and feed him . . . Only gradually could I "unfreeze" towards him inside,' and she went on to tell how she had remained 'detached' from the baby for 'over a year'.

One woman said of this experience: 'I've had it taken from me like a prize wisdom tooth by the dentist,' and another: 'I felt intensely estranged when the baby was brought to me eventually.'

It was not only the sight or sound of the baby, but physical contact, which was a clear signal in the bonding that took place between mother and newborn, and which in those accounts which described the meeting-through-touch of mother and baby obviously initiated a rush of feeling. A mother who had had a Caesarean section woke up to find the baby waiting to be put in her arms, and holding her baby, 'washed him in tears of joy'. Another said, 'I didn't feel any emotion when I first saw Catherine lifted out and heard her cry, but as soon as they gave her to me to hold a few seconds later I thought she was fantastic.' The mothers themselves often wanted to touch most of all: 'I did so want to cuddle and touch her before she was wrapped'.

Women sometimes described how they tried to put the baby to the breast, but it was 'grabbed', or 'snatched away', or how the midwife 'did not believe in it' or 'was shocked', told the mother she must not do it as it would 'make the baby sick', or took the baby away because she said she had to weigh, bath, Apgar-rate, clothe it, put it under a heater or give it to the paediatrician. Other mothers said that they were not allowed to hold their babies immediately because 'they were too busy with the placenta'. These mothers clearly surrendered their babies reluctantly, and some experienced helpless anger.

The most positive expressions of emotion about the baby occurred in those reports when the mother saw the head as it was being born, or even before it had fully emerged: 'I sat up and leaned forward to watch the head being born. Fantastic!' and in which she felt the baby moving against her thigh or lying on her abdomen immediately following delivery. Here again, it seems to be a matter of physical contact reinforcing sight and sound, and being perhaps the most significant element in attachment to the neonate.

Some of the mothers who had epidural anaethesia, so that they had little or no sensation in the lower half of their bodies, said that it was like watching a scene on film or a TV documentary. 'I felt terribly detached watching in the mirror, and a little guilty because I felt that everyone expected me to be overwhelmed with joy,' said one woman who suffered from post-partum depression for several months after. Another, completely without sensation from an epidural which had been topped up, delivered spontaneously in a labour ward bed, without realizing it, and with no awareness of the baby except that she said that the Sister called out for someone to come and help, at which point she heard a baby screaming and then saw the Sister pick one up from between her legs. She said that she could not believe that it was her child, and felt bound to ask the Sister whether it was really hers. In other reports where epidurals had worn off for the expulsive stage, these mothers too used words descriptive of touch such as 'wet', 'slippery', and 'kicking'. In some accounts the baby was removed at birth, but the all-important contact had already been made, and the mother felt and *knew* that the baby belonged to her, and she to it.

Induction and active management of labour can occasionally be a life-saving procedure. It is clear, too, that some babies need to be given special care after delivery, although in many cases perhaps this might be done at the mother's bedside, in the way that is being done at present in some progressive maternity hospitals.

But even though a minority of mothers and babies benefit from the sequence of events which starts with induction, continues with obstetric intervention, and culminates with the baby in the intensive care unit, it is questionable whether this is justification for submitting the majority of women to what many of these mothers described as the misery of enforced separation from their infants, and whether society should permit modern technological innovations in the culture of childbirth to risk interfering with the basic human patterns of attachment between parents and their young.

Whether or not labour is induced, the time immediately after birth is treated by many hospitals not as a special period in which important psycho-biological needs of the mother are served by the staff, and in which she takes care of and gets to know her baby, but primarily as one during which both mother and child are medically screened and processed and must pass tests before they can be pronounced 'not at risk' and discharged back into society. This is taken to be the main function of the hospital not only in industrialized but also increasingly in developing societies. The traditional ways of birth and the culturally accepted manner in which the mother first relates to the baby and the baby to her, are destroyed and replaced with Western methods. The focus of obstetric and neonatal care is almost exclusively on disease and potential disease. One of the effects of this is to reduce the perinatal mortality rate. What we do not know is the effect that such wholesale replacement of traditional institutions and culturally reinforced patterns of caring has on the quality of family life.

The West exports its technology with as much vigour as the Victorians did their religion and forms of administration. We tend to believe that if a machine to regulate labour or an obstetric procedure is right for one woman whose baby is at risk, therefore it must be right, too, for all women whose babies are not at risk. It is part of the same kind of confused logic that if it is advisable to separate *some* babies from their mothers for paediatric observation in a central nursery, then it is right to separate *all* babies from their mothers. And the obstetrician adds, 'All babies are at risk unless proved otherwise'.

Many mothers are persuaded that only if every new technique and every available machine is used are they giving their babies the best chance, and fathers are often even more readily convinced. One consequence is a failure of confidence in handling and relating to the infant, a basic lack of trust in the ability to mother one's own baby. This is such a familiar syndrome in the West that we hardly comment on it any more, anticipating that the new mother will be awkward, unsure of herself, anxious and readily distressed. But this particular psychological reaction to motherhood is almost unknown in peasant cultures, where birth takes place at home and where the new mother cares for her baby from the moment of delivery with the help of other women members of her own or her husband's family.

If there is anything to be learned from the studies to which I referred earlier the time immediately following birth may include some of the most important moments of the baby's, and also, perhaps, of the mother's life, because mother and baby are literally 'getting in touch' with each other. As we become more concerned about the quality of parenting in our society and about the neglect or maltreatment of babies, including the psychological battering which can harm a child no less severely than can physical assault, we ought to pay more attention to these important moments in which attachment between the mother and her baby begins to dawn, and both parents have the opportunity to a basic psychological 'tuning in' to the new baby.

Even in the West, when births take place at home as

many still do in the Netherlands, a quiet time for meeting with the baby occurs naturally after delivery. Although it may not come so easily in hospital, it is possible to provide this opportunity for mothers and fathers. It is up to couples to ask for it and to enquire in advance whether, if everything is straightforward, they will be allowed at least half an hour in the delivery room alone with their baby.

Close holding and the spontaneous stroking and massage which occurs when parents explore the new baby, first touching it lightly with their fingers, and then cuddling it, feeling the firmness of the limbs, stroking its silky hair and 'breathing in' its reality involves emotional 'work' which may be no less important than the physical work of labour, and it is one which we should not allow to get crowded out by the busy activity of a hospital. Mothers do not need to be told how to do it. They do need, however, to be handed the unclothed baby, to be left alone and in peace, and to be free to do what comes naturally.

8

Learning to be a Mother

Adjusting to parenthood
Childbirth of course is not the grand finale but one point, albeit a very dramatic one, in the process of becoming a mother.

The first baby
The birth of the first child is almost invariably a crisis for the parents in terms of their own emotions and their sense of the enormous challenge they face. When 46 American couples were asked whether they estimated that the birth of the first child entailed a crisis for them, 38 said that it did, and that it was a severe, or extensive one.[1] They explained this was because of tiredness, not being able to get out of the home, reduced social contacts for those women who had worked outside, loss of satisfaction in their jobs, and of course, loss of their incomes. They also described the sheer hard work of having a baby, feelings of guilt and inadequacy about being a good parent, the load of responsibility for the new life, the decline in housekeeping standards, and the woman (and occasionally the man) felt that she had 'let herself go' and was not bothering about her appearance in the same way. Some women were experiencing secondary frigidity, husbands were worried about financial matters, they did not have time to be alone together, and

[1] E. E. Le Masters, 'Parenthood as Crisis', *Marriage and Family Living* Vol. 19, 1957.

there were worries about birth control and a general
sense of disenchantment. 'We knew where babies came
from,' said one woman, 'but we didn't know what they
were like.' These couples were not unusual; nearly all the
babies had been wanted, their marriages were estimated
as happy, and they saw themselves as having 'average' or
better personality adjustment. Another study[2] disclosed
that the birth of the first child frequently cut conversation time between husband and wife by half.

In interviews that I have conducted with new parents
a few weeks after childbirth, couples often talk about the
shock at disruption of established living patterns connected with having a baby in the house. 'We were never
really prepared for this' . . . 'We were ready for the birth
but we didn't think how it would be after' . . . 'My whole
life revolves around the baby, attending to her needs,
worrying about her, trying to find out why she's crying,
trying to do things *right*' . . . 'I hadn't realized how much
work a new baby was. How do women with more than
one child ever manage? My time is completely taken up
just with one. I sometimes don't know whether it's day
or night. All I know is that he's either asleep or awake.
If he's awake he's plugged in and sucking. If he's asleep
I'm snatching the time to get the nappies washed or trying to catch up on sleep myself', and 'I have never felt
so tired in my life. I had no idea it was like this!'

The three months immediately following birth are
particularly challenging ones which necessitate adaptation to the demands of the new baby. Psychologically the
mother experiences a period in which she is tied to the
baby by an invisible emotional umbilical cord, and when
the baby needs what has been called 'primary maternal
preoccupation'.[3] The mother's complete centredness on

[2] Harold Feldman, *Development of the Husband-Wife Relationship: a research report*, Cornell Univ. Mimeograph, 1964.
[3] D. W. Winnicott, *The Child, the Family and the Outside World*,

the infant, who is more helpless than any other animal baby, and is utterly dependent on its loving caretakers, is clearly an important element in the survival of the species. In fact, the few months after birth together form a fourth trimester of pregnancy, in which the mother and baby are still united in a symbiotic bond (and particularly if the mother is breast-feeding, as of course most mothers are the world over) and in which the wellbeing of one is inextricably linked with that of the other.

Such symbiotic interdependence of mother and child is well recognized in most peasant and hunting societies, where the child is held close to its mother's body, day and night, almost like an extension of herself, and where suckling takes place in a casual and spasmodic manner, with the baby frequently dropping off to sleep while still at the breast. It is almost a marsupial phase of existence for the baby, who has emerged from the uterus into an extra-uterine stage, but it is still thought of as being a part of its mother. Just as the baby kangaroo comes out of the pouch but still clings to its mother, so the human infant is slung or cradled on her back or hip, in the folds of her shawl or other garment or in a basket or carrying net. Since nutritional survival depends on breast-feeding in these societies, and the baby fed on artificial milk is likely to get infective diarrhoea and die, this marsupial stage of infant existence has obvious survival value.

Under these conditions the mother is also able to learn from and about her baby in a way that is much more difficult for the woman who places her infant in its separate nursery, attending to it only when it sends out distress signals. One important element in maternal learning in the first weeks and months after birth is this symbiotic co-existence of mother and infant.

Penguin, and *Collected Papers: through Paediatrics to Psycho-analysis*, Tavistock, 1958.

196 Women As Mothers

There are two contrasting mothering styles between which mothers in the West can choose today. On the one hand is the mother who lives relatively independently of the newborn baby. Having given birth to it, it starts its separate existence and she continues hers as before. Her breasts, arms and body are her own. On the other hand there is the mother whose baby is attached to her like a limpet, who becomes herself the baby carrier, the baby nourisher, the baby comforter, the child's life growing out of hers and physically contiguous with it. There are, of course, many points along the continuum between these two extreme positions. Each mother may at times feel guilty or anxious that she is not mothering in the other way. The woman who goes back to her job leaving the baby with other caretakers can be guilty about not breast-feeding and tending it herself. But so may the one who gives herself to the baby without restrictions. She may feel guilty about sudden and uncontrollable resentment at being so sucked into and taken over by motherhood.

Sharing Parenthood

In many societies the responsibilities and pleasures of parenthood are spread. The baby's life may be enriched by relationships with other people too which can develop as early as a few weeks after birth. The extent to which this happens depends, of course, on the opportunity presented to the baby to interact with other people. There is a distinctive culture contrast between those societies in which the baby is required to relate to only one or two individuals, as is frequently the case in British families, and other societies, such as in Africa, where many mother substitutes are available, where all of them mother in approximately the same way, and where groups of women meet regularly to share household chores or work in the fields together. In such societies attachment soon grows in breadth, and although a child is always aware who his mother is, and has a special relationship with her, the range of affectional bonds established early in childhood reduces the risks of maternal deprivation when a mother is for some reason inadequate. Even when the biological mother is absent, other mothers are available, and although they cannot take her place, they act in much the same way, and are bound in the same close web of relationships in the community.

In these societies too, there is a powerful bond between siblings and others who behave 'as if' they were brothers and sisters. The bonding of members of peer groups is significant throughout the individual life cycle. For the small child it shapes the world in which it moves. The baby is already surrounded by other children who are its brothers and sisters or cousins, and at each phase of development there are groups of kin to whom it is bound by ties of affection and loyalty.

Evidence from ethology suggests that this may be a vital element in a healthy social environment for the growing child. Harlow's experiments with rhesus monkeys[4] showed that the presence of other youngsters was important for normal development, and that in the absence of a mother, siblings provided the social releasers which made for a well adjusted adult monkey capable of becoming an adequate parent in its turn.

This is the main pattern of child-rearing practices in the Israeli *Kibbutzim*, which we shall be looking at more closely in chapter 13. Children are brought up for the

[4] H. F. Harlow and G. Griffin, 'Induced mental and social deficits in rhesus monkeys', in *The Biosocial Basis of Mental Retardation*, S. F. Osler and R. E. Cooke, editors, John Hopkins Press, 1965.
 H. F. Harlow and M. K. Harlow, 'Effects of mother-infant relationships on rhesus monkey behaviour, in *Determinants of Infant Behaviour*, edited B. F. Foss, Methuen, 1969.
 H. F. Harlow and M. K. Harlow, 'Developmental aspects of emotional behaviour, in *Psychological Correlates of Emotion*, edited P. Blacker, Academic Press, 1970.

most part in the children's houses, and looked after by
professional nurses. In babyhood they are in groups of
half a dozen or so, and at three years enter larger groups
of twelve to eighteen children. They grow bound firmly
to their brothers and sisters of the *kibbutz*.

Older children are often involved with the care and
teaching of younger ones rather as if in a peasant society
they were mothering younger siblings. But in the *kibbutz*
this care is institutionalized through the babies' and
children's houses. The emphasis is not on the emotional
ties between the members of the nuclear family, although
these may be strong, but on the larger family of the
kibbutz.

Such a system contrasts with the accepted patterns
which run through all Western cultures, and it is remarkable that Jews coming from these cultures to Israel
are so often able to make the great psycho-social adjustments to function in and feel a part of the *kibbutz*
society.

The nuclear family.
The urban family into which a baby is born in other
industrialized societies is likely to be small; the baby
has one or at most two siblings. The kin network is
widely dispersed and even close relatives outside the immediate conjugal family form a collective unit only on
ritual occasions when their relatedness is celebrated, such
as at birthdays, Christmas and funerals, and, perhaps, for
a meal on Sundays. In a study done in 1960–4,[5] it was
discovered that for 62 per cent of middle-class London
informants the effective kin set – that is, those with whom
there was regular contact – stopped at first cousins or
closer relatives. Even in the major life crisis of the birth

[5] Raymond Firth, Jane Hubert and Anthony Forge, *Families
and their Relatives: kinship in a middle-class sector of London*,
Routledge, 1970.

of a baby a couple may cope alone. In the same study it was found that 40 per cent of couples receive no kin help at the time of a confinement. The woman's mother was the person most likely to come to help, which she did in 50 per cent of cases, whereas the husband's mother assisted in a few cases only. The woman's sister gave help in less than 10 per cent of cases because she was often employed or busy with her own home. Help from relatives was often not wanted, or considered 'of dubious value'. The authors comment:

> For a woman pregnancy and confinement is the period when she feels perhaps most of all the need for mobilization of her resources. Utilization of kin services is part of her strategy. Failure to utilize such service may indicate the lack of close kin or a calculation that on balance the strains are likely to be more severe than the benefits received.[6]

While a certain degree of moral responsibility is felt to visit and remember relatives, the actual physical contact with them is often slight and even where couples have elderly parents living with them, for instance, emotional ambiguity may be expressed.

We may have an idealized view of how families once were – in a *Cider With Rosie* style rural England that was always sunny. The comfortable solidity of the large interacting kin group was a luxury of the Victorian middle and upper classes, but less often a reality for the poor. Once the Industrial Revolution was under way there was little time for working-class families to bother with relatives, or any relatives not directly involved in the economic unit of the immediate family, and men, women and children worked throughout the daylight hours, and often at night too, whether in factory or cottage industry.

[6] op. cit.

But whether there is evidence of a dramatic change away from a vital, interacting extended family system generally throughout English society is not here the question. There is certainly a great contrast between the Western way of family life and that of most of the rest of the world. Since mothers initiate their children into the society's culture, and particularly prepare them for parenthood in their turn, and since the ability to do this is dependent to a large extent on the experience of having been loved and cared for oneself, unhappy families tend to perpetuate themselves. Compensation can be made later in life, and may come through being loved and loving as an adult, but the growth of a woman as a mother able to nurture an infant in a way that is satisfying both to the child and to herself normally begins *in her own infancy and childhood*. It is not something that is learned in parentcraft classes or from a book, but is part of the developmental process. 'In relation to her own child,' says Deutsch, 'woman repeats her own mother-child history.'[7]

This is why the breaking of the cycle of deprivation in those families which are at the bottom of the socio-economic scale in Western societies depends not on rescue work *after* the deprivation is already noted, but on working with an eye on the future, and providing extra support for parents in the hope that even though there may be limited results in the present generation, their children will grow up able to be better parents. It is a long term project, and one which brings few immediate rewards.

Education for parents in pre-industrial societies
In peasant societies the care of small children traditionally takes place in women's groups focused on the performance of a domestic or other productive task. Women

[7] Helena Deutsch, *Psychology of Women*, Vol. 1, Grune and Stratton, N.Y., 1944.

kneel by the river rubbing clothes on the stones and pounding and pummelling them while at the same time caring for children. They spin and weave with the children beside them, or prepare food for cooking, sew skins for garments, build dwelling huts, or work in the fields, and all the time the small child is an observer of the inter-action not only of adults but of mothers with children. The distinction, marked in our own society, between com-munality and privacy, does not exist. The lessons of mothering are there for all to learn.

In many hunting and gathering societies dwellings are shared by several families. The Nootka of the American Northwest coast had large cedarwood houses common to four or more families. Each corner was inhabited by one family and others were ranged along the sides. Apache extended family groups shared one large tepee. The Ongre Negritoes of Little Andaman Island have enor-mous oval thatched houses, also shared by several families, each of which has its own fireplace, and Indians of the Amazon basin still live communally in dwellings of this type.

Even where families do not live completely in common, they frequently have inter-connecting houses. The Ainu of Japan sometimes had pit houses which were linked with each other by tunnels. In these dwellings the family life of each member was evident for all to witness, and children absorbed information about babies and their needs and how to satisfy them without requiring formal instruction.

In agricultural as in hunting societies, children are the responsibility of all adults. The children of the band, tribe or village are 'our' children. Mothers share child-rearing tasks. Andamanese women pass babies round and cuddle them, and each lactating woman may suckle the child whilst it is on her lap. Should any girl prove inadequate as a mother there are always other women willing to take over the mothering role. Surrogate mothers

are often grandmothers, or other women of the grandmother generation. In some societies children are sent to
the grandmother's house to be weaned. In Jamaica, where
women work in domestic service and in shops and offices
in the town, it is customary to send first born children
back to 'me mada in de country' who by the time she
reaches middle age expects to have a second family consisting of her grandchildren to rear, and who although
she grumbles about the responsibility and hard work sees
this as providing social insurance for her old age. In
societies such as these, children learn what mothering
is not only from their own mothers and women of her
generation, but also, and even primarily (as is frequently
the case in the West Indies) from their mother's mother.

Every peasant child has the experience of caring for
still younger children, siblings or cousins. As soon as a
child can walk easily she may have a baby strapped to
her back, and small 'mothers' play, run, jump, imitate
household tasks and help their mothers with babies
permanently clinging to them. The peasant girl learns very
early what it is to have a baby almost as an extension
of her own body. This is particularly the task of girls,
but boys too are expected to do their share of baby-
minding. For the girls, however, the tasks persist long after
the boy has left home and joined peer groups of other
boys intent on adventure, whether these are neighbour-
hood gangs or formally constituted age sets or as in primitive societies. In many cultures the boy even sleeps away
from home with the men, or in special huts in which
he learns what it is to be a man in his society. Girls
tend to be much more home-centred, whether from choice
or necessity, and close to their mothers, who provide for
them a pattern of motherhood.

Once contact with other cultures changes the patterns
of family life and child-rearing, the old continuity in
mothering is destroyed and mothers try to adapt to new
challenges and to use new techniques. This is nowhere

more evident than in immigrant families. A gulf develops between what West Indian immigrant mothers in Britain for example, call 'the old time way' and the instructions and advice that they receive at Health Clinics. The conflicting experiences of mothering are a cause of family dissension, and the children often get caught in the crossfire. But more is happening even than that. These children are being provided with multiple models of mothering, and ones about which conscious decisions have to be made. The traditional completely spontaneous mothering is no longer possible.

Yet it would be wrong to suggest that no explicit instruction is given the expectant and new mother in pre-industrial societies. There is a wealth of folklore to teach her how to keep the child healthy, to use herbs and correctly enact ritual, as well as giving guidelines to the normal development of a child. But this is the common currency of women, and simply confirms what they all know already. The Jamaican peasant mother *knows* that she should put a little washing blue in the water to keep the *duppies* away, or failing this, a few drops of Dettol. She remembers that that is what her mother did, and her aunty and granny. It is common knowledge. It is only if the child is ill that she will seek advice from the nurse at the clinic, or if it does not soon recover, the Obeah practitioner (the witchdoctor, male or female). In crises the peasant mother seeks help from ritual agents in the society, whether these represent the old rituals of witchcraft, magic and religion or the new, potent rituals of science and medicine. But in day-to-day family life she acts without reflection or doubt.

Images of parenthood in Western society
The expectant mother in contemporary industrialized Western society may never have touched, or even seen, a newborn baby before. The appearance and needs of a tiny baby may be as much a mystery to her as the breed-

ing of giant pandas. She will probably have read the occasional article in a magazine and have seen a photograph or two, but she is well aware that in having a baby she is starting to do something about which she knows nothing. She could go to her own mother for information, but this is often impossible in a highly mobile society in which the couple starting a family may be hundreds or thousands of miles away from the homes of the prospective grandparents. She may feel, too, that this is not a subject about which her own mother could be up-to-date, and given the speed of technological change associated with baby care, she is probably right. Our educational and child-rearing systems put great emphasis on the development of individuality and self-direction. The young pregnant woman wants to do things *her* way, and even if her mother is available she may not wish to ask for help. When expecting the first child the couple may not yet know any others with babies, and although they see parents in the supermarket or the High Street they have no idea of what it feels like to have a baby in the house, or how it may affect their own relationship.

The expectant mother may worry about her lack of technical information, and many of the requests for advice which are made to me as a childbirth educator come at first couched in terms which are essentially requests for facts. She often does not know that even more important than the technical know-how is some understanding of the emotional, relational, and self-image changes inevitably involved with rearing a child.

Although women's magazines, TV and radio, have some function in sharing reality with the mother and in offering education for parenthood, there is little in the education of children in our society to prepare them for parenthood. Of course, girls have their dolls, boys may have Action Man, and both boys and girls have animal toys, puppies and kittens to love and tend. There is the horse stage, more pronounced for girls than for boys, which for middle-class English girls may last from the pubertal years till marriage or after, with its combing down and mucking out, training and caring. English schoolgirls rehearse motherhood with their ponies. But there is little opportunity to find out what real babies are like, of seeing them at first hand and learning how to cope with the almost off-hand nonchalance of the peasant child with four or five younger brothers and sisters. A few schools tackle the emotional aspects of sex and childbirth as part of education in 'family living' or 'human relationships', but this tends to be a short course designed for fifth or sixth formers in the week after examinations are over, when the staff are busy marking papers and do not know what to do with the rest of the term. Nobody takes it very seriously.

Motherhood myths

Moreover every new mother in Western society is brought face to face with a reality often far removed from the fantasies of pregnancy. Kellmer Pringle[8] believes that an important function of education for motherhood should be that it 'deglamorizes' parenthood. Certainly even women who have ample experience of other women's problems in learning to be mothers may themselves find adjustment difficult during this 'fourth trimester'. A psychiatric social worker who had a baby when she was already in her forties was thrilled with her child and fascinated by her new role, but after some months realized that she was suffering from the constant fatigue and over-concern for the baby which she described as 'subclinical postnatal depression' and put it graphically when she said to me, 'I have come to the end of the lollipop, and all I've got left is the stick.'

The myth of maternity which is commonly accepted in our own society – a myth which asserts that mothers

[8] Mia Kellmer Pringle, *The Needs of Children*, Hutchinson, 1974.

have loving, tender feelings about their babies, that as a consequence of the biological act of having given birth women become different from their former selves, are selfless and giving and experience supreme satisfaction in sacrificing themselves in this way, is crystallized in the image of the Virgin Mother sitting in placid serenity with her infant Son on her lap. She is untouched by anxiety or passion, and represents the purity of woman given in service to her child.

We express our own infantile view of the mother as the property of the baby when we create this dichotomy between real feelings and the idealized vision of sanctified motherhood. At the back of every image of the mother as goddess is that other mother who personifies all the hatred which has been repressed. She is the witch, the wicked stepmother who gives her child a poisoned apple to eat or commands the shepherd to kill her and bring her the heart.

When sexuality is divorced from the emotions involved in mothering, and an antithesis is created between them, a romanticized model of motherhood is erected with which women cannot possibly identify. They then experience the hopelessness and failure of trying to act a part which they know they cannot play and for which they feel temperamentally unsuited: 'I haven't any real maternal instincts'. Alex Comfort[9] contributes to this false antithesis between sexuality and motherhood when he makes statements which imply that parenthood is incompatible with exultant sex, such as: 'The best modern sex is unreproductive . . . The development of a recreational erotic life needs privacy. Sexual freedom just isn't compatible with a childbearing lifestyle.'

In spite of the reality of the presence of their own mothers, children grow up clinging to this romantic

[9] *The Joy of Sex*, Simon and Schuster, 1972.

version of how a mother 'should' be. In adolescence the image begins to be shattered once and for all, and boys and girls have come to terms with their flawed mothers, and establish a new relationship with them as human beings, and not just as 'mothers'. At the same time parents have to learn that their children are not simply their children, but people. One of my daughters said to me, with evident surprise in her voice, having come to a carefully considered conclusion about me: 'I didn't realize that mothers had personalities! I thought they were just mothers, and the main thing about them was that they were motherly.'

Mothers who cannot mother

No one knows how much violence is expressed against children in pre-industrial societies. It would be quite wrong to take it for granted that it does not exist and there is a good deal of evidence from societies like those of the Caribbean to suggest that physical punishment is often a normal part of family life. The phenomenon of repeated violent assault on a baby or small child because a mother or father have lost control of themselves is, however, something which, although well recorded for our own society, has not been commented on by anthropologists working in pre-industrial societies. Even Colin Turnbull writing about the Ik, probably the most unpleasant people an anthropologist has ever had to study, although describing how mothers shrugged their shoulders when a baby was devoured by a wild animal and urged on the men to kill it as it would now be fat with the child and therefore make a good meal, did not suggest that there was any baby battering of the kind we know so well in the West.

When I interviewed mothers in Jamaica one of the subjects I was interested in was how you 'grow a child right'. Although these women all thought discipline was important if the child was not to grow 'rude' (the neighbour's children were usually provided as an example of this) everyone stressed that a child should never be slapped till it 'knew sense', and that meant that he or she was talking well.

I met mothers who were depressed and suffering from other forms of mental illness, and whose children were neglected, but never one whose inner turmoil found expression in violence against a baby. Perhaps such women existed, but in a peasant society it is impossible to seal the doors and windows and conduct one's family life in privacy behind the walls; neighbours and relatives would soon become involved and would certainly take over care of a baby if the mother proved incapable of mothering her child. Perhaps this is the important thing about a peasant society: family life is lived out in public, and social sanctions created and exercised by the larger community control and to a certain extent safeguard actions within the family.

The very high levels of child abuse in Western society may be partly the result of intolerable social conditions, inadequate education for parenthood and the social isolation which comes from living in small family units.

Many women grow to love their babies even though they started off fairly cool, and, perhaps, slightly alarmed at their own reactions. Babies have personalities. Some obviously do not make it easy for a mother to love them. A 'good' baby helps; a crying baby may make it just too difficult for its mother. One mother of a screaming baby said:

I fell into a deep sleep and after about ten minutes he began to cry. I went to the cot and shook him and shouted 'Shut up for God's sake!' I felt I *had* to sleep and sleep. That was the most important thing, he yelled so much and I was shattered.[10]

[10] Reported in 'My world became the size of a baby', Catherine Ballard and Hilary Hackett, *Spare Rib* 47, June 1976.

There are babies who are unpredictable, and others who are mentally retarded, hyperactive, or who are suffering from a handicap which makes it difficult to 'warm' to them. This is why child abuse is often directed only at one child in a family, who is the one picked out as 'bad'. Sometimes this is the child who is different because he or she is especially intelligent or bright and lively. In one survey of 26 children:

> In nine instances, the children were thought to be 'slow' in development or mentally retarded, and six additional children were described as having been 'bad', 'selfish', 'defiant' or 'hard to discipline'. It has been our clinical impression that within the latter group may be children who are, relative to their siblings, hyperactive or intellectually precocious.
> We also have seen several instances where the intellectual endowment of the child appears to so exceed that of one or both parents that his inquisitive behaviour makes him vulnerable to parental abuse. Thus, there appears to be a group of children whose behaviour makes them particularly vulnerable to abuse . . .[11]

In all this the woman's relationship with the father of her child is important. If the marriage is sound and she feels she is getting loving support from him the task of coping with a difficult baby is made simpler, and as she learns to handle the relationship her mothering skills develop. But if the relationship is poor or there is no man to accept responsibility, she can reach breaking point quickly.

Depression can lead to inability to love a baby. But equally, failure to love a baby can result in depression, because a woman then feels a failure and may seek a

[11] C. Henry Kempe and Ray E. Helfer, eds., *Helping the Battered Child and His Family*, Blackwell, 1972.

quality in the relationship with the baby, a rewarding warmth coming from the baby to her, which manifestly is not there. She can feel as if bereaved of the baby of her dreams, the child she hoped for and whom she sheltered in her body, and encounters instead a complete stranger who appears in its place.

Although we may think of mothers who use physical violence against their babies as cruel monsters, in fact they are often sad, pathetic and terribly vulnerable. One depressed mother told me:

> The baby's cry makes no sense to me. Nothing is passing between us. We are not exchanging. There was a time, after the birth, when we were offering things, but I have turned full circle. I have done some awful things.

When I asked what things she confessed, quietly and with shame, she had 'thrown the children on the floor', and added that her husband was afraid to discover what had happened when he returned from work at the end of each day. In this case the husband, who desperately wanted things to 'work out' and 'come right somehow', without him having to do anything about it, or their inability to cope being made public, was, like so many partners, colluding in the child abuse. The distress which both of them were feeling was itself a product of an unhappy marital relationship: 'All we do with each other is to look at each other to see how we are. We have had three conversations that I can think of ever since we were married. We seem to be paralysed with each other,' the wife said.

When a mother (or, for that matter, a father) actually uses violence against a baby, there is always a specific crisis which acts like a trigger. It may be something minor, but it comes at the end of a long road of frustration and irritation. The authors of *Helping the Battered Child and*

His Family[12] say that it can be 'a washing machine breaking down, a lost job, a husband being drafted (in the armed services), no heat, no food, a mother-in-law's visit and the like' and add that 'it would seem most unlikely for the crisis to be the *cause* for abuse, as some would like to believe; rather it is a precipitating factor'.

Parents who are specially 'at risk' of battering their children were often themselves maltreated as children and came from families in which there is a history of violence. They tend to be people who are at odds with society, facing a multitude of other problems besides those involved in bringing up the family, and who are generally social casualties. For unhappy families often perpetuate themselves through the generations. Brandon[13] has described these families as being disorganized ones 'in which violence pervades every aspect of their lives' as well as including individuals with hysterical traits, who perform an act of violence and then flee from the scene, abandoning the child in its pram in a street or in a shop. Although a few battering mothers may be real sadists who get relief from their own tensions by inflicting pain on others, the vast majority are 'vulnerable women under stress' who deeply regret the injuries they have inflicted and say things like 'When I hit him I then pick him up and cuddle him'.

Except in certain special areas, often near big teaching hospitals where there are psychiatric departments involved in research in baby battering, there is little support for the mother who is in danger of physically abusing her child, and a great deal of depression amongst new mothers goes unnoticed and neglected. It has been estimated that between 4000 and 5000 children a year in the United Kingdom are battered at one time or another; about a

[12] op. cit.
[13] Sydney Brandon in a lecture to the North Western Regional Health Authority, reported in *The Times*, November 27, 1974.

tenth of them die of their injuries, and 400 may suffer
permanent brain damage.[14] In a few hospitals there
are mother and baby units where mothers, and fathers
too if they can, are able to come in with their babies, so
that not only can the staff learn more about the problems facing the mother and observe her behaviour with
the child, but there is also an opportunity for her to learn
in a facilitating environment which gives care not only
to the baby but also to her. It may be that these unhappy
women will only be able to mother when they have been
mothered themselves.

Being able to mother is something which is learned
from infancy on. Most cultures seem to manage this
education extraordinarily effectively. We are only just beginning to be aware of the diffuse but important skills
which our post-industrial society has neglected.

Learning how to be a mother is not a matter of adopting a certain set of attitudes, but of expressing one's own
personality in the task of responding flexibly to the child's
needs. Each woman brings a unique combination of skills
and experience to motherhood. There is no such thing as
the 'perfect' mother, if only because the role only achieves
meaning when it is part of a growing dyadic relationship
with a child, and if there are other children in the family,
the relationship between all the children and their mother,
and between each and every combination of them. The
mother sees herself in their eyes, as she must do also in
the eyes of her husband. What she is and the way she
conceptualizes her own role is to a large degree a product
of all these images of the self, which, especially in a large
family, in each day and every hour of each day are subjected to kaleidoscopic transmutations, depending on the
situation and the actors.

Motherhood is, in fact, never really learned. It evolves.

[14] Conference on baby battering held in Chester, reported in
The Times on November 26, 1974.

In our own society grandmothers are above all ex-mothers. They are people who have finished doing a task. They may be allowed to have a hand in mothering, and be permitted to re-enact their own mothering experience spasmodically and in a modified way with their grand-children, but they in effect 'play' at mothering only on occasions when this is agreed by the real mother, or in situations of crisis when their help is sought because of the inability to cope or absence of the real mother.

When a girl gives birth to her first baby she replaces her mother, who then retires into being a grandmother, per-mitted to indulge in nostalgia about her own former ex-periences, but basically inactive as a woman in relation to children. The grandmother's overtures to the grandchild may be accepted with varying degrees of tolerance. Some-times they are rejected outright: the sweets she offers will ruin the child's teeth; she is spoiling the baby, or trying to potty-train it when the mother has decided that the baby will be allowed to be clean in its own time, neglects the important task of teaching the two year old to read, or has other outmoded ideas about child-rearing.

Particularly when the grandmother is the man's mother rather than the woman's, intense conflict may develop and a triangular relationship between husband, wife and his mother causes problems not only in relations between mother and child but also in the marriage. In fact, many husbands' mothers stand back, since this is accepted to be the territory of the wife's mother and because she is already warned by the stock music hall figure of the mother-in-law and the ridiculing of her role in the form of numerous jokes. As a result overt conflict in fact develops over child-rearing more often between mother and daughter.

This is one of the subjects that couples expecting their first baby are apprehensive about during the woman's pregnancy, and I find that in discussion groups in preparation for birth and parenthood a question which frequently occurs is, 'How shall we deal with Mother?' The husband is concerned as to how he can protect his wife from her mother, and she is anxious lest her mother shall upset her husband:

'Her mother is the dominating type'; 'We have to hide the car round the back of the house because Mother says I shouldn't be driving while I am pregnant'; Mother worries about how well I'm feeling really all the time, and I couldn't bear to have her around when the baby is born'; 'I know that Martin won't feel it's really his home if she comes to stay, and yet I realize that she is feeling shut out'; 'Mother has been dropping so many hints for such a long time about when are we going to start a family that I don't feel it's our baby any more, and I know if she comes here she'll take over'; 'Roger would like to opt out, and leave me with my mother, but I'm grown up now and I need him, not her. How can I get him to see this?'; 'She's a very busy lady, Ruth's mother, and she likes to organize things. I'm having to put my foot down.'

One interesting phenomenon is the number of calls for help which first-time mothers make to advisors and counsellors after a grandmother has come to stay or when the mother has been visiting her. In my own experience of postnatal counselling it is immediately following family reunions that urgent requests for assistance with breast-feeding or distress signals connected with anxiety about the baby and the woman's ability to mother flood in. Easter and Christmas are peak periods for mothers to lose their confidence and need someone with whom they can talk.

We have not discovered what to do with our ex-mothers. They are a social liability rather than an asset. They themselves know that they are not wanted, and for those women who have never had the opportunities of education which will fit them for later careers, who are not easily employable outside the home, or who lack the initiative and confidence to seek outside interests, the 30 years they can expect after mothering is over may be very empty and purposeless. In 1850 a woman's age when her last child was 11 averaged 47. By 1950 it had gone down to 37.[1] Mace describes the crisis of coming to terms with the reality of 'the empty nest',[2] and other counsellors[3] advise that husbands and wives should help each other by 'recognizing, supporting and sharing each other's need to mourn'.

In women mental illness is far more common after the age of 40 than before, and there is an insidious kind of depression which occurs at or soon after the menopause associated with grieving for the loss of youth and the meaningful family role the woman once had, which accounts for thousands of women of this age being permanently on tranquillizers. It is this age group which has the hidden problem of domestic alcoholism, the sherry or whisky bottles under the sink, as the woman seeks to retreat from the long lonely hours in which she is no longer needed by anybody. In the United States and increasingly in Britain these women hope for a new lease

[1] Michael Young and Peter Willmott, *The Symmetrical Family*, Penguin, 1975.
[2] R. David Mace, *Success in Marriage*, Hulton, 1958.
[3] Howard J. Clinebell and Charlotte H. Clinebell, *The Intimate Marriage*, Harper & Row, New York, 1970.

of life with hormone replacement therapy, which seems to promise a return of fading physical charms and the possibility of new love. The magic potion cannot itself cause them to find satisfying activity in the world beyond the four walls of home. The foundation of their depression lies not so much in their endocrine glands as in the social situation of the mother who is no longer wanted.

In a study of the life cycle of American women as wives, housewives and mothers, Lopata[4] asked housewives to rank a woman's different roles in the family in order of importance. Whereas 45 per cent thought that the combined roles of wife and mother were important, only 3 per cent attached importance to her role as a grandmother. Women in American society do not see themselves functioning as grandmothers with any meaning, and their response to the shrinking social circle resulting from the children leaving home is to try to become competent in new areas of life outside the home.

In pre-industrial societies, in contrast, the role of the grandmother is frequently of major importance, and it is often not until a woman becomes a grandmother that she attains full dignity and authority as a woman, can speak as an elder, have a hand in the cultural traditions of her people, and represent a value system to her daughters and daughters-in-law. A peak point in a woman's life is when she becomes a grandmother or matriarch. The Chinese veneration for old people is well known. Traditionally, a son's most important obligation is to ensure that his parents have a happy and comfortable old age, and elderly people are afforded something approaching reverence.

The same respect for age exists throughout Africa. Among the Kgatla of Bechuanaland young couples always start off their married life in the home of either the

4 Helena Z. Lopata, *Occupation: Housewife*, OUP, 1971.

usband's or the wife's parents, and are subject to the uthority of the head of that household. If it is the wife's arents' house the husband visits only stealthily at night. f it is the husband's parents' home, the wife must be ubmissive and behave like a servant in the house. The woman's mother cares for her daughter in childbirth, or when she is ill, and advises her constantly. The grandmother 'tests and trains'[5] her son's wives when they are .ving in her compound: 'Her interest in the welfare of er children does not cease till the day of her death, for ven as an old woman she continues to serve them as well s she can'.

It is the responsibility of married sons to assist their arents with the ploughing, to give them occasional resents and help them in any way they can, whereas narried daughters help particularly with gifts of food nd clothing and help in the household. There is a great mphasis in honouring and obeying parents, and young eople consult them before embarking on any new venture or coming to any important decision. Thus the Kgatla grandmother is a person with dignity, responsibility, . continuing stake in her children's and grandchildren's rogress and welfare, and through her children's fertility as work to do and an established place in society recogized by all.

The strong emotional bonds between mothers and daughters and between daughters and their grandmothers that is, between direct uterine descendants) which exists mong the Ndembu of Zambia, a matrilineal society, grows ut of early childhood, for children are reared in their naternal grandmother's households from the age of three or four until just before puberty.[6] This practice has a ignificant effect on Ndembu religion. The mother and

Schapera, op. cit.
[6] V. W. Turner, *The Drums of Affliction*, a study of religious processes among the Ndembu of Zambia, OUP, 1968.

grandmother ghosts are those who most often visit women
first afflicting them, and later helping them, whereas the
ghosts of the husband's mother and grandmother hardly
ever put in an appearance. It is the dead mother and
maternal grandmother whose power is most involved
in all cases of infertility, even though they may have
been completely non-threatening in life, and who guard
as it were, the entry to the uterus. When their power
has been given public recognition and they have been
suitably propitiated, they confer their benevolence and
permit the woman to conceive.

In the ceremony of Nkang'a, the girl's puberty ritual
the young girl is taken away from her mother in order to
bring back grandchildren, and at the very end of the rite
the novice is led to her grandmother's hut before she is
taken to sleep with her bridegroom. The girl is only
separated from her maternal lineage in order to go out
get children, and then return them to the lineage of which
the grandmother is the representative.

In North American pre-industrial societies, too, the
grandmother has great dignity and authority. The maternal
grandmother is head of the Hopi Indian household, which
normally consists of a woman, her daughters, their husbands and their unmarried sons and married and un
married daughters. A man usually refers to his mother's
rather than his wife's home as his own. On feast days
he always goes to his mother's home and later, after his
mother's death, to his sister's, while the wife continues
to celebrate the feast in her mother's home. In a similar
way the Navajo have what has been called 'matrilocal
grandfamilies'.[7] When a couple marry they live either
with the husband's or the wife's mother, but the pull is
always stronger to the wife's mother. It is the grand
parents who decide such matters as when the sheep should

[7] Gary Witherspoon, 'A new look at Navajo social organisation'
American Anthropologist 70, 1970.

be dipped or sheared, and who constitutes the final authority in all matters concerning agriculture. The Navajo grandmother does not so much impose her decisions on the household as 'serve as a focus for communication and of organizing co-operation'.[8] She does not need to work *through* men, but is a mediator *between* them.

This pattern of authority invested in the senior female member of the family is common in many societies even though they do not necessarily have a matrilineal descent system. It means that a woman's life cycle unfolds towards the achievement of status as a grandmother controlling the family.

In Atjeh, on the northern tip of Sumatra, women own the houses, and even where men own the land, the women work it. On it they grow the rice which is not only the staple food, but the essential ingredient for sacrificial rites, so that the men cannot sacrifice to the gods without the women's co-operation. The tie between a mother and her children and grandchildren is the most powerful in the community, and husbands are treated as guests who often outstay their welcome.[9] (The divorce rate is about 50 per cent of all marriages.)

The grandmother is of central importance in ex-slave societies, and her position is often reinforced in conditions of urban poverty today. Among poor black Americans there is great emphasis upon the strength and resourcefulness of women. Households frequently consist of a three-generational unit made up of a woman, one or more of her daughters and her daughter's children, along with any men with whom the women may be living. Because of poverty, women with children have no alterna-

[8] Louise Lamphere, 'Women in domestic groups', *Woman, Culture and Society*, edited Michelle Zimbalist Rosaldo and Louise Lamphere, Stanford Univ. Press, 1974.
[9] James Siegel, *The Rope of God*. Berkeley, California, 1969.

tive but to live with their mothers and to share availabl
resources. The sons who are out of work may also co
tinue to live with their mother.

The grandmother's power is also institutionalized in th
Caribbean, where grandmothers frequently rear their gran
children from the time they are weaned. In Jamaica th
peasant woman does not expect to marry until she ha
established a long and fertile relationship with a ma
who provides for her and her offspring. Older wome
anticipate having a second family consisting of the
daughters' firstborn children and other children born ou
side regular unions to rear when they are themselves i
middle age. They usually still have children of their ow
living at home, and siblings, aunts and uncles are brougl
up together. Although they grumble about this, it is co
sidered highly desirable for a woman to have health
children around as she gets older, who can run errand
fetch the water and firewood, and help in the hous
with horticultural work and with 'higgling' or sellin
market produce. As the grandmother ages the girls grad
ally take over more and more responsibility for th
running of the household, and by old age a woman ex
pects granddaughters to be caring for her in her turn.
is thought to be a dreadful thing to leave old wome
without young people to help them, and when I was d
ing my own field work I interviewed in two household
where it was claimed by proud grandmothers that youn
men who were emigrating had deliberately impregnate
girl-friends so that there would be a baby to leave wit
their mothers when they left. So in some cases th
father's and not only the mother's mother also rear
grandchildren.

On the other hand, maternity without paternal obliga
tion is heavily sanctioned in Jamaica (a concept quit
different from that of illegitimacy). When a girl become
pregnant the mother will not 'quarrel' provided there i
a man to 'response' for the baby, but if there is no on

to accept financial responsibility the girl may be flogged and turned out of the house. Maternal relatives then intercede with the mother to take her daughter back, which she usually does after a decent space of time. The baby is born in the grandmother's house, and the girl cares for it with the help of her mother for nine months to a year, and then goes off to seek work in the town, leaving the baby with her mother. The pattern is remarkably similar to that of the Ndembu of Zambia: the girl only goes out from her mother's house to get children to bring back to give to her mother, and the flogging and turning out constitute a transitional ritual to mark the girl's passage into motherhood, a ceremony in which she, as it were, 'pays' for the right to sexuality and motherhood, and one point in the cycle by which new children are added to the grandmother's household, and continue her line.

Raymond Smith[10] makes the point that in certain sections of Guiana men have little authority, not only over households, but also in other spheres of economic and political life, whereas women have a clearly defined status as mothers. As mistress of a household the grandmother exercises power not only over her own children, but over children who are not her offspring. He says that a child born to a daughter living at home often grows up calling its grandmother 'Mama' and its own mother by her first name, as if she were a sister, especially if the grandmother has young children of her own. This has to be the case or there would be great confusion because 'the older woman could hardly act as disciplinarian to one set of children and as an indulgent grandmother towards another set living within the same household.'

This raises an interesting point about grandmothers

[10] Raymond T. Smith, *The Negro Family in British Guiana*: family structure and social status in the villages. Routledge, 1956.

generally. They are not usually seen as disciplinarians but as indulgers of children. Anthropologists call this the 'equivalence of generations'; that is, alternate generations are structurally equal, and can therefore behave towards each other in a more relaxed way than can consecutive generations. In Guiana, too, there is a normal grandchild-grandparent relationship of this kind, which is one of 'affectionate indulgence, and a kind of equality'.[11] A grandmother often identifies with her grandchildren and takes their side in quarrels with the mother. When a young girl wants to go to a dance, and has been forbidden by her mother, the grandmother may plead for her.

Grandparents and grandchildren can joke with each other in a way which is often impossible for parents and children to do. Grandchildren can tease or even disobey their grandparents without meriting punishment. Perhaps this is why grandmothers often say that they can 'enjoy' their grandchildren more than they ever could their own children. The grandmother does not have to justify her right to be a mother or prove her ability to rear the baby and can see the problems of crises of family life in perspective from the vantage point of experience. She can relax and enjoy the child.

The grandmother who is indulgent with her grandchildren can at the same time be authoritarian and even tyrannical with her daughters. In Taiwan young women living with their mothers-in-law have a high suicide rate. The ghost of a suicide is believed to be powerful and revenges the death on the person who caused it. But most women and their mothers-in-law 'settle down to a pattern of occasional bickering',[12] and the younger woman soon realizes that having the older woman in the household means that she is free to go and visit her own parents

[11] Smith, op. cit.
[12] Margery Wolf, Women and the Family in Rural Taiwan, Stanford Univ. Press, 1972.

and that the mother-in-law is a help with the children. It sounds, in fact, as if they usually develop something of the relationship of sisters living in the same house, intermittently nagging at each other, but perhaps quite enjoying it, and in this case, both competing for the attention of the male, who is the son of one and the husband of the other. One of the subjects which can cause stress is a dispute between the two women about the discipline of the children. Grandmothers often criticize their daughters-in-law for punishments which they consider too harsh, even though they may have punished their own children in a similar way.

The grandmother in Taiwan also engages in matchmaking, planning who the children shall marry when they are grown up. The daughters-in-law tolerate this, knowing that the grandmother is unlikely to be around when such decisions have to be made. The grandmother visits round from house to house in pursuit of her plans, and acts as paid intermediary between families; she may also arrange adoptions, settle family disputes, and negotiate 'face-saving compromises for quarrels of various kinds.'[13]

All the big family ceremonies involve great expenditure of woman-power, and the grandmother's help proves very useful on the occasions of birthdays, weddings, funerals and religious festivals. Margery Wolf[14] says that these celebrations are much easier to organize if the younger woman can draw on the older one's experience and her memory of how things were done last time: 'For many a woman in her sixties, this lingering responsibility, the recognition by sons and daughters-in-law of her continued competence, is a source of great satisfaction.'

Some grandmothers are consulted by others in the village on matters relating to family, marriage and child-rearing problems and become known as the wise women

[13] Wolf, op. cit.
[14] op. cit.

of the community. They frequently engage in a little commerce, selling from their own flocks of chickens and ducks to neighbours or in the market, or becoming money-lenders at a high rate of interest. Margery Wolf[15] comments that in many communities the *hue-a*, or short-term loan associations, are completely dominated by old women, and it is from these families often have to borrow in order to have enough money to arrange a wedding or funeral. Another favourite occupation of grandmothers and especially of those who were formerly prostitutes, is gambling at mah-jong or cards, and it can become a major concern of each family to keep its grandmother from gambling away the family savings.

In old age there is also more time to become involved in religious activities, and the grandmother may go on tours round religious centres, combining sight-seeing with worship of the gods. Occasionally temples are restored, and the project is run by grandmothers who raise money for repairs and organize the eventual celebration. Religious festivals are linked with outdoor opera or puppet shows, and 'just as many American women become addicted to soap operas', so, says Wolf, older women who can escape the burden of daily household responsibilities sit for long hours watching both afternoon and evening performances of folk opera. The most successful programmes on Taiwanese television are these lengthy opera and puppet shows, and interviewing was impossible at any time when one of these programmes was showing.

Although childless couples were common in the Japanese village described by John Embree[16] in the forties, fertility, and in particular the bearing of sons, is so important in the traditional Japanese family that if a couple have no male heirs to carry on the family name, to tend the ancestral tablets when they die, and also to look

[15] op. cit.
[16] John F. Embree, *A Japanese Village*, Kegan Paul, 1946.

after them in old age, they adopt a young boy – often a brother's son – and bring him up as their own. Virtually every old person therefore becomes a grandparent.

In Japan entry into the last and oldest age-group, at sixty-one, is celebrated with a party. From this time on a grandmother must be treated with great consideration; everything she asks for must be given her, her opinions listened to with respect, and she should never be criticized. The equivalence of generations is here given powerful symbolic representation, and an elderly person can again wear red, the colour of childhood. In recognition of having attained the full social status of the elderly grandmother she may now wear a crimson underskirt. Old age is thus not a disability which a person tries to ignore, but a triumph, and a vantage point attained at last at the end of the long road of child-rearing.

We need to find a more positive role for grandmothers in our own society, and to discover a new dignity and potential for creative achievement in the woman who has brought up her family who, because of all she has learned from this experience, may have a great deal to contribute to society.

10
Women as Polluters and Creators

In Chapters 4 and 5 we began to look at the darker
side of motherhood, and at women's feelings about themselves as mothers. Men, too, have conflicting feelings
about women as mothers.

In most societies woman is a paradox. She is dangerous, mysterious and an unclean thing but also, as a
mother, the most revered. As a non-mother and erotic
object she represents the forces of darkness, of animal
nature which draws men away from the spiritual, a
polluting agency which threatens to emasculate men's
vital powers. St Paul's highly negative view of women
as tempters of men is not really very different from the
leitmotiv running through many Eastern philosophies
and Persian and Greek ethical writings. These ideas were
not introduced by Christianity, but grew out of a long
tradition in which the world was seen as divided into
opposites, black and white, evil and good, flesh and spirit,
the profane and the sacred. Women ensnared men and
tempted them to desert the noble goals they sought. The
theme occurs throughout Greek mythology, as does the
myth of 'the toothed vagina' which traps and threatens
to mutilate the hero in the mythology of many primitive
peoples.

The early Christian church developed this theme in no
half-hearted way. St Jerome warned that women were the
gateway to the devil. St Thomas Aquinas called them
'defective – ill-formed males', John Damascene castigates
them as 'the outpost of hell', 'sick she-asses' and 'hideous

tapeworms', and Pope Gregory the Great went so far as to state that they had two uses only, prostitution and motherhood.

As mothers, on the other hand, women are the fount of creativity and love, embodiments of charity and sacrifice. In this chapter I want to look at men's ideas about women as mothers and non-mothers and the contrasts between them. Perhaps it may suggest some of the reasons for the unattractiveness of birth control, or failures in its use, in those cultures where children are born not only to support their parent in their old age, or even to carry on the lineage, but because without them a woman is nothing.

Women as mothers have been put on an altar for so long and in so many different cultures that there is a tremendous gulf between men's and their own perception of the ideal mother and the real women who try to live up to this impossible ideal. This may help us to see some of the stresses inherent in being a mother.

Mothers in India

In India a woman is considered a subordinate, spiritually inferior and handicapped person whose salvation can be found only through implicit and unquestioning obedience to her husband, whatever his character and however he treats her. She must revere him even though he be evil, and can sacrifice, fast or make a vow only through him as a religious intermediary. In her are incarnate the unbridled forces of earthly existence, the passions of the flesh, attachment to possessions and occupation with the petty things of this world, and when she snares a man she drains his capacity to achieve ascetic contemplation and spiritual strength. Indian myths abound in stories of women who have misled ascetics and even gods and have ensured that they never escaped from the eternal bondage of sexual desire. That is why a wife's role must be one of implicit obedience to her husband's will and why she must worship him as a god. Moreover, she is an agent of pollution by the very fact that she menstruates and that matter regularly issues from her body. She lives in isolation for four days every month, so reminding everyone in the household of her inferior status and her carnal bondage.

As a *mother*, however, the woman is revered and the concept of motherhood is emotionally evocative and significant throughout Indian culture. The mother's power and influence over her children is reinforced by the segregation of women, in particular by the custom of *purdah*, and by the traditional withdrawal of the father from interests in domestic activities. Richard Lannoy, in his powerful study of Indian society,[1] stresses particularly the strength of the affective relationship between mother and son, which has existed since the establishment of the joint family systems of late Vedic times and still operates in the modern middle-class nuclear family. He emphasizes the ambivalence and duality of her role as wife, and therefore sexual being, and as the mother who is venerated. While on the one hand 'she seduces her husband away from his work and his spiritual duties' and is a threatening figure, who because of her fatal sexual attraction and her insatiable lust lures a man to gratify his desires, makes seminal thrift impossible to attain and so weakens him both psychologically and physically, on the other hand, she is idealized and 'raised to the level of a goddess in the home'.

In one study of the urban Hindu family,[2] family members were asked to rate the strength of their emotional ties with other members, and of a sample of 157, 115 said that the greatest emotional intensity existed in the

[1] Richard Lannoy, *The Speaking Tree*, OUP, 1971. I am drawing particularly on Lannoy's material in this section.
[2] Aileen Ross, *The Hindu Family in its Urban Setting*, Toronto Univ. Press, 1961.

mother-son relationship, and the other rates were: brother-sister 90, brother-brother 75, father-son 74, father-children 24, husband-wife 16, sister-sister 5. The significant thing here is that the husband-wife relationship, although not the last, is relatively low on the list. It is only as a mother that a woman assumes power in her household.

It is especially in relation to the firstborn son that the Indian woman attains this status. Adult men may wax eloquent about their mothers, using religious imagery to describe their purity, wisdom and self-sacrifice:

It seems to me that if God is love, He should be conceived of as a Mother and not Father . . . There was a time in my youth when I made myself sick with love of God . . . I . . . concentrated on the face of my mother, believing that if God was, he must be a supreme image of my mother's disinterested love.[3]

Richard Lannoy[4] comments on the ambivalence in the home, ascetic, punitive, authoritarian paternalism contrasting with indulgent, permissive and tolerant attitudes on the part of the mother. The child is bucketed into an environment alive with inconsistencies and contradictions which on the one hand reflects 'relaxed flexibility in child care' but on the other must be very confusing because it involves pampering and indulgence in early childhood, followed by excessive prudery, meticulous cleanliness and parental rejection. The 'nest warmth' of the joint family system does not necessarily provide the child with great security, and from the nostalgic vantage point of our own nuclear family system we may overestimate its advantages.

Children's learning takes place through direct observa-

Krishnalal Shridharani, *My India, My America*, Duel, Sloan and Pearce, New York, 1941, quoted in Lannoy, op. cit.
op. cit.

tion and participation in the extended household. Little
instruction is given, and when it is it tends to be conflicting, since the many adults around and range of mother-
surrogates available means that each individual may
direct the child in a different and contradictory way.
The small child is merely a 'passive observer of the busy
courtyard life'[5] and never knows the experience of accept-
ing individual responsibility for anything.

The code of child-rearing puts great emphasis on the
warmth and intensity of mother-child relations. But whatever the Hindu child-rearing ideal, it is only high caste
Hindus who live in the conditions in which it is practically
possible to indulge and cherish a child. One out of every
ten Indian babies dies in infancy, and endemic diseases like
malaria, dysentery and smallpox take their toll of health
as well as life. This means not only that children are more
or less taken for granted, but that the doctrine of rebirth gives meaning and justification to the high death
rate. As a consequence no child is unique; each is part
of the great stream of life flowing through the universe.

The Indian family, says Lannoy,[6] embodies a 'patterned
ambivalence' which reflects

the human dilemma caused by the environment in
which, for example, climatic conditions are extreme
and which cause great suffering to babies, from prickly
heat and other rashes, the pervading cloying damp-
ness of the monsoon season, mud, insects, flies, rodents,
dust and in the winter piercing cold. Jackals cry in
the night or adults in the close packed family quarrel
loudly and disturb the child's sleep. During the day
adults bicker and argue and tempers get frayed between the pent-up, jealous women. As seasons change

[5] Leigh Minturn and John T. Hitchcock, *The Rhajputs of Khalapur
India*, Wiley, New York, 1966.
[6] op. cit.

storms build up or scorching desert winds blow, the child's routines have to change without warning, and the boy or girl grow up to anticipate all change as painful and to feel that no actions of theirs can have effect on the conditions of existence or reduce the individual's vulnerability to the raw forces of nature.

The mother is the mediator between the child and its environment, but she can never protect the infant from it completely. When she puts it down it is cocooned in swaddling clothes from head to toe, and simply lies there with few or no toys, nothing to handle, but only the possibility of watching or of contemplating its own body and internal states. She tends to handle the baby impersonally, with a formal aloofness, a neatness and economy of action which preclude any unnecessary cuddling or emotional outpourings. When the baby is cleaned, however, the mother is likely to rub it quite roughly. Concepts of pollution lead to the baby being handled brusquely when it is bathed and a good deal of friction is applied to skin which may be already sore and sensitive from rashes.

When a baby is born the mother and child are isolated in an inner room in a state of ritual impurity for several days, during which time the baby's horoscope is prepared. The house is purified, but the woman does not go back to all her household and other tasks for a period of another 34 days. The baby is fed on demand, and babies are not left to cry as it is thought to be weakening. Breast-feeding continues for two years or more, and weaning is gradual. The baby is in flesh to flesh contact with its mother's body astride her back, or that of a mother surrogate, until it is able to run around independently, and in some rural areas the baby is carried like this under the mother's sari. The baby is never left alone, and when the mother is working she does so whilst continuing to carry her baby or lays it down close to her.

The Hindu ideal supports the symbiotic interdependence of mother and baby. In practice, extreme poverty, primitive technological conditions and maternal malnutrition or even starvation, all limit the loving care which is available to be given to the baby, however, and impoverished mothers find that their milk dries up when they are hungry and undernourished themselves, or they have to work so hard carrying fuel, cooking, cleaning or working in the fields, that the baby must wait a while before it is attended to.

Bowel and bladder training is relaxed, and this is in striking contrast to the taboos relating to pollution and the 'washing mania' which the adult Hindu observes. Perhaps this is so because at this stage the baby is seen like an extension of the mother's own body, but as yet without spiritual and ritual responsibility. Because the baby is so close to her own body the mother becomes aware very early on of the exact point at which to pick the baby up and hold it out so that it can defecate. Then she wipes up after it and washes it. At about two the toddler is taught to go out into the yard to squat down and begins to learn the strict regulations regarding faecal pollution, and at five the child goes to the fields with a pot of water or in the middle-class household uses the lavatory. The mother begins to teach the child from about the age of two that his right hand is 'clean', and that he should wipe his bottom only with the left, which is 'dirty'. At the same time he is taught about the permanent and collective pollution of low caste, so that values relating to personal hygiene and to temporary, individual defilement are immediately associated also with status in the social system and with a wider system of values.

The Indian baby remains a baby for a long time, and sleeps with its mother for the first four or five years. Everything possible is done for the small child; he is fed by hand, bathed and dressed. No one tries to teach him to walk or to talk; he simply does both when ready. The mother makes little conscious attempt to mould her child's behaviour apart from the gentle, reiterated and consistent emphasis on the clear distinction between the clean and the unclean, the sacred and the polluted. There are few rewards for good behaviour, but a casual slap or formalized scolding for behaviour which according to custom is considered bad or polluting.

There are always older children and adults around on whom the small child can depend for help, so there is no need to learn to be self-reliant, and since the whole extended family lives and works together, no need to compete with anyone else, but rather an implicit assumption that the child will conform to the rhythms and lifestyle of the family, without change or experiment.

Mothers have particular problems in disciplining and controlling the growing boy. They themselves are under the control of superiors, and must obey their husbands without question, and children soon learn this. A rebellious little boy can exploit his mother's situation and become very demanding. The boy does not come under his father's direct control until he is five, and from three to about seven he may take full advantage of his mother's subordinate position in the hierarchical system of the family to resist her authority, to run away outside the house to areas which are not under her control and where she may not herself be allowed, and whines, cajoles and pleads until he gets what he wants. He quickly learns that temper and tantrums are effective, and the violent outburst of rage remains a potent and effective method of controlling the behaviour of anyone of uncertain status in adult life.

The mother scolds her naughty child and tells him that it will be outcast, or is an 'Untouchable'. She threatens ghosts or witches, and that Kali the goddess of destruction (who represents the dark side of the mother image) will come and harm him. If scolding is ineffective, she may lock the child in a dark room, and Lannoy says that this is a terrifying experience for the small child, and that it is significant that one of the techniques used by holy men is meditation in a dark room, which is regarded as a severe spiritual ordeal.

But however the child exploits his mother, in later life she is looked back on with something approaching veneration. The great Vedic purification sacrifice, the Soma, embodies the adult's conceptualization of motherhood. To be 'born into divine existence'[7], the suppliant must first return to the womb and become himself a fetus. He must once again become dependent on his mother, the ground of his being, and by implication, hence also on the body social. The Soma sacrifice crystallizes ideas about the relationship of men to their mothers and also of men to society. The human body is 'the lotus of nine doors',[8] always vulnerable to pollution from outside and inside, which retains its wholeness only when a balance is maintained between different parts of the body, and between different parts of society. The Soma sacrifice embodies and dramatizes an infantile attitude, and retains the image of the mother and return to her in fetal dependence, as one of superordinate value in attaining purification.

Traditional attitudes are changing rapidly in the Indian middle class, and women are taking on more authority in the home, as well as often taking on jobs outside it. In the towns the nuclear family system has largely replaced the extended family system, removing some of the old stresses, but replacing them with new ones. One of the problems is that whereas in the joint family there is an unbroken chain of occupational uniformity, and the young learn exactly what to do by emulation of their elders, once such a system has collapsed young people have to go outside the family to learn new occupations,

[7] H. Hubert and M. Mauss, *Essay on the Nature and Function of Sacrifice*, Cohen and West, 1965.
[8] The Athar-Veda, quoted in Lannoy, op. cit.

and this is accompanied by a greater degree of individuality and striving for independence, freedom, and an
improved standard of living. It is often women who agitate
to break away from the joint family and who persuade
their husbands to leave. But all this entails great psychological adjustment to operating alone, in the relatively
isolated husband and wife unit, without the support of
the joint family. Without other women able to play the
part of mother surrogates for the growing child the
maternal role is intensified, and this may produce special
difficulties in the mother-son relationship, where the
mother has a hold over her son and a concentrated emotional dependence which produce tensions for the boy
when he leaves home. One result is that the traditional
serenity, calm and poise of Indian life is being replaced
by 'nervousness, restlessness, and a hard, desperate, sullen
feeling of a world bereft of love'.[9]

However, women in India are not, as yet, competitive
with men to the same degree that they are in the West,
nor do they demonstrate what Lannoy rather quaintly
calls 'masculine traits of behaviour which are familiar in
their counterparts in Anglo-Saxon countries'. For the most
part they do not need to seek success outside the home,
because they have quietly assumed complete and un-
contested power inside it. The modern Indian mother is
supreme.

The Jewish ideal
The powerful, enveloping and sometimes suffocating love
of the Jewish mother for her children is a theme reiterated in modern novels. In this section I want to look
not at social pathology, however, but at the Jewish ideal
of motherhood, and see how this has been expressed
historically.

The traditional Jewish family has been called 'a walled

[9] Lannoy, op. cit.

garden',[10] the basic unit of the Congregation of Israel, the home, its temple, the father, a priest, the children acolytes, and each meal a holy communion. Nearly every Jewish ritual concerns the family and almost every family gathering has an associated ritual. The patriarchal principle is embodied in the person of Abraham, and the overriding obligation of the father to instruct his wife and children. The first commandment is 'thou shalt be fruitful and multiply' and to extend the family onward into time and to reinforce its unbreakable links back into history, 'the rocks whence you were hewn, and the hole and the pit whence you were digged'.

In ancient Hebrew culture the wife's most important task was to produce male heirs and her status as a woman depended on her ability to do this. A man could divorce a barren woman, and as his wife aged he might take another wife. Still today among the strictest orthodox Jews women are second-rate members of the congregation and whereas there are great celebrations on the birth of a son, the birth of a daughter is marked hardly at all. Although the Talmud instructs that a father should 'look on the birth of a daughter as a blessing from the Lord', the implication is otherwise. The morning prayer of the devout Jew is 'Blessed art Thou, O Lord our God, King of the universe, who hast not made me a woman'.

It is recorded that Rav Eliezer ben Hyrcanus was tackled on a point of scholarship by a clever woman, but became impatient, and protested: 'A woman has no learning except about the spindle. Let the words of the Torah be consumed in fire, but let them not be transmitted to a woman'.[11]

A woman's body is like a vessel, the orifices of which

[10] Chaim Bermant, *The Walled Garden; the saga of Jewish family life and tradition*, Weidenfeld and Nicholson, 1974, to which I am particularly indebted for information contained in this section.

[11] Quoted by Chaim Bermant, op. cit.

must be kept closed, but from which regularly polluting matter seeps. Woman as a sexual being is an agent of impurity because of menstruation: 'And if a woman have an issue, and the issue in her flesh be blood, she shall be in her impurity seven days'.[12]

> If a man shall lie with a woman having her sickness, and he shall uncover her nakedness – he hath made naked her foundation, she hath uncovered the fountain of her blood – both of them shall be cut off from among their people.[13]

Even if the blood should leave a stain 'no bigger than a mustard seed' the woman is unclean, so the seven days were extended by the Rabbis to twelve for safety. The *Baraita de Niddah* stated that the breath of a menstruating woman was poisonous, her glance was harmful, and she polluted the air around her. 'She was regarded as the ultimate in corruption, a walking, reeking, suppurating pestilence.'[14] It was not uncommon for women to consult the Rabbi for his advice on whether stains on their underclothing would be considered as rendering them impure or not, and to visit him clutching the stained garments for him to examine, which he did with the impersonality of a doctor making a careful clinical examination.

The Laws of the Shulchan Aruch instruct the woman to be responsible for taking precautions that her husband shall not touch her by mistake when she is in this defiled state. In Orthodox homes the double bed is unknown, and has been much criticized by some Rabbis as a symbol of depravity. Following separation the purification ceremony of the ritual bath must be performed and the woman must immerse herself three times in moving

12 Leviticus 15:9.
13 Leviticus 20:18.
14 Chaim Bermant, op. cit.

water, whether this be that of the special *miqvah* bath or the water of a river or the sea. It is obligatory on husband and wife to have intercourse on the night after her immersion, which tends to correspond to the time of ovulation and therefore to be the woman's most fertile period. If after ten years it is evident that the woman is barren or if the couple have been using birth control and so have borne no children, then they are considered to be living in sin by the ultra-Orthodox. Jews as a whole, however, practise birth control and the two or at the most three child family is the norm. The use of the condom is considered sinful and to be tantamount to the sin of Onan. The woman assumes responsibility for contraception, and the Pill is accepted as complying with doctrine.

The Talmud lays down the duties of a wife to serve her husband, including washing his face and pouring his drink into the glass, and Maimonides added many other services which he had acquired from observing behaviour in the Moslem cultures in which he lived. One duty he emphasized which is relevant to the area on which we are focusing in this book is that she should breast-feed her children herself.

It is incumbent on both parents to ensure that their children are properly educated, daughters in the arts of the housewife so that they can marry well and sons so that they become wise and govern their families well, and there is an emphasis on academic excellence and on the scholarship which makes for a good Rabbi. There exists only one specifically Jewish lullaby in the English language which mothers used to sing to their babies and it embodies the ideal of education as part of the serious business of life:

> O, hush thee my darling, sleep soundly my son,
> Sleep soundly and sweetly till day has begun;
> For under the bed of good children at night,
> There lies till the morning, a kid snowy white.

We'll send it to market to buy *sechora* (supplies),
While my little lad goes to study Torah.
Sleep soundly at night, learn Torah by day,
Then thou'll be a Rabbi 'ere I've gone grey,
But I'll give thee tomorrow ripe nuts and a toy,
If thou'll sleep as I bid thee, my own little boy.[15]

Parents borrow and save so that the son can go to university and become 'my son, the Doctor', who by virtue of his education and of the new social world he has entered has different friends, interests and beliefs, and then may become a source of disappointment and perplexity, of mingled pride and despair. Chaim Bermant[16] defines the special quality of *naches* which a Jewish parent hopes to get from children, 'a mixture of gratification, pride, joy, thankfulness, a sense of beatitude, the feeling that God is smiling down assentingly', and says that 'if a parent says reproachfully, "I only want you to be happy", he means all I want from you is *naches*, and *naches* is best gained if the child does what his parent would have done had he been in the child's place.'

Academic education is traditionally considered suitable for boys, however, and the parents' pride in daughters consists in them becoming wives and mothers. For it is only in motherhood that a woman fulfils herself completely and that the inherited taint of female sexuality is overcome and transmuted.

The Orthodox Jewish woman's province is the home, of which she is in charge and with which she is identified. A Rabbi commented, 'I never called my wife "my wife". I called her "my home".'[17] Her primary task is to create 'peace in the house' and a stable family life. As families have become smaller the tireless energy, determination

---

[15] Solomon Schechter, *Studies in Judaism*, Philadelphia, 1903.
[16] op. cit.
[17] Chaim Bermant, op. cit.

and concern for her children's welfare is concentrated on a few and can produce the stifling 'smother love' which results in anxiety and neuroses as the growing children try to break away from her enveloping pride in them.

The mother of a family has always had an important ritual function in the home, but in contemporary Jewish life the role of the mother is becoming ever more ritually significant. As the demands of modern non-Jewish life reduce opportunities for living according to Jewish faith outside the home, her role in making the home the centre of Jewish culture becomes more important. Frequently household members find it too complicated to bother with *kosher* dietary regulations outside the home, but rely on the mother to observe *kosher* within it. In the modern world the mother has therefore assumed a unique ritual role. It is she who is there to see that traditions and ceremonies are carried on, that Jewish customs are upheld, and that Judaism is represented to her children in an immediate and correct way such as occurs in the Sabbath lighting of the candles. As a result in the Jewish family the mother is becoming more and more the individual on whom the transmission of the culture exclusively depends. It is she, rather than the father, who becomes the embodiment of Jewishness to her children.

The basic physical impurity of having been born a woman is thus transcended, and she represents the historical link of every Jew with his past.

The Mediterranean Ideal

For the Greek peasant woman too, motherhood is fulfilment; but even more than that, it is redemption from the sin of having been born a woman. Women are considered weak and sensual creatures who must fight a constant battle against the innate spiritual disadvantages of having been born female. They must also be forever on their guard to maintain their chastity and to defend themselves against male sexuality. Virtue lies in 'shame' and it is said, 'Better to lose your eye than your reputation'. When God ordered the universe he gave man intellect, but he left women unreasonable, emotional, predisposed to quarrel and make trouble in the village, talkative and silly. 'Men are intelligent,' they say, 'but women are gossips.' They are all 'Eves'.[18]

Menstruation is evidence of female impurity and a woman in this condition must refrain from engaging in ritual activities such as making the Christmas sausages, baking bread for the liturgy or remembrance food, lighting the church candles, kneeling in front of icons or lighting the sanctuary lamp. The word used, 'to take', is that used about plant grafting too; if a woman does these things, the act will 'not take' – it is pointless, for the grace cannot flow. Men, however, are 'pure', and this makes them innately more responsible and able to relate to God effectively and to contact the divine world without hindrance. De Boulay[19] lists the qualities associated with male and female nature to show the bipolar contrasts between masculinity and femininity:

Man	*Woman*
Adam	Eve
Superior	Inferior
Right	Left
Closer to God	Closer to the Devil
Intelligent	Unintelligent, 'stupid'
Strong-minded	Credulous
Cool-headed, brave	Fearful
Reliable	Unreliable
Strong	Weak (seen also in the aspect of sensuality)
Responsible	Irresponsible

[18] See Juliet de Boulay, *Portrait of a Greek Mountain Village*, OUP, 1974, to which I am indebted for much of the information in this section.
[19] op. cit.

A woman also possesses an additional quality, that of
sexual shame and modesty, and it is this which saves her
from giving way to all the negative qualities. She bears in
trust not only her own self-respect as a woman, but also
the honour of her family. Campbell[20] points out that the
mother symbolizes the solidarity of the family and that
its honour and integrity depend on her virtue:

> A mother who is thought to have lost her virginity
> before marriage or, afterwards, to have been guilty of
> adultery, or even an apparent inclination towards it
> infects her children with the taint of her dishonour,
> and however closely these children may conform to
> right ways of behaviour, they cannot retrieve the repu-
> tation of their family.

He describes a woman who always laughed and joked
in a manner considered unseemly because of her poverty;
she ought to have been conscious of many worries.
Everyone agreed that her daughter, Chrysanthe, was
modest and hardworking, but, nevertheless, the whole
village was waiting 'with some confidence' for her moral
faults to reveal themselves.

From the age of 17 or so a girl must behave 'as a
maiden of virtue who is acutely sensitive to shame'.[21]
If she does not preserve her virginity untarnished she
faces possible death, or at any rate dishonour and a dis-
honourable marriage to a widower or a man of ill repute.

Immodesty marks woman's abdication of her femininity,
the betrayal of her nature and therefore of her divinely
prescribed role, of her family of origin or marriage

[20] J. K. Campbell, *Honour, Family and Patronage: a study of
institutions and values in a Greek mountain community*, Clarendon
Press, 1964.
[21] Campbell, op cit.

which, of necessity, entrusted her with its honour, that is with its most precious possession.[22]

Men's shame is rather different; it is no sexual shame, but shame at failure to fill the role of a man in the culture. For a woman shame is the one means of salvation, and without it she succumbs to a mere animal nature. All the men of the family must be concerned to protect their wives and children from shame, for their own honour is based on their ability to safeguard their dependants from shame.

It is precisely this sense of shame which both links each woman with the transgression of Eve, the prototype of woman, and which also retains within it the capacity to uplift her from being a mere weak woman and to fulfil the highest role accorded to a female – becoming a wife and mother. It is this, too, which 'allows for the creation in society of the ideal marriage relationship, that of symbiosis, or, as the villagers put it, one in which both husband and wife are equally necessary'.[23] Marriage alone, says de Boulay:

makes possible for woman the transcendence of her nature which is a part of her social and metaphysical heritage. For it is then that a woman has a home of her own and it is through the home that she expresses herself. While girls and unmarried women are treated as underprivileged by neutral members of society, and widows as dangerous and disruptive embodiments of the darker powers of feminine nature, to the married woman alone is given the charter to . . . tame and conquer those elements by which society is threatened.

[22] J. G. Peristiany, 'Honour and Shame in a Cypriot Highland Village', in *Honour and Shame*: the values of Mediterranean Society, edited by J. G. Peristiany, Athens, 1965.
[23] De Boulay, op. cit.

And this it is which the mother of a family does; her task is to tame the wayward and unruly natures of her children and to so express herself in the lives of children and grandchildren that she finds fulfilment through them, and in particular through the honour of her sons and grandsons. One village woman said of her grandchildren: 'I am now as far as little Christos. We live as far as little Christos',[24] which is all the more significant because she ignored his younger sister, Tassoula.

The mother 'holds the house together' and her proper sphere of activity is the home. It is not only her practical work, cooking and cleaning, baking the bread and making the cheese, caring for the goats and hens, carrying the water and looking after the children, which is important, but also the way in which she makes of the house a sanctuary from the cares of the outside world, and this is partly due to her careful observation of the correct ritual actions. She must observe religious fasts, attend church regularly, as a representative of the house, observe memorial services, make remembrance food, and count the strands in the home-made candles which commemorate the dead of both her own and her husband's families. She is the link with the historic past, because it is she who remembers *for* the others, symbolically revealing the continuity of the family and the community of kindred, both dead and alive.

She is considered closer to her children than is their father. He 'threw them out of his belly', but they come from her womb. Since the husband is occupied throughout the daylight hours outside the home, the woman is solely responsible for child care, and small children see little of their fathers except on feast days.

The Greek peasant woman, like the traditional Jewish woman, is identified with the house, and the Greek word for 'wife' is interchangeable with that of 'house'. If a

[24] De Boulay, op. cit.

woman is long away from her home it is a kind of 'spiritual infidelity'. 'Without the housewife', the villagers say, 'the house cannot function'.[25] In the house a woman expresses her creativity, and the home is the justification of womanhood. The order and pattern of the sacred world is reflected in the order, generous hospitality, love and peace of the home, and the mother is the guardian of this household shrine. There must be food in plenty for all who come, a warm welcome, and a sharing of the harmony of spirit of which the home is ideally the fountain. The home represents the sacred world in microcosm, and the mother is its priestess.

In the three societies at which we have looked in this chapter a woman has little value until she becomes a mother. She has uterine potential, and is appreciated for this reason, but can only justify her existence when she marries and bears children. If women in such societies are expected to limit their families and a curb is to be put on the population explosion, something else will have to take the place of uterine worth, and these and similar cultures must change so that women are valued for qualities which can be realized other than through childbearing and rearing.

Traditionally the ideal of motherhood has enriched society. It has embodied concepts of tenderness, compassion, generosity, selflessness, love, harmony and creativity in the face of other more aggressive and self-assertive quintessentially 'male' qualities like courage, power, fighting spirit, justice and technical achievement. But we live in the late twentieth century. Society is changing and we can no longer afford to value motherhood above barrenness. In passing through this cultural revolution qualities associated with motherhood have to

[25] De Boulay, op. cit.

find expression other than solely through maternity.

The danger is that in the absence of motherhood, or with childbearing restricted to a small section of the population, we overvalue the masculine and underestimate the 'feminine' which seem less rational and therefore suspect. Perhaps we have to rediscover just those values which motherhood has traditionally represented, and to find them not only in the biological figure of the woman as mother but in all of us.

11

The Changing Face of Motherhood

Like just about everything else in social life, motherhood has been experimented with and shaped to fit prevailing fashions and fads, or subordinated to a great social ideal which has entailed radical change in its form. Sometimes these experiments have involved only a few people or a small section of society. There was a cult in the United States in the immediate post-war period which asserted that if death and illness were never mentioned to or in front of a child it would have immortal life. So members of this sect tried to rear an infant in a closely guarded, isolated existence and a state of verbal asepsis, without meeting other children, or having access to TV or radio, surrounded only by beautiful things and people with loving thoughts, who revered the child as a future redeemer who would lead humanity away from pain and sorrow. This was, of course, too precious and specialized a task to be left to the mother, so the child was reared by worshippers who were at the same time its jailers. He could not have pets in case they died or were injured, or even get used to one person in case he or she became ill or died and then he would learn about pain, sickness, suffering and death. Bliss was the only permitted experience.

But most recorded experiments have been part of a larger social goal.

Motherhood in Utopia
One of the most important 'experiments in motherhood'

took place in the Oneida Community, which was created by a religious visionary, John Humphrey Noyes, in the mid-nineteenth century in America. A significant element in the community was peer group criticism in public and anyone unsure of their ground or the wisdom of a course of action voluntarily submitted themselves to criticism from all in meetings held regularly for that purpose. The Perfectionists, as they called themselves, based their organization on communism and on what later became known as 'free love', although Noyes warned his followers concerning sex of 'the temptation to make a separate hobby out of it. One should share all things in common and avoid attaching oneself to individuals'. This allowed for free 'circulation' and exchange of 'magnetic influences'. Sexual intercourse was the most intimate and powerful means of 'laying on of hands' and should not be restricted to one partner only. Girls were initiated into sexual love when they were about thirteen, often by Noyes himself. In 1848 he instituted a system of 'male continence' or *coitus reservatus* which he taught was health-giving, which constituted an effective means of birth control in the community. In 1869 a 'stirpiculture experiment' was started which the Perfectionists hoped would ultimately transform American society and the world. Anyone had a right to refuse to have intercourse with anyone else, but only those chosen by Noyes had a right to breed, and even when a couple had started a baby they were not supposed to be specially attached to each other, but had to give way to other members of the community and not become 'sticky'. The young women of the Community issued a statement saying that:[1]

We have no rights or personal feelings in regard to child-bearing which shall in the least degree oppose or

[1] John McKelvie Whitworth, *God's Blueprints: A sociological study of three Utopian sects*, Routledge, 1975.

embarrass him (Noyes) in his choice of scientific combinations . . . we will, if necessary . . . cheerfully resign all desire to become mothers, if for any reason Mr Noyes deems us unfit material for propagation. Above all we offer ourselves 'living sacrifices' to God and true Communism.

In practice, since Noyes believed in the inheritance of acquired characteristics, particularly from the father, whom he thought had a greater genetic influence than had the mother, and, because a principle was adopted to draw the fellowship upward', it was often older, highly honoured 'spiritually minded' men in the community who fathered the children, and it was said that many of the babies were fathered by Noyes himself.

It proved very difficult for couples to separate, as they were supposed to when a baby was on the way, and in one contemporary account written by a visitor to the Community[2] a painful incident in which a young man was publically 'criticized' for his attachment to the woman who was bearing his child is described, and it is recorded that he was instructed by Noyes to let another man sleep with her. It was perhaps because of such incidents that a system developed whereby couples lived together before and for a short time immediately after a birth, and then parted. Mothers cared for their babies until they were nine months old, and at night till eighteen months. After this time the 'stirps' (the babies) visited their mothers twice a week, but both mothers and children were publicly criticized if they showed signs of being unduly attached to each other. Love between mother and child was not the only suspect attachment; children who got too fond of their friends were also criticized and separated. No one was supposed to 'stick' to

Charles Nordhoff, *The Communistic Societies of the United States*, Dover, New York, 1966 (first published by Harper & Row, 1875).

anyone else; there was to be no possessiveness, no ex clusiveness, in fact, no commitment between individuals, only a commitment to the community, and exclusiveness from the world outside. Pierrepont Noyes, the son of the founder, wrote of his childhood: [3]

> We Community children lived in a little world bounded on all sides by isolation. We believed that outside those walls were philistine hordes who persisted in religious errors and social formulas under which they sinned and suffered. When I was a child the world 'outside' was a world of taboo.

When the children had been weaned, at about two years, their care was taken over by male and female nurses in the nursery, and from the age of three or four they ate with the adults, but at their own special table. Their education and discipline was conducted not by their mothers, who had given up their children and had no rights in them, but by the entire Community.

The Oneida Community invented a system in which attachment between mother and child was not only ignored but in which a deliberate attempt was made to eradicate it. The comments that one rather perplexed visitor to the Community made foreshadow some of the observations made by Rene Spitz[4] and John Bowlby[5] about the effects on children of the lack of a one-to-one relationship with an adult:

> The children I saw were plump, and looked sound; but they seemed to me a little subdued and desolate, as though they missed the exclusive love and care of a father and mother. This, however, may have been

[3] *A Goodly Heritage*, New York, 1958.
[4] René Spitz, 'Anaclitic Depression', in *A Psychoanalytic Study of the Child*, Vol. II, International Universities Press, 1946.
[5] John Bowlby, *Attachment & Loss*, Penguin, 1971.

only my fancy; though I should grieve to see in the eyes of my own little ones an expression which I thought I saw in the Oneida children, difficult to describe – perhaps I might say a lack of buoyancy, or confidence and gladness. A man or woman may not find it so difficult to be part of a great machine, but I suspect it is harder for a little child.[6]

We are never told what the women felt about having to part with their children. Research done on Rhesus monkeys[7] suggests that for those who grew up in the movement and had themselves experienced 'maternal deprivation' and a deliberate withdrawal of love as children, all attachments to other individuals later in life may have been difficult, and this may have made it easier for them to hand their children over to the Community without distress.

Communist China

Some of the most dramatic changes in the role of the mother have occurred in Communist China. Since 1949 the Marriage Law has been the basis of family organization replacing the system of feudal marriage which preceded it. It proclaims the equality of husband and wife and the duty of each to rear their children. Men are not permitted to apply for divorce during a woman's pregnancy or within a year after she has given birth. In fact throughout the 1950s divorce became increasingly difficult for couples who had children.

On marriage, as in the past, a woman frequently goes to live with her husband in his parents' household, so that her relationship with her mother-in-law is central to her life, and affects the way she brings up her children.

[6] Nordhoff, op. cit.
[7] H. F. Harlow, 'Development of affection in primates', in *Roots of Behavior*, edited by E. L. Bliss, Harper, New York, 1962.

Delia Davin[8] says that the tensions between these two
women form the subject of much recently published
fiction, and that they fill the pages of problem pages in
newspapers, more so than any other problems about
marriage and the family. Whereas in the past the mother-
in-law used to be the superior authority in the house and
supervise her daughter-in-law's work, the younger woman
now often goes out to work and the older one has to do
all the menial tasks previously done by the younger. Some
mothers-in-law escape from this into work outside the
home, and the two women share chores in it. Others
refuse to do housework or to care for children, or cook
for their son only, and refuse to feed his wife. Such
problems may be referred to the cadre of village women
responsible for supervising the revolution at local level.
Often the solution is for the *grandfather* to take on child
care while both women go out to work.

In spite of changing edicts from on high about the role
of women in society, actual systems are worked out on
an empirical basis. In the countryside families still live
and eat together and work in the same agricultural team.
Peasant women have for a long time been accustomed
to helping to cope with the crisis of harvest, and the
babies and small children are left behind in the care of
an older woman or one whose feet had been bound and
was therefore incapable of doing agricultural work.
Communal child minding on a regular basis was an extension of this system. In one village, for example, in
which women were 42 per cent of the labour force, a
meeting was held at which it was decided that since
mothers were worried that their children were not being
cared for adequately, and since some of the child minders
were anxious about the responsibility they had taken on,

[8] Delia Davin, *Woman — work: women and the Party in revolutionary China*, OUP, 1976. I am grateful for material from this
book used in this section.

a proper nursery should be set up, and that the elderly women of the village and children over ten should run it, along with a rota of mothers should they be needed. Simple rules were drawn up, including one to the effect that the minders were not to allow chickens to scratch the faces of the babies, and vegetables, leaves, clay and empty match boxes were used as play materials.

Men were supposed to withdraw from their children from about the age of six years old, lest they get too intimate and unruly with them, but whereas the father became authoritarian, the mother went into league with her children, and particularly with her sons, using her husband's isolation from them to form firmer bonds of affection, acting as the interpreter of their father's behaviour, negotiating to get them off punishments, and acting generally as intermediary. 'For the children,' says Margery Wolf of the traditional family, 'the final evidence of their uterine family, in opposition to the family defined by their father, may well be the fact that father beats not only them but mother as well.' Thus

'women in modern China are not shiny new models turned out especially for the new society. A silent, oppressed population of women did not turn overnight into an energetic, astute body politic. In fact, the family system that ignored them for centuries also equipped them well to participate in the revolution and the new society. They were far more experienced than their brothers at shaping opinions, sensing changes in attitude, evaluating personal advantage and disadvantage in sets of circumstances. It is not their skills that are new but the appreciation of those skills'.[9]

[9] Margery Wolf, 'Chinese women: old skills in a new context', op. cit.

In the cities, the members of the nuclear family are usually separated during the day, but meet as a family after work, having picked up the baby from the crèche. Couples rely a good deal on the help of grandparents after the birth of the first child, even though it is accepted that the man shares the housework, laundry and child care, and though there are many crèches at places of work. Women invite a mother or mother-in-law to come and live with them when the baby is born. The fact that both the man and the woman are working outside the home has the effect of strengthening family ties and cementing the bonds between parents and grandparents. Even when there are adequate nursery facilities it helps to have a grandparent available who can take the child to and from the crèche and can cope with school holidays, and also if it gets ill. It may come as a surprise to realize that maids are also employed, although only a minority of working women can afford them. Davin stresses that no mass movement to sever child care from the family was ever attempted and far from causing disintegration of the family the Communist Revolution in many ways reinforced it. 'After a decade of change in its structure,' she adds, 'Chinese society remained firmly based on the family.'[10]

The Kibbutz
The other great modern experiment which affects motherhood is, of course, the kibbutzim of Israel.

The ideal which led to the creation of the kibbutz had little to do with motherhood, but rather with building,

A new way of life in a very old and hostile land. True, the raising of a new generation to this new way of life was soon of crucial importance, but of necessity it took

[10] Delia Davin, op. cit.

a second place. Because unless the first generation created the society, how could it shelter any new generation?[11]

As the earth was sown, the harvest seen, the economy boomed and the immigrants at last felt the land their own, however, the kibbutz ideal concentrated on the nature of the relationship between the whole community and its young, the hope of the future. The kibbutz started as an alternative to conventional family life with a highly diffuse and unemotional form of multiple mothering, but the relationship of parents and children has now assumed central importance.

In the beginning, all the primary tasks of child-rearing were taken over by trained personnel, *metapelets*, in the baby and children's houses, while the mother was released for productive work. This was in part a reaction to the traditional female role of the ghetto in which a woman's whole life was devoted to her husband and children. It was considered that the woman pioneer, or *chalitzah*, had to be really free and equal with men, and this could only be so if she were liberated from the tasks of motherhood and shared guard duty with the men, drove tractors, built houses and dug roads alongside them. In fact, few women took on heavy agricultural labour to the extent that men did.

But the ideal of the elimination of role differentiation between the sexes was there. Moreover, it was necessary to utilize all available man and woman power towards the common goals of establishing and maintaining the kibbutz. No one could concentrate on private interests. The kibbutzim were a result of the radical rethinking of sexual roles as well as of community goals.

In the early years of the kibbutzim child-rearing was

[11] Bruno Bettelheim, *The Children of the Dream: Communal child rearing and its implications for Society*, Thomas and Hudson, 1969.

characterized both by an institutional as opposed to a
personal pattern of care, and by intermittent mothering
and regular changes in the *metapels* caring for the child
in the children's houses as he or she moved up from one
to another. Bruno Bettelheim saw this as resulting, for the
mothers, in feelings of guilt at not caring for their own
children as their mothers had done, and also, in women
who had been brought up on a kibbutz themselves, in a
certain emotional detachment from their children.[12] Even
so, some couples left the kibbutz on the birth of a second
and third child because the mother wanted to care for her
own baby, although because of the lack of confidence in
her ability as a mother, she had been happy to surrender
the care of her first.

Babies in kibbutzim are normally breast-fed, and when I
was in Israel I visited one kibbutz where flags are hoisted
so that a woman working in the fields or elsewhere
can see by the colour of the flag that her baby needs
feeding. Six months is considered quite long enough for
this, however, and mothers do not expect and are not
permitted to breast-feed longer. This may be because the
metapelet has ample time to concentrate on feeding the
babies with solid food, whereas the mother tends to hurry
feeds, or at least to feed with one eye on the clock, because she has to get back to work. This is not a situation
which favours happy breast-feeding or easy lactation.
Bottlefed babies are usually weaned on a cup at four
months. This is part of a system in which the baby is
urged forward away from infantile dependence on its
mother to be trained to work towards the communal goals
of the kibbutz. It may be for the same reason that babies
as young as six weeks are placed in high barred cots on a
white, flat surface, with space around them on all sides,
and are not nestled in cradles or carriers as are small

[12] Bruno Bettelheim, op. cit.

babies in many other societies.

The pattern in many kibbutzim is for the parents to spend two hours a day, often between the hours of five and seven p.m. with their children, while the rest of the time they are cared for in the children's or baby houses. Originally all children slept in dormitories and did not return to their parents' home at night, but in some kibbutzim children now sleep in their parents' homes. Longer periods are spent with the parents on the Sabbath. Nowadays the scene in the kibbutz on a Saturday was described to me as 'like a family convention', and this is accentuated by the fact that there are in some of the older kibbutzim four generations of family living, from the age of seventy-five or so down to the newborn baby. The kibbutz, in fact, is perhaps more than any other society today, based on the family. It results in a social situation which can be especially difficult for those who are childless, who may face a peculiar kind of loneliness in these periods of each day and during the Sabbath when the whole community is engaged in what is in effect a celebration of the family.

Because the time spent with children is devoted entirely to them there tends to be greater concentration on active relations between parents and children in the kibbutzim during the family hours than exists in a society like our own where a mother is likely to have a couple of youngsters underfoot all day, and struggles to do her housework and cooking without the toddler getting into the coal skuttle and the baby into the golden syrup tin. In the kibbutz the mother is less apt to be the tired, irritable woman who hopes that the children will not provide too many interruptions so that she can get on with her work, and tends to be the fairy godmother who belongs to the child for a limited period of time, but during that time is bountiful with gifts and with love.

In our own society fathers who return from work to see the children only when they are bathed and ready for

bed sometimes fill this role, and may be resented by
mothers who feel that they have to be sole disciplinarian
and educators. But in the kibbutz both parents can con
centrate exclusively on the children and lavish affection
on them during the limited times with them. Chaim
Bermant says:

> The whole ritual is vaguely reminiscent of the practic
> of nannies bringing the children downstairs from the
> nursery to have tea with papa and mamma . . . In the
> kibbutz one's parents become a species of grandparent
> or Dutch uncles – smiling, indulgent, generous
> Discipline, instruction, chastisement are received else
> where; the sacred hours are for love and affection
> for fun and games, for being spoiled. And indeed every
> home will have its games' cupboard for the occasion
> as well as a store of sweets and biscuits and an endless
> supply of drinks. The parents are entirely at the disposal
> of their children.[13]

People do not call on each other during these hours, and
all debates and social activities stop. They correspond
to what in the United States is sometimes called 'fun
time'.

The children form the centre of the social life of a
kibbutz, and the whole community revolves around them
the symbol of the future which can redeem the evil and
sufferings of the Jewish past. They are the focus of all
communal festivals, both the traditional ones like
Chanukah, Purim and the festival of the First Fruit, and
the newer ones which have developed out of the life
of the kibbutzim, such as the sheep-shearing festival. In
discussion about motherhood in a kibbutz I was struck
by the number of times informants referred to 'our
children not as the children of a certain pair of parents

[13] Chaim Bermant, op. cit.

ut as the children of the whole kibbutz. When children re successful in some venture – pass examinations, or vin travel scholarships or a place in an orchestra, it is not nly the proud parents who are glad; the triumph is one or the whole community. When a young person dies in attle in the sudden outbreaks of conflict between Arab nd Jew the whole kibbutz mourns because they have ost a son, and the young people grieve for a dead brother. oth because of the crises of the political situation and ecause the kibbutz is a large family, the system has estored to its members of all ages the experience of death s a normal life crisis, of facing bereavement and mourn- ng together, which for most of us has not existed since he nineteenth century.

The pull of the nuclear family and its interests in some vays undermines the communal identity of the kibbutz nd a fine balance exists between allowing for a certain onconformity and freedom and the maintenance of group oyalty. In some kibbutzim the communal dining halls, ymbolic of the common interests of the whole kibbutz, re less and less used, and in place of the great gathering ogether after work to talk through all that has happened uring the day, people carry off triple-deck saucepans full f food to their own dwellings, using the dining-room nore like a soup kitchen or Chinese takeaway.

However the kibbutz changes, the children in many vays have become its reason for existence. The modern ibbutz is a child-focused society, and the qualities of the ood parent are those called upon in every adult. It has nstitutionalized responsible parenthood, and stemming rom it, the love and loyalty of siblings as the main bonds velding individuals together in a new social unit. As I tarted to write about the kibbutz a woman wrote from srael to say that she and her family were soon to move nto a kibbutz, 'because,' she said, 'we want to see more of ur children, and this is not possible in the city'. In spite f the children's houses or perhaps because of them, the kibbutz may have rediscovered motherhood.

Communes

Janet passed to me what Louise passed to Janet
and Louise passed to Janet what some woman
passed to Louise, And I pass to you what Janet passed
    to me.
And somehow in the loving and sharing and the pass-
    ing
we are loving everyone.
One family.
Home to my family at last.

It was dark and wet in the place where I was labour-
    ing.
I was surrounded by women.
We all held hands and raised them up and down
to signal the rising and falling of the water.
And we breathed and we chanted and we sang:
One family.
We are all one family.
Home to my family at last.

I disappeared into a slit in the sky.
The world opened and took me in
and I was lying, legs spread,
on the roof of everything,
the tears streaming down my face,
my mouth open for the scream but no scream came.
And from all around me I could hear the chanting of
    my friends.
They were chanting:
One family.
We are all one family.
Home to my family at last.

Yea, yea, it was all incarnated in me.
I was sexless.
I was colourless.
I was faceless.
I was the one family.
We are all one family.
Home to my family at last.[14]

There are probably as many kinds of communes as there are families. There are town and rural communes, those that seek to be self-sufficient, others in which many of the members are on a permanent drug trip, and still others founded on strict religious beliefs. The important thing about them all from the point of view of this study is that they are seeking alternative solutions to the isolated nuclear family.

The religious commune has firm rules of conduct and often a carefully defined internal structure, with authority vested in elders or a leader. In a Moslem commune in central London, for example, the senior members apply the test of the Koran to everyday problems confronting the community, and to questions of conduct concerning marriage, pregnancy, birth and child-rearing. Men and women eat, worship and pass most of their days separately. I was able to learn something about this when I had the pregnant members of the commune with co-members who were supporting them in antenatal classes. The participation of husbands was discussed, but the woman who with her husband founded the commune, herself childless, was firm that Moslem doctrine did not permit men to participate in childbirth. This caused great unhappiness to one expectant mother who could not come to terms with the decision. In discussion the women stressed that the father was sharing in the birth in that it was his prayers,

[14] Janet Brown, Eugene Lesser, Stephanie Mines, *Two Births*, Random House, 1972.

recited as he stood outside the labour room, which would assist the delivery of the child, that he could come in immediately the baby was born, and that his special task was to place a piece of date against its lips to introduce it to the sweetness of life. Infant care and child-rearing was seen as the mother's occupation with the help of the community of women of which she was a member. The male role was to act as a bridge for wives and children between the commune and the outside world and between the profane and the sacred.

In contrast male participation in birth is considered of superlative importance in many of the Californian and other American communes. Here there is a strong emphasis on preparation for birth and parenthood. It is not only the father who shares in the experience, although his is a central role, but all the other members of the commune, both female and male.

Birth is the greatest trip of all, an occasion for transcendental meditation and ecstatic communion. The labour is often accompanied by music made by the commune members who lie around the mother as she gives birth on the floor, on cushions or a mattress, and she and they may smoke grass as well as sipping herb teas and honey or eating macrobiotic porridge of wholemeal grains. Care is usually given by a lay midwife. There may be readings from Kahil Gibran, poems written in the commune and mystical works, together with singing, chanting and praying and incense is often burned. Children of members as well as other children of the couple having the baby are frequently present. The naked mother is massaged with oil, and all in the room may join in her rhythms of breathing as she handles contractions. The community of feeling immediately after the delivery contributes to a postnatal 'high'.

The little girls were watching and Heraclitus, the cat was standing on his hind legs at the foot of the bed also watching . . . Dennis, Bob's close friend, poured champagne . . . and Cathy served the birthday cake.[15]

The woman is encouraged to adopt different postures, and in some cases delivery is effected with her on all fours. Great emphasis is put on nontraumatic delivery of the baby and a gentle welcoming into the world, according to the teachings of Leboyer.[16] The mother may herself deliver the child, drawing it up over her body assisted by the father. In some communes the father lifts the baby out and presents it to her with the words 'Take this our child' or words to that effect. He often bathes the child in warm water as Leboyer advises.

The expectant mother has often made a birthday cake in early labour, or before it begins, and after the delivery there is a party with all sharing in a piece of the cake and drinking wine. Couples in these communes are concerned to reintegrate birth into the world of natural things and to see it as part of the ebb and flow of the whole of life.

In some communes the placenta is divided and shared between all those present, and is either eaten raw, with something of the significance of a holy communion, or cooked and eaten as the only unkilled meat, rich in protein and minerals, to be consumed by vegetarians. *The Birth Book*[17] contains a recipe for Placenta Stew.

  1 fresh placenta
  flour and oil
  onions, carrots, potatoes or rice
  stew spices
  tamari wine.

[15] *Two Births*, op. cit.
[16] Frederick Leboyer, *Birth Without Violence*, Fontana, 1977.
[17] Genesis Press, undated.

Cover stew size pieces of placenta with flour and sautée in a stew pot with onion and oil. Placenta has no fat in it, make sure you use oil. When the pieces are brown and the onion golden brown, add sliced vegetables and water to cover and stew for about one hour. Add some spices and wine and tamari and let cook more until tastes good.

One of the difficulties in a commune may be to work out what exactly the relationship of each member is to be to the child. Although in some everyone is eager to share in child care, in others there are members who want nothing to do with children, and when babies are born they may be suspicious that the childbearing couples are taking over the commune. In some groups the new parents start tidying up and cleaning and organizing their lives in a way which they did not think necessary before the baby came, thus making demands on the other members and usurping territory. The new mother sometimes anticipates that she will be cared for and nurtured by other members of the commune, and they are not prepared to do this. In some communes the couples with children become fairly stable, keeping the commune running, while other unattached individuals drift in and out depending on them in much the same way as a small child depends on its parents. Sometimes, too, the mother resents other people 'interfering' in the way she is bringing up her child and cannot trust the way they deal with it.

Parents also have to consider that the communal family may be shortlived and that it may be difficult to cope with constantly changing membership, not only for the permanent couples in it, but also for the children. The commune is not necessarily an easy answer to the challenges inherent in motherhood, since although it solves some difficulties and although learning to live together can prove an exciting adventure, it produces new diffi culties and involves a commitment to shared responsibility from the group.

In some of the American communes heavily permeated by the drug culture the women are peripheral to the central drug-hooked male core, and are called 'chicks' – a term which suggests that they are not fully fledged as women, but rather something between an object and a pet.[18] Although some of these very passive, acquiescent girls do not cook or housekeep, once there are babies they become more concerned about the environment and often make demands on the men to improve it. Perhaps they see their babies as extensions of themselves, and although they feel unable to make demands on their own behalf, are able to do so for the child. In one commune of this type nearly every woman was monogamous, although the overall pattern was one of serial monogamy, and pregnancies were usually unplanned, so as not to interfere with nature. There was a good deal of petting of the man by the girl, and of the babies by the men. The author comments:

> The men seemed to affectionately treat the babies as pets. The networks without babies had an immense and growing number of cats all of whom were known by name but few of whom were other than haphazardly cared for.[19]

He remarks on the pervading air of depression in these communes in Philadelphia. This depression probably grew out of the tendency to exploitation which characterizes them, the girls and boys exploiting each other and both exploiting the parent society. The men in these male-orientated communes hang together because they are essentially passive and need other men to reinforce their

[18] Ross V. Speck, *The New Families*, Tavistock, 1974.
[19] *The New Families*, op. cit.

masculinity, and the women need a group of men to re-inforce their identities in a general situation in which they are treated as sexual toys. The group is so passive that even sex is reduced to a carnal game, and sexual exploitation hardly seems important any more.

There is a peculiar paradox about the place of women in commune living, and in a way the role of the mother has come full circle, for, he says, in the Philadelphia communes: 'The girls were a parody of their middle-class mothers . . . more compliant, more masochistic, more submissive, and less autonomous than the parent culture.'[20]

Perhaps a woman does not escape the traditional mothering role that easily after all.

So we can hand children over to grandparents, can go in for intermittent mothering, leaving children in crèches all day while their mothers are in employment, or we can get women to become mothers to a whole community. We can use other people, amateur or professional, as surrogate mothers for long or short periods, or to take over the mothering role entirely. Or we can continue as we are, more or less locked up in our homes.

But there is another way. Our society could use fathers more. The gain would be not only for mothers, but for children and men as well. Young couples today are evolving new kinds of shared parenting, and are finding that they enjoy it.

For this to happen reorganization is necessary at the level of management in offices, schools, hospitals and factories, so that fathers and mothers can share in bringing up their children and have rewarding jobs too.

This is starting in Scandinavia and parts of the USA. The roles of men and women are undergoing dramatic change to suit modern lifestyles and goals, and institutions are changing to accommodate them. Couples are

[20] *The New Families*, op. cit.

getting employment which gives each of them 50 per cent time at work and 50 per cent at home.

At Stockholm University I was struck by the number of men wheeling prams or with baby carriers attached to their backs as they did research or taught students. This happens because when parenthood is shared not only do fathers come into the home, but babies go out of it more and mobility becomes a prime requisite. The gulf between home and workplace disappears. This must have been more like it was for the hunter who carved arrowheads as his toddler watched or the fisherman who mends nets as the children play beside him. Children can gain much from participating in the world outside the home, not only in planned play groups and carefully controlled child-centred environments, but in the hurly burly of adult activities. After all, they are going to grow up to become adults themselves.

In Swedish universities it has become a normal and accepted part of life. Employment possibilities of this kind are limited, and are largely in education, but gradually the system is spreading to other parts of Swedish society.

Shared parenthood means that each partner is equally responsible for domestic work. It is not a question of the man just 'helping' when he sees his wife too irritable or exhausted to carry on. Gronseth[21], in a study of Norwegian couples sharing parenthood, discovered that they all felt they had gained a lot, and this sense of being enriched is the main characteristic of all such partnerships studied so far. Though some experts have warned that men will become impotent if they surrender their traditional masculine roles, this does not seem to be the case,

---

[21] E. Gronseth, 'Work-sharing families: adaptations of pioneering of families with husband and wife in part-time employment', quoted in Rhona and Robert N. Rapoport and Ziona Strelitz, *Fathers, Mother and Others*, Routledge, 1977.

and couples say that sex is better. They also say they enjoy having more time with each other, as well as with the children.

Perhaps shared work and parenting can produce a pattern for the future which will allow both parents to have the best of both worlds.

When a woman is feeling ground down by the repetitive daily chores of motherhood, with wet and dirty nappies, mashed banana on the floor and sticky fingers everywhere, broken nights and sniffles and grizzles, bringing up children can seem a never-ending and thankless task, and one which is destroying her as a person. There are times when every mother wonders why on earth she has chosen to live like this. Even for those couples who seek education for parenthood, children, glimpsed from the other side of pregnancy, have a rosy hue, and it is only the reality of actually coping with them day and night that deglamorizes parenthood.

It is mothers who spend most of their time with the children, and, motherhood, however romantic its image before the children come, can easily seem sheer mindless drudgery. Instead of bringing fulfilment and satisfaction, the woman feels she is deteriorating into an exhausted, frustrated, irritable shrew whose only language is baby talk or conversation about Timmy's teething and the two year old's tantrums.

There are lovely moments even so, when the baby is sleeping blissfully, the washing is out blowing in a spring breeze, the baby wakes and smiles in glad recognition, or when the man she loves comes in at the end of the day and she has somehow managed to get through the housework and cook a meal and they can share an evening together. A good deal that is written about being a mother is about general principles and methods and types

270 Women As Mothers

of relationship (there is plenty in these pages, I know), but misses out on the quality of the hours that follow one on another through which the woman has to live day to day, and through which she comes to get an image of herself which is either diminishing or enriching. This is not only affected by, but is for most couples largely dependent on, the man's estimation of his wife's worth in her role as a mother.

When a man does not value his wife as a mother, or competes with the children to be mothered by her rather than giving her support in her relationship with the children, she is forced to walk a very lonely road. More should be done in the education of boys, especially, to help them see value in the qualities exemplified in good mothering as well as those associated with success in jobs outside the home and in earning ability and economic and political power. For as we have seen, mothers are made by the culture in which they have to operate.

Motherhood has been twisted into a great many different shapes to fit different social goals. Perhaps mothers themselves should now begin to say what kind of society they want so that they can function most effectively and what needs altering to help parents do a better and more satisfying job of bringing up children.

Western society is organized, for the most part, for workers in factories, offices and shops. It is not organized for families. Mobility with small children is extremely difficult. There are all sorts of things that are impossible to do with children in tow because it is made clear that, like dogs, they are not welcome. Public libraries, art galleries, restaurants, even hospital waiting rooms, rarely cater for children. They are there, if at all, on sufferance.

It is not a matter of making concessions to women with children, a pram park here and a baby changing room there, but of working out the conditions which have to be met for mothers to be able to put their best into mothering and for families to have the kinds of environment in which they can flourish. It means that maternity hospitals will have to become places in which mothers know that their babies really belong to them and not to the hospital, and where loving support and freedom is given them to create their own setting for labour and their personal styles of childbirth and to work out their own ways of caring for and relating to their new babies.

It means, too, that some mothers will choose to get out of the home more, and that some fathers will choose to be more in it, and many may choose shared work and parenting. For this to work, employment opportunities will have to be provided so that each parent can work only half time out of the home, and this entails re-thinking personnel policies and the whole deployment of labour in our society.

Many mothers may decide to stay at home while the children are young and be full time mothers. Yet girls are educated as if they could *either* have jobs or be wives and mothers. We have not yet come to terms with a society in which most women have finished childbearing by the time they are 30 or one in which women can expect 20 or 30 years of active life after the last child has left home. The woman who tries to get back into a profession after having her children finds that obstacles are continually put in her way. Yet it should not be impossible to devise methods of continuing education for women and for seeing professional education in terms of two stages, the first being a more general introduction perhaps, and the second stage one of greater specialization, in many cases drawing on the varied experience most women have gained while bringing up children.

Any reorganization of society which focuses on the needs of women as mothers must involve a re-evaluation of what is important about the mothering role for the community as a whole. Young people growing up should learn that mothers are not second-class citizens, doing a job anyone can do, but individuals who require special skills to perform what is perhaps the most important task for which any human being can prepare themselves, creating the society of the future. The exciting thing about being a mother, or a father who is able to be with the children a good deal, is the very close observation of unique human beings as they develop and the chance to participate in this physical, intellectual and emotional growing. Life holds other opportunities of helping things grow, of course, whether they are gardens, clay pots, books or music, and for both parents enjoying other activities and having interests and responsibilities outside the home can enrich the environment for the children too. But sharing in the unfolding of human life is especially satisfying and just because it is possible for so many people it should not be undervalued.

It does not stop once the children are no longer babies, but continues and hots up in pace as they enter a social world and start to use their inventiveness and adaptability in relations with other children and adults. It gets even more exciting, even if rather alarming, as they become adolescent and see-saw between being grown-up and children again with quite astonishing rapidity. There is probably no other work which is more demanding and which involves the whole person in the same way.

Being a mother, and for that matter being a father, is depreciated in our society. It is something intelligent women who have education and jobs are supposed to fit in to a very limited part of their lives or to do almost in their spare time. This is fine if this is how they really want to do it. But it does not have to be done like that. Being a mother is an exciting occupation which demands all one's intelligence, all one's emotional resources and all one's capacity for speedy adjustment to new challenges. There is no reason why a woman should not want to have another career as well, but it is a pity that she should feel she ought to because she is 'only a mother'. Mothers

A World Fit for Mothers? 273

have underestimated themselves for far too long and too often have been crowded out by the professionals who give advice, tell them how children ought to be brought up and often criticize them when things go wrong. Experts can often help, but women might take a good deal of advice with a pinch of salt and find out what works for them.

There is more than one way of being a parent, too, as I hope I have shown in this book. A man and woman do not have to have the same kind of partnership as the ones next door or exactly like anyone else. It is worth making experiments, and indeed very important to do so to adapt to children's different needs. As they grow the children make their own experiments and act out different roles in preparation for the world outside their homes. The family is a sort of crucible in which human beings coalesce, separate, reform in a different way, and spark off diversified reactions. The crucible holds danger certainly, but also, for both parents, a quite incredible fascination and promise as they share in the ultimate creative processes.

The advantage of seeing mothering from a cross-cultural vantage point is that the observer quickly realizes that instead of one ideal of mothering there are many permutations of the motherhood role. No one of these is universally right. Each is the product of women's empirical experience in a specific culture and is finely adjusted to the value system of that society. What works in one probably would not work in another.

In so far as we are concerned about what kind of society we have, the quality of our corporate life, we ought to think about the role of women as mothers in it. A new Jerusalem cannot be built only by altering schools, laws, economic systems and public institutions. Its foundations lie in the quality of interaction in the family from its very beginnings with a man, a woman and the baby they are bearing. Nor is it just a matter of educating and supporting parents when they already have a child; pregnancy is an important time of preparation, and even before that, the way the parents were reared themselves has significance for the kind of family life they are able to produce.

It is for this reason that societies which we think of as 'simple' may have something to teach us in the West about the quality of family life. The skills of mothering in such cultures cannot be simply transplanted unmodified to our own culture. But the living substance of what goes on from day to day in the home, in particular through the shared lives of women, and the unself-conscious mothering which is caught rather than taught as each girl grows up to become herself a mother, these things may have lessons for us.

We have organized a society in which responsibility for healing, education and birthing has been handed over to the professions. As a result the motherhood role has become impoverished. All too often the only personal satisfaction and social recognition that a woman can find is in a job outside the home. We have lost something precious. For being a mother is one of the most important jobs anyone can do. The future lies in the hands of the mothers of today.

NDEX

Index

Acholi (Uganda) 179
Adivi (S. India) 179
adjustment to society 24
adult status 52
advice from others 18–20, 22–3, 32, 204
Ainu (Japan) 201
anaesthesia 159–61
Andamanese 91, 201
antenatal clinics 138–9, 145–6
anxiety 26, 99–102 *see also* stress
Apache Indians (USA) 201
Arapesh (New Guinea) 83–4, 122
Arms, Suzanne 95

Banaro (New Zealand) 58
Bang Chan (SE Asia) 122
Bantu (S. Africa) 58, 133–8
Barcia, Caldeyrio 114
barrenness 237–8
Bechuanas (Africa) 134
Bemba 88
Bermant, Chaim 239
Bernard, Jessie 45
Bernstein, B. 31–2
Bibring, Grete 96
body-image 35, 108
bonding 53, 163–70, 195, 197
Boulay, Juliet 241, 243
Bowlby, John 250–1

breast-feeding *see* lactation
Buber, Martin 27

Campbell, J. K. 242
caring 26, 36–7
Carpenter, Genevieve 175
Cartwright, Ann 79
Catholic mothers 41–2
child abuse 66, 207–12
childbirth
  ritual 109–14
  psychology of 111–13
  posture 114–17, 152
  men and 119–23
  in Jamaica 127–32
  in South Africa 132–8
  in East Germany 138–41
  depersonalization during 146–62
  use of anaesthetics 159–61
  as crisis 193
child-minding 252–4
China 251–4
class 23, 39, 58, 115
cleansing 117–19, 147–8, 232
Comfort, Alex 206
communes 260–6
competitiveness 67
consensual courtship 58
contraception 25, 29, 75–80, 238
control *see* discipline
cultural anthropology 14
cultural background 20, 42, 105–7, 163

Dahomey (Africa) 73–4
Dakota Indians (USA) 99, 116
Dally, Ann 68
Davin, Delia 252

emerol *see* Pethidine
pendence 65–6
personalization 146–62
pression 45, 209–10, 215
scent groups 104
scipline 69, 140–1, 222, 229, 233
sease 74 *see also* infant mortality
vorce 251
eutsch, Helene 63
ctor-patient relationship 142–3
ouglas, Mary 125
eams 100–2
usun (N. Borneo) 179

ster Islanders 115
ucation for parenthood 15–18, 28, 30–1, 98, 136, 138, 200–3, 205
nbree 224–5
notional attachment and responses 17, 31, 38–9, 161, 172–3,
    188–9, 249, 256
docrine changes 170–1
idurals 159–60
ans Pritchard, E. E. 14
xtended family 54–5, 56, 60, 230
e contact 174

ther's role 39–40, 57, 83, 97–9, 122–3, 140, 148–50, 262
eding 33 *see also* lactation
minine behaviour 61–2, 63
rtility 58, 73–4, 82, 84–5
rceps delivery 161

andfathers 252, 254
andmothers 66, 180, 202, 213–25, 254
uatemala 84, 89
ilt 29–30, 39, 193

arlow, Harry 166, 174, 197

Havik Brahmins (S. India) 64–5
healers 123–4
helpers 38
Hopi Indians 218
hormone changes 170–1
housework 37, 45–6, 257

Ila (Rhodesia) 88
illegitimacy 57–8
imprinting 164–5
impurity 237–41
inadequacy 23, 34, 37, 193
induction 94, 154–8, 169, 184–6
infant mortality 74–5, 117, 124–5, 190, 230
infanticide 79, 124–5
insecurity 34
instinct 104–5, 163
interactive system 167
isolation 33–4, 35, 56, 96, 181–2, 199, 231

Jamaica 63–4, 66, 90–1, 100, 113, 118, 127–32, 148–9, 180–3, 202, 207–8, 220
Japan 224–5
Jewish mothers 41, 69, 235–40
joint family 234

Kellmer Pringle, Mia 205
Keneba (Gambia) 92
Kennell, John 173, 184
Kgatla (South Africa) 75, 81, 83, 216–17
kibbutz 198, 254–60
kinship 104
Kipsigis (Kenya) 82
Klaus, Marshall 173–84

labour 146–62
lactation 18, 70, 77, 168, 231, 256

language 62
Lannoy, Richard 228–30
Lazare, Jean 102
Leboyer, Frederick 263
Lele (Central Africa) 87, 125–6
Liedhoff, Jean 21
Lopata, Helene 34, 38, 216
love 65–6, 68–9 *see also* emotional attachment

Mace, David 215
Macfarlane, Adrian 173, 175
magic 109–14, 123, 125, 133, 203
male-female roles 24
Manus (New Guinea) 112, 114, 116
Marquesan Islanders 54
maternal mortality 107
maternity assistants 38
maternity hospitals 136–7
matrifocality 57
Mbuti (African Congo) 81, 91–2
Mead, Margaret 14
Mendez-Bauer, Professor 114
menopause 215
menstruation 61, 88, 119, 237, 241
Merbentyl 159
metapelets 255
Mexico 118
miscarriage 107
mobility 36 *see also* isolation
monogamy 55
Morgan, Patricia 39
Mossi (Sudan) 86
mother-daughter relationship 64–5
mother-father relationship 32, 33–4, 37, 45, 54–5, 81–4, 97–8,
    209, 229, 251
mother-son relationship 228
mother-in-law 83–4, 251–2, 254

motherhood
  psychoanalytic approach to 15
  norms of 16, 24, 139, 142
  interaction with child studied 18
  advice on 18–20
  and social pressure 29
  as anti-social activity 29–30
  isolation from society 33–4, 35, 148–9
  as an interruption 35
  and social pressure 35
  ideals and images of 38, 42–4, 46–7, 70, 203–5, 206 *see also*
    inadequacy
  as a trap 44
  working mothers 48–9
  right to 51
  and dissemination of culture 63
  repeated patterns of 63–4, 87, 163–4, 200
  competitiveness in 67
  adaptation during 67–8
  and instinct 104–5, 163
  in Jamaica 180–3
  emotional response 187
  and young girls 202
  myths of 205–7, 227
  men's concepts of 226–46
  in India 227–35
  Jewish ideal of 235–40
  Mediterranean ideal of 240–5
  in Oneida Community 248–51
  in Communist China 251–4
  in kibbutz 254–60
  in communes 260–6
Mundugumor (New Guinea) 89–90

Navajo Indians (USA) 218–19
Ndembu (Zambia) 178, 217, 221
neurosis 45

Newson, J. and E. 31–2
Nootka (USA) 201
norms 16, 19–20, 24, 139, 142–3
Noyes, John Humphry 248–51
nuclear family 53, 55–6, 60, 198–9, 254, 259
Nuer (Sudan) 74
Nyakyusa 87

obstetrics 95, 144–5
Oneida Community 248–51
Ongre Negritoes (Little Andaman Island) 201

pain 100, 159, 186
parental authority *see* discipline
Pethidine 157–9, 186
Pethilorfan 158
physical contact 21–2, 163–5, 167–8, 172–3, 178, 187, 188, 192,
      196
pollution 226–8, 231
polyandry 54
polygony 54
Prechtl, Heinz 166
pregnancy
   and physical appearance 51
   as force for social cohesion 81–4
   as ritual state 84–7, 92
   and status 86
   and taboo 87–92
product-orientation 34, 41
purification 117–19, 147–8, 232, 234

recognition 175–6
relation-orientation 41
religion 86, 112–13, 126–7, 181, 203, 244
right to motherhood 51
ritual 51, 84–7, 92, 93, 99, 106, 109–14, 117–19, 133, 147–8,
      161, 221, 231, 235, 238, 241

Scandinavia 16, 157, 266–7
segmented societies 132–3
separation of mother and baby 22, 177–80, 187–90, 196, 237
sex 17, 25, 52, 58, 62, 91, 97
sexual roles 61–5
shame 242–3
shared parenthood 266–8
shared responsibilities 45–6, 97, 196
Sia Indians 115
Siberian nomads 115
Smith, Raymond 221
social pressure 35
social values 24
South Africa 132–8, 178
Spitz, Rene 250–1
stimuli 165
Stopes, Marie 78
stress 44–5, 94
Sumatra 85
superstition *see* ritual, taboo
Switzerland 157

taboo 87–92, 97, 99, 183, 237
technology 24–5, 152, 183–92
Thompson, Barbara 107
Tikopia 74
Todas (India) 54
Turnbull, Colin 207

unmarried mothers 57–8
USA 54, 57, 58, 103, 184
Usiai (New Guinea) 116
uterine family 253

witches 85, 123–7, 203, 233
Wolf, Marjery 223–4, 253
Wolff, P. H. 174

women's movement 48

Xhosa (Transkei) 83

Zulus 80, 134
Zuni Indians 112–14

Fontana books about childbirth

The Psychology of Childbirth
AIDAN MACFARLANE

In remarkable detail and using the most recent research, Aidan Macfarlane traces how a relationship develops between a mother and her baby from conception to the first hours and days after birth. He discusses the influence of a mother's feelings during pregnancy on the behaviour of the baby in her womb, examines the question of pain relief, especially psychoprophylaxis, and looks at the current debate over modern obstetric technology. He describes the mother's reactions to her new-born baby and indicates how much the baby can see, hear, feel and smell in the minutes after birth.

Birth Without Violence
FRÉDÉRICK LEBOYER

The doctors smile, the mothers smile, but almost all newborn babies cry bitterly. Blinded by harsh lights, deafened by intolerable sound, abandoned in an incomprehensible environment, they screw up their faces and howl. But does birth have to be as painful for babies as it usually is? Dr Leboyer thinks not. And in this human study, he advances a radically new concept – birth without violence. In words and pictures, he shows how we can treat babies as human beings and ease them from the womb gently and with respect.

THE DEVELOPING CHILD

The First Relationship: Infant and Mother
DANIEL STERN

Within the first six months of his life, a baby learns virtually all the basic patterns which he will follow in the interpersonal relationships throughout his subsequent life. Dr Stern describes the behaviour of parent and baby which formulates these processes of social interaction, evaluates their importance for development, and gives parents fascinating insights into the relationship with which they are so familiar.

What is a Child?
NICHOLAS TUCKER

Psychological discussion of development almost always focuses on the child *now*, in twentieth-century Western society. Yet a child for the Victorians, in the Middle Ages, and other cultures today, and as depicted in fictional writings across the centuries, is a very different creature. So what is a child? What is it that distinguishes a child from an adult? Why do the definitions alter, and from where has the twentieth century derived its particular account?

Forthcoming
Memory ANN BROWN
Perception and Attention JEROME BRUNER
Learning Disabilities SYLVIA FARNHAM-DIGGORY
Child Abuse HENRY KEMPE
Moral and Social Development ELLIOT TURIEL

THE DEVELOPING CHILD

An Open Books/Fontana series edited by Jerome Bruner,
Michael Cole and Barbara Lloyd

The Perceptual World of the Child
TOM BOWER

This book describes and analyses the full range of visual,
auditory, and tactile abilities possessed by babies and small
children – the complex knowledge and skills with which they
are born, the abilities that develop, those that have to be
learned, and those which, absent at birth, have to be
compensated for by other senses or by artificial aids.

Distress and Comfort
JUDY DUNN

Why do babies cry? How can we determine what upsets them,
and how can we best comfort them? Judy Dunn shows how
recent research has provided answers to such questions, and
presents the conclusions, together with a multitude of new
and illuminating insights into the world of the infant.

Play
CATHERINE GARVEY

The significance of play to a child has long puzzled parents
and social scientists alike. For the first time, the author
analyses the meaning of play for children primarily between
the ages of 2–5, and makes clear the vital ways in which play
helps the child develop and learn about the world in which he
or she lives.